CROSSBILL GUIDES

Southern Morocco

Crossbill Guide: Southern Morocco
First print: 2023

Text and research: Martin Pitt
Editing: Dirk Hilbers, John Cantelo, Sean McKay, Kim Lotterman
Illustrations: Horst Wolter
Maps: Alex Tabak, Dirk Hilbers
Type and image setting: Oscar Lourens
Print: ORO grafic projectmanagement / PNB Letland

ISBN 978-94-91648-21-2

This book is made with FSC-certified paper. The printing process is CO2-neutral through carbon-offsetting. To compensate for the CO2-emissions of the printing processes, we've invested in the project 'Sustainable farming for the future'. For more information, see www.southpole.com under the listed project. You can find the certificate of the carbon-offseton our website under 'downloads' on the Southern Morocco Guidebook page.

© 2023 Crossbill Guides Foundation, Arnhem, The Netherlands

All rights reserved. No part of this book may be reproduced in any form by print, photocopy, microfilm or any other means without the written permission of the Crossbill Guides Foundation.

The Crossbill Guides Foundation and its authors have done their utmost to provide accurate and current information and describe only routes, trails and tracks that are safe to explore. However, neither the Crossbill Guides Foundation nor its authors or publishers can accept responsibillity for any loss, injury or inconveniences sustained by readers as a result of the information provided in this guide.

This book is published in association with KNNV Publishing.

www.crossbillguides.org
www.knnvpublishing.nl

KNNV Publishing

CROSSBILL GUIDES FOUNDATION

This guidebook is a product of the non-profit foundation Crossbill Guides. By publishing these books we want to introduce more people to the joys of our beautiful natural heritage and to increase the understanding of the ecological values that underlie conservation efforts. Most of this heritage is protected for ecological reasons and we want to provide insight into these reasons to the public at large. By doing so we hope that more people support the ideas behind nature conservation.
For more information about us and our guides you can visit our website at:

WWW.CROSSBILLGUIDES.ORG

Highlights of Southern Morocco

1 Visit Souss-Massa National Park for the iconic and endangered Northern Bald Ibis.

2 Head for the snow-capped peaks of the High Atlas Mountains around Imlil or Oukaïmeden for the dramatic scenery and endemic species.

3 Explore the atmospheric sand seas on the edge of the Sahara at Erg Chebbi or M'hamid in the Drâa and walk the palmeries at Rissani, Merzouga or in the Drâa to experience traditional life on the desert edge.

4 See hundreds of pink Greater Flamingos and other waterbirds in the ephemeral desert lake of Dayet Srij.

HIGHLIGHTS OF SOUTHERN MOROCCO

5 Scour the high gravel plains around Boumalne Dades for the charismatic Fat Sand Rat and a plethora of wheatears and larks.

6 Visit the Souss Valley for its endemic Argan forests and their organic produce and the source of 'our' Painted Lady butterflies and the start of their wondrous migration.

7 Wander the Souks and Medinas of historic Marrakech and seek Barbary Partridge, Barbary Ground Squirrel, Maghreb Magpie and Moussier's Redstarts just outside the city walls.

8 Cross the barren hillsides of the Anti-Atlas Mountains, wondering at the stark landscapes and the tectonic folds that formed them.

ABOUT THIS GUIDE

About this guide

 boat trip or ferry crossing

 car route

 bicycle route

 walking route

 beautiful scenery

 interesting history

 interesting geology

This guide is meant for all those who enjoy being in and learning about nature, whether you already know all about it or not. It is set up a little differently from most guides. We focus on explaining the natural and ecological features of an area rather than merely describing the site. We choose this approach because the nature of an area is more interesting, enjoyable and valuable when seen in the context of its complex relationships. The interplay of different species with each other and with their environment is astonishing. The clever tricks and gimmicks that are put to use to beat life's challenges are as fascinating as they are countless.

Take our namesake the Crossbill: at first glance it's just a big finch with an awkward bill. But there is more to the Crossbill than meets the eye. This bill is beautifully adapted for life in coniferous forests. It is used like scissors to cut open pinecones and eat the seeds that are unobtainable for other birds. In the Scandinavian countries where Pine and Spruce take up the greater part of the forests, several Crossbill species have each managed to answer two of life's most pressing questions: how to get food and avoid direct competition. By evolving crossed bills, each differing subtly, they have secured a monopoly of the seeds produced by cones of varying sizes. So complex is this relationship that scientists are still debating exactly how many different species of Crossbill actually exist. Now this should heighten the appreciation of what at first glance was merely a plump bird with a beak that doesn't close properly. Once its interrelationships are seen, nature comes alive, wherever you are.

To some, impressed by the virtual familiarity that television has granted to the wilderness of the Amazon, the vastness of the Serengeti or the sublimity of Yellowstone, our nature may seem a puny surrogate, good merely for the casual stroll. In short, the argument seems to be that if you haven't seen a Jaguar, Lion or Grizzly Bear, then you haven't seen the "real thing". Nonsense, of course.

But where to go? And how? What is there to see? That is where this guide comes in. We describe the how, the why, the when, the where and the how come of Europe and North Africa's most beautiful areas. In clear and accessible language, we explain the nature of Southern Morocco and refer extensively to routes where the area's features can be observed best. We try to make Southern Morocco come alive. We hope that we succeed.

How to use this guide

This guidebook contains a descriptive and a practical section. The descriptive part comes first and gives you insight into the most striking and interesting natural features of the area. It provides an understanding of what you will see when you go out exploring. The descriptive part consists of a landscape section (marked with a red bar), describing the habitats, the history and the landscape in general, and of a flora and fauna section (marked with a green bar), which discusses the plants and animals that occur in the region.

The second part offers the practical information (marked with a purple bar). A series of sites and routes (walks and car drives) are carefully selected to give you a good flavour of all the habitats, flora and fauna that Southern Morocco has to offer. At the start of each route description, a number of icons give a quick overview of the characteristics of each route. These icons are explained in the margin of this page. The final part of the book (marked with blue squares) provides some basic tourist information and some tips on finding plants, birds and other animals.

There is no need to read the book from cover to cover. Instead, each small chapter stands on its own and refers to the routes most suitable for viewing the particular features described in it. Conversely, descriptions of each route refer to the chapters that explain more in depth the most typical features that can be seen along the way.

In the back of the guide we have included a list of all the mentioned plant and animal species, with their scientific names and translations into German and Dutch. Some species names have an asterix (*) following them. This indicates that there is no official English name for this species and that we have taken the liberty of coining one. We realise this will meet with some reservations by those who are familiar with scientific names. For the sake of readability however, we have decided to translate the scientific name, or, when this made no sense, we gave a name that best describes the species' appearance or distribution. Please note that we do not want to claim these as the official names. We merely want to make the text easier to follow for those not familiar with scientific names. An overview of the area described in this book is given on the map on page 15. For your convenience we have also turned the inner side of the back flap into a map of the area indicating all the described routes. Descriptions in the explanatory text refer to these routes.

 interesting flora

 interesting invertebrate life

 interesting reptile and amphibian life

 interesting mammals

 interesting birdlife

 site for snorkelling

 interesting for whales and dolphins

 visualising the ecological contexts described in this guide

Table of contents

Landscape — 11
  Geographical overview — 13
  Geology — 17
  Hydrology — 24
  Climate — 26
  Habitats — 30
  Low Arid Steppe — 32
  The High Atlas Mountains — 34
  High Arid Steppes — 43
  The Sahara — 47
  The Anti-Atlas Mountains — 55
  The Souss Valley — 57
  The Coast — 61
  History — 65
  Nature conservation — 74

Flora and Fauna — 79
  Climate history and speciation — 81
  Flora — 85
  Mammals — 95
  Birds — 101
  Reptiles and amphibians — 119
  Insects and other invertebrates — 126
  Marine life — 134

Practical Part — 137
  Routes in the High tlas Mountains — 138
  Route 1: Oukaïmeden — 139
  Route 2: Imlil — 143
  Route 3: Escale forest — 148
  Route 4: The Sub-alpine zone above Zerkten — 151
  Route 5: Source de Tichka — 154
  Additional sites in the High Atlas — 156
  Routes in the High Arid Steppe — 160
  Route 6: Ouarzazate Reservoir — 161
  Route 7: Dadès Gorge — 165
  Route 8: Plains of Boulmane Dades — 168
  Route 9: Gorges near Imiter — 171

TABLE OF CONTENTS

Additional sites in the High Arid Steppes	173
Routes in the Sahara	176
Route 10: Desert well near Jorf	177
Route 11: Erg Chebbi and its environs	180
Route 12: The southern Route – Tazarine	185
Route 13: The Drâa Valley	187
Route 14: M'Hamid	191
Other sites in the Sahara	193
Routes in the Souss valley	196
Route 15: Iriri fields and Tiouiyine	197
Route 16: Crocus fields of Ighri and Tinfat	200
Route 17: The Argan forest	202
Route 18: Aoulouz barrage and river	205
Additional sites in the Souss Valley	208
Routes in the southern Anti-Atlas	212
Route 19: Tafraoute	213
Route 20: Tissint	217
Route 21: Taghjijt	220
Additional sites in the southern Anti-Atlas	222
Routes near the coast	225
Route 22: Tamri	226
Route 23: Paradise Valley	229
Route 24: The Souss Estuary	232
Route 25: Oued Massa	235
Additional sites near the coast	240
Tourist information and observation tips	**245**
Birdwatching list	**264**
Acknowledgements	**272**
Picture and illustration credits	**273**
Species list and translation	**274**
List of text boxes	
The Moroccan Town	12
Khettaras – irrigating the desert	23
The Argan Tree	92
Crest to the Test	108
The plight of the Houbara	110
The Bald Ibis	114
Painted Lady – portrait of a nomad	128

LANDSCAPE

Regardless of the point of entry, from your first steps in Morocco it is clear that this country is very different from any part of Europe. As soon as you step out the airport you are thrown into a melee of unfamiliar sights and sounds. There are men in flowing Djellaba robes, Arabic script and unfamiliar languages surround you. Everything appears hectic. If there is a system, it is not clear to the first-time visitor. However, the noise and bustle on the streets hide a rich culture of tolerance and hospitality.

Move on from here and you'll soon notice points of familiarity. The European influence, a hang-over from the colonial era firstly under Spain and then France, is still just under the surface. Latin script on road signs, advertisements and businesses are all commonplace.

Morocco has a history that matches any of the dynasties at home. This is a thriving and internationally focused country and the infrastructure is improving year on year.

Although it is wonderful to immerse yourself in the colourful city life, most naturalists will soon want to look beyond. Only exceptionally do any of the towns hold any attraction to the nature lover, and although visits are unavoidable for amenities and supplies, it is the countryside where it all happens. Not far outside the busy urban centres, you will find yourself amidst a wonderful mix of orchards, palmeries and arable fields, the latter grown either for fodder or directly for food. Fields are always close to water sources or in river valleys. In fact, nearly all valleys have been modified, their rich alluvial soils put to best use. Where valleys are not 'used' for agriculture, they are often flooded to hold water for irrigation or water supply. The barrages range from simple weirs and cisterns providing small pools up to modern day high concrete dams holding back massive reservoirs, and everything in between.

In the cultivated valleys, trees are plentiful. They provide the shade needed to prevent desiccation of the arable crops. This managed shade is particularly important on south facing slopes and away from the mountains. Often these trees are crops in themselves, such as pistachios, almonds, and south of the High Atlas Mountains, date palms. The latter are clustered into palmeries. For centuries, the fruits provided the ideal food for the desert crossing camel trains, thereby supporting the trans-Saharan trade routes. Away from human habitation, the hillsides and steppes are almost barren. Natural vegetation is concentrated in small pockets but wherever it can be found it provides the vital home and food for wildlife. Despite the

Erg Chebbi, one of two sand ergs near the Algerian border.

INTRODUCTION

> **The Moroccan town**
> Diving into any town or city will show that despite modern development of the outskirts the traditional streetscape and urban planning of the centres have remained largely unchanged. The central area, or Medina is a mass of tiny streets with shops spilling out onto the street where people mix with carts, bicycles, mopeds, motorbikes and sometimes trucks competing for the same space. The souks, as shops and markets are called, are arranged zonally, with types of goods, be it food, spices, clothes etc., each with their own area and competitors close at hand. Virtually nothing is visibly priced and shopping is a process rather than a simple transaction. Within part of the medina will be the Kasbah, the fortified heart of the town which is the refuge for the townsfolk in the time of unrest. These Kasbahs are often now used as the administrative centres or converted into hotels. In some strategic towns you'll find the more functional *Ksar* which look identical to the Kasbah, but historically functioned as a military base. The Medina's streets are narrow, shaded and away from the traditional ornately carved wooden doors offer nothing to the street. Its townhouses are *riads*, whose design surrounds the perimeter of the plot with the occupied rooms, leaving a central courtyard or garden (riad being the Arabic word for garden).

Ait Ben Haddou, a preserved Ksar and World Heritage site.

predominance of exposed rock and small shrubs, the whole landscape is made up of a mosaic of differing ecological nuances driven by the factors of geology, hydrology, altitude, temperature, and orientation to the sun. Those nuances are often remarkably subtle and learning to read the differences in habitats and discovering the characteristic flora and fauna of each ecosystem is one of the attractions of this area. Unlike in the majority of Europe, much of the flora and fauna here are consists of niche specialists, requiring a particular mix of conditions. Understanding the basics of the habitats and requirements of each species helps enormously in the success of finding them.

For the naturalist this is a land of contrasts and adventure. There is always a feeling of going somewhere less travelled and the potential for seeing something new. The flora and fauna may be poor at a single point, but by moving through the landscape and its niches it collectively becomes rich and exciting.

This guide is designed to help you explore the variety of Southern Morocco's ecosystems and to discover the flora and fauna that live there.

GEOGRAPHICAL OVERVIEW

Geographical overview

Firstly, we need to clarify what is meant by Southern Morocco, as there is no clear line or province that defines the extent of the book. Our aims are to provide a guide and travel companion to the southern part of Morocco. We have chosen the practical approach to concentrate on most attractive areas that can be reached from Marrakech or Agadir, both of which have an international airport. Our area stretches out west, east and south to the border with Algeria. It does not include the southern province historically known as Western Sahara. To the north, the area of this guide stops short of the Middle Atlas.

Mountains dominate Southern Morocco and two ranges cut through this region. The High Atlas Mountains loom over both Marrakech and Agadir and, as the name suggests, is the highest of the two ranges, with peaks of over 4000m. Further south is the parallel range of the Anti-Atlas Mountains, which mainly tops out below 3000m. Separating the two ranges is a plateau lying at around 1100m above sea level which we refer to in this book as the High Arid Steppe. A similar plateau, the Low Arid Steppe, is to the north of the High Atlas Mountains. It is around 300m lower and much more cultivated (see page 32).

The area south of the High Atlas Mountains is dominated by two river systems, namely that of the Souss and the Drâa. Both rivers rise in the High Atlas Mountains and run to the Atlantic, but that is about all they have in common.

The Drâa, together with its tributaries of the Dadès and Imini, has cut the north-south valley that provides access to the northern edge of the Sahara.

The Toubkal massif is the highest part of the High Atlas range.

LANDSCAPE

GEOGRAPHICAL OVERVIEW

After the confluence of the two tributaries near Ouarzazate, the Drâa runs south of Anti-Atlas Mountains down to the sand sea at M'hamid. This is the ancient route to the Sahara, and travelling it takes you back to a time of caravans and palm-filled oases, when the trade was by camels and the journey was a perilous adventure. Even today the journey is one of adventure and the human impact becomes lighter as you travel south into the desert itself. It is only at the far south, close to the Algerian border that the classic image of desert becomes a reality. Rolling sand dunes are relatively rare in this area, but a visit to Erg Chigaga, 40km beyond the end of the road will get you to an area that provides or even surpasses that vision. Most visitors access similar desert landscapes via Erfoud, 200km to the east, where the dunes of Erg Chebbi feature on many tour itineraries, both of naturalists and other travellers. In either location, the remoteness and stark beauty makes these areas the highlight of any trip and give access to species that are the things of dreams. Birders have been making this pilgrimage for a few decades and a network of guides has become established with the knowledge (and the 4x4s) needed to find the special birds around Erg Chebbi, and more recently also M'hamid. Other animal groups are not yet as well provided for, but things are changing quickly.

The Souss is both a river and a district and the term is used interchangeably in Morocco. The triangle of relatively low-lying land formed between the High Atlas, the Anti-Atlas and the High Arid Steppe is collectively known as the Souss Valley, even if much of it is actually some way away from the river. This triangle of fertile land is bounded by the Atlantic to the west and has a subtly different climate

GEOGRAPHICAL OVERVIEW

from that of the rest of the country. On the one hand, the Souss valley has been heavily settled and adopted for high intensity agriculture (this is the premier agricultural zone for exported fruit and vegetables), but on the other, it supports a unique ecosystem – the Argan forest. This is an open park-like habitat dominated by the endemic Argan tree – a species that is ecologically, socially and economically important (see box on page 92). The coastal strip is a distinctive ecosystem in its own right. Within our region, it changes character as you move from the north to south. Classic, Mediterranean-style maquis covers the northern zone, whilst heading south from Essaouira to Agadir and beyond, the coast becomes warmer and succulents typical of the Canary Islands join the mix. Further south the coast becomes truly Saharan in character.

River estuaries punctuate the coastline and form the majority of Southern Morocco's small but important wetlands. These are sensitive habitats and fortunately three are protected as part of the Souss-Massa National Park.

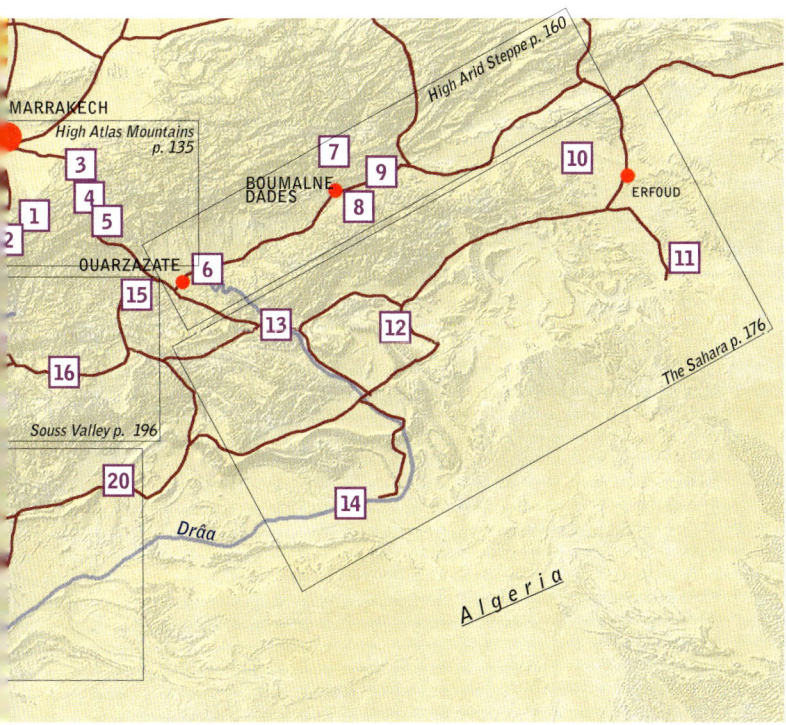

The numbers refer to the routes described on page 138 and further.

LANDSCAPE

GEOGRAPHICAL OVERVIEW

The stark landscape of the southern Anti-Atlas.

Round trip

The area covered in this guide is huge, and to gain the best from your visit you need to cover ground in order to visit the various distinctive sites. The first challenge is to decide which you want to visit in the time available to you, and then to decide on a route that covers these. The most logical round trip when starting in Marrakech is to go via the High Atlas to the High Arid Steppes and the desert on the south side of the mountains, before swinging over to the coast and following it up north again (or vice versa). Since there is only one road along the coast and (only) four roads crossing the High Atlas Mountains (via passes called *tizis*), the defining choice is which tizi to take. Any journey begins by picking the crossing points. Once on the other side, there are few towns and connecting roads, so options are limited.

Most visitors wanting to see a good cross section of the habitats and species make a round trip starting with a visit to the High Atlas Mountains, crossing over to explore the High Arid Steppes on their way over to the far east to explore the Sahara including the dunes of Erg Chebbi. For the return visitors cross over to the coast via the Souss valley to Agadir to explore the Souss-Massa National Park and finally take the coastal road back up to Marrakech. This guide is organised in this way to facilitate this circuit, but of course the zones can be taken in any sequence to suit your needs or points of access.

Keep in mind that away from Marrakech and the coast, the population is sparse. The roads are delightfully empty of traffic making travelling a pleasure, unless you are in need of help. Make sure you take the necessary precautions when travelling here (see page 246 and further).

Geology

Southern Morocco is dominated by the High Atlas and these mountains are the result of tectonic movement that began in the Jurassic period and continued through two eons. The folded rocks were then overlain by sediments, that often were then further folded. This resulted in heavily broken bands of rock which can be best seen along the major roads across the High Atlas, especially on route N9 from Marrakech to Ouarzazate.

The Mountains

The High Atlas Mountains define the geology and landscape of much of Southern Morocco. Their direct impact on the climate influences the ecology of the area covered in this book.

These mountains form one of four parallel ranges in Morocco that run in a general northeast-southwest direction. All were formed by the northward movement of the African tectonic plate into the European plate; the same process that gave rise to the Alps, Pyrenees and most Spanish ranges. From south to north, the four Moroccan ranges are the Anti-Atlas, the High Atlas, the Middle Atlas and finally the Rif, which lies on the country's northern coast. Only the High Atlas and Anti-Atlas Mountains lie within the range of this book.

The multiple folding events that formed both mountain ranges mainly occurred in a period of over 100 million years through part of two eras – the Jurassic (200-145 million years ago) and the Cretaceous (145 million to

The folding events in the mountains are best seen in the Anti-Atlas where the ridges have subsequently been eroded by wind and temperature.

LANDSCAPE

GEOLOGY

65 million years ago). Prior to this the landscape was primarily flat or part of the prehistoric Tethys Sea. The sea was punctuated by a series of *inselbergs* (literally island-mountains), which are standalone volcanic mounts that erupted during the Pre-Cambrian era (over 600 million years ago).

As part of this ancient seabed, many strata of sedimentary rocks were deposited over the whole of the African plate, and it is these that were pushed up during the folding events and form the Atlas and Anti-Atlas Mountains. The volcanic inselbergs were subsumed into both ranges during these mountain building phases.

Mighty as these mountains remain today, in terms of altitude, they must be a shadow of their former selves. The predominance of relatively soft sedimentary rocks has led geologists to conclude that these ranges were once much higher. Both the speed with which the mountains rise and the speed with which the rocks erode can be estimated. Once they were probably as high as the current Himalaya (i.e., 7,000m). In terms of drama, erosion also added to the landscape. It has cut gorges, cliffs and bluffs in the bedrock, often leaving extensive scree slopes below. The harder volcanic inselbergs are now the highest points of these ranges.

Between folding events, the area became submerged by the sea. Further layers of sedimentary rocks were deposited during this time. These new strata were then themselves folded as the next folding event arrived. The overall result is a complex mix of deposits and fault lines and the heavily broken strata of rocks we see today.

The highest mountains in southern Morocco are pre-cambrian igneous inselbergs.

Today, the High Atlas is by far the highest of all four of the ranges and it is also the most extensive. It runs nearly 2,000 kms from the Atlantic coast in the west all the way across the country and then through Algeria to Tunisia. The width of the range varies from 50 kms to almost 100 kms. The highest point is Jebel Toubkal, (*Jebel* being the Arabic word for mountain), which at

GEOLOGY

The bare rock faces show the evidence of folding, and often subsequent deposition and refolding.

4,167m is the highest African mountain north of the Sahara and lies only 39 kms south of Marrakech. The massif here (basically a large inselberg) contains three peaks of over 4,000m and its unique combination of elevation and geology means that it holds a special mix of flora and fauna. It is also high enough to have snow cover throughout the summer in some years. Oddly, however, it is difficult to view these high peaks clearly except when you hike from Imlil up the mountain (see route 2). From other directions, nearer peaks of the massif block the view.

The Anti-Atlas has a similar structure. Like the High Atlas, it consists mainly of folded sedimentary rocks, but again many of the main peaks, including the highest point, Jebel Sirwa (3,304 m), is of Precambrian volcanic origin. The Anti-Atlas lies wholly within Morocco and runs for 500 kms eastward from the Atlantic. It is not a single range, rather a fragmented series of sub-ranges that lie in a zone around 50km wide.

Both on the north and south side these ranges rather abruptly give way to the steppes. This sharp transition is the result of distinct tectonic fault lines. The fault line to the southern edge of the High Atlas is both extensive and active and is the main reason for the continuing geological instability in the area. Earthquakes are common and although most are small, they can on occasions be destructive. The 1960 earthquake in Agadir was the worst in Morocco's history and flattened the city, killing around 15,000 people.

GEOLOGY

Different rock types

In addition to the ancient igneous (volcanic) and more recent sedimentary rocks there are other rock types to be found.

As the bedrock was folded, the heat and pressure were in some places so intense that the original material changed its structure and 'metamorphosed' into shales and slates. In the most actively folded areas, the pressure extended all the way into the deep earth crust. In places, the pressure became too strong and the crust ripped open, allowing hot magma to rise up from the earth's mantle. These so-called igneous dykes cooled to form 'veins' of very hard rock. Both of these rocks are best searched for near the fault lines and are most easily seen in the Anti-Atlas, were the lack of vegetation makes them very visible.

At the other end of the hardness spectrum are the most recent and very unstable sedimentary layers. These are close to the surface and as they haven't been folded, they nearly all bed horizontally. These include soft sandstones, mudstones and particularly sedimentary conglomerates – rock made up of boulders that are locked in soft sediments, much no doubt material from the high peaks as they eroded. In places these conglomerate layers are over 70m thick and form unstable hillsides, especially in the High Atlas. These zones are very susceptible to landslides making the road building difficult as the soil is soft and friable.

Across the whole region, sedimentary rocks from the Cretaceous era are incredibly rich in marine fossils. Belemnites, trilobites, ammonites and other prehistoric species are amazingly common and often can be found simply lying at the base of bluffs and cliffs. A whole industry has sprung up collecting, preparing and selling these to tourists and you will see stalls and shops in all the towns offering them for sale.

Steppes

The original strata that formed the mountains are present to the north and the south of the mountains as well, but they remain horizontal as they are unaffected by the folding of the mountain ranges. Although originally of the same strata the area to the north of the fold zone is 300m lower than those on the south. On the north they are covered by what we call the Low Arid Steppes in this guide and to the south are the High Arid Steppes.

As with the mountain zones there are Precambrian outcrops of igneous rocks in the steppes as well. These are particularly prevalent at the fault zones around the edges towards the coastal area and the edges of the continental plates and become less frequent as you move south and east.

GEOLOGY

As most of the rocks are sedimentary, and some of these very soft indeed, the main features of the arid steppes are the bluffs from fault lines and the carved gorges that hark back to a time when the environment was wetter and rivers regularly flowed down from the mountains. These wadis have persisted and have been enlarged by the rare, but sometimes violent, flash flood events that can follow rainfall in the steppes and the nearby mountains.

Sahara

Further south, the Sahara edge is also relatively flat and lower still at 750m above sea level. If the steppes can still be said to be impacted by water, the Saharan landscape is defined by wind. Most of the wider Sahara is a sedimentary depression but in the northern edge there is a number of bluffs at the fault lines, rippling southward from the mountain ranges. There are, however, few water-created features such as gorges or wadis. The typical landscape along the Sahara edge is the gravel plain. The surface is matrix of rock fragments that have previously eroded from the bedrock and supplemented by the erosion from bluffs and outcrops, including the mountain ranges to the north.

Sand is created by thermal erosion of exposed rock. The extreme temper-

The Sahara is mainly gravel plains interspersed with bluffs

LANDSCAPE

GEOLOGY

ature fluctuations, in combination with the wind, peels the sand off the rock like cells from a skin. The sand has been blown here from all over the Saharan depression. The southerly winds frequently blanket the area with new deposits, mostly as small mobile dune systems that 'flow' over the gravel below. Rarely, these aggregated to form 'ergs', or sand seas. By definition, an erg covers at least 125 square kilometres and forms very impressive dunes, in places reaching over 150 m high. The sand dunes of Erg Chebbi are the finest and most accessible example of this classic Saharan landscape. Another large sand sea is around M'hamid, with another large dune at nearby Chigaga.

As with higher up in the steppes and the mountains, the desert edge too has its share of Cretaceous limestone rock at the surface. As higher up, fossils are plentiful in the bedrock. They are continuously exposed by the process of exfoliation, the peeling back of the rock face by expansion and contraction due to the massive temperature ranges here. As fossil hunters are less frequent, there are still places where visitors can find fossils simply scattered around on the ground.

Desert rivers can only be seen after rains and over impervious rocks, where the water is forced to the surface, as here near Tizzint.

Khettaras – irrigating the desert

Whilst on the surface the land may seem dead and dry, there is a flow of life-nurturing water flowing underground, well-shielded from the desiccating powers of the sun. The water runs largely through man-made underground canals, the *khettaras*. Although there may be not be much to look at in the field, you can marvel at the ingenuity of these constructions.

Khettaras is the local name of the ancient Persian technology of *qanats* (canals), that are dug between well-shafts to divert water flows. The khettaras were initially formed to improve existing oases. With growing sophistication, they were used to create man-made oases and irrigation channels.

In Morocco, the khettaras system is quite complex as it has to follow the heavily folded and faulted permeable rocks. More shafts were needed and tunnelling between shafts was required to initiate the flow. In addition, water was actively captured at the base of mountain slopes to encourage as much water as possible to enter the khettaras. In places, cisterns were dug to increase the amount of water stored in the system and ensure that during drought at least some water was available. The khettaras needed almost constant maintenance as they are prone to silting up, and the flow would divert over time into unwanted directions. However, the success of the system can still be seen today in the extensive palmeries in the two valleys leading to the Sahara – the Drâa River valley and further east around the Tafilalt-Rissani area. These have relied on khettaras water for irrigation since the late 14th century.

There is little to see on the surface, but an ad-hoc 'museum' to this has been set up near Jorf (see route 10). Between Rissani and Erfoud the line of spoil heaps follows the old road, unfortunately looking more like fly tipping than a historic relict.

Hydrology

In more northerly areas such as Europe, transpiration from vegetation and evaporation from lakes and rivers drives (in part) the cycle of water. Tree leaves and surface water makes the air humid, clouds are formed and rain falls, often not too far from where the water evaporated in the first place.

In such an arid and barren region as Southern Morocco, there is little surface water or vegetation, and this local hydrological circle does not exist. Water is only available if it is carried into the region by the large-scale weather systems, nearly exclusively from the nearby ocean. Here, it is only the highest of mountains that are able to force humid air upwards high enough to form clouds that provide the life-giving rain and snow. Therefore, it is the High Atlas that dominates the hydrology of the region. The Anti-Atlas Mountains, just a little lower and a hundred or so kilometres to the south, are too low to create sufficient clouds and are substantially drier.

Even so, the High Atlas Mountains are not big generators of rain, in part because the offshore Canary current prevents the ocean winds from travelling inland (see page 27). In the mountains rain and snow are almost wholly limited to the cooler winter months. There are no icesheets or glaciers and the snow fields rarely persist through the summer months. This means that there are no permanent sources for streams and rivers and nearly all water courses are liable to dry out during the summer months. Away from the High Atlas Mountains, many valleys are called 'wadis', meaning that they hold water only immediately after rain. Where they run over permeable rocks they wash out, the water disappearing into the bedrock rather than continuing to flow towards the sea.

There are four key rivers in the area, and all spring in the High Atlas Mountains. Running towards the south are the Drâa and the Souss, and to the north the Tensift and its tributary the N'fis. Most of them are heavily modified with multiple dams to keep the precious water as long as possible. The Tensift brings water to the increasingly intensive agriculture of the northern low steppe. The water is divided over so many channels and irrigates so much land, that there is not much left of the original river system.

The Souss flows east to west, reaching the Atlantic just south of Agadir and dominates the low lying plain between the High Atlas and the Anti-Atlas. This triangular area, that opens to the Atlantic in the west is both wetter and hotter than the surrounding parts of Morocco. The Drâa picks

HYDROLOGY

up flow from the Dadès and Imini Rivers and heads due south before flowing through the Sahara zone on the Algerian border to finally reach the sea near Tan-Tan. This is Morocco's longest river at about 1,100km. Again, it has been adapted for agriculture and the Dadès is famous for its Damask Roses. South of the Anti-Atlas, palmeries stretch along the Drâa's banks providing the classic oasis feel to the landscape. In the harsh environment of southern Morocco, the river valleys are about the only places that can be cultivated. For centuries, the locals have stored and modified the available water to attempt to provide a more consistent flow for growing crops. There are also cultural reasons for the extensive water management of the river valleys. With the arrival of Islam that values water in its view of 'heaven on earth' the technology of irrigation increased with the skills and expertise that they brought from the Middle East. With large areas of permeable rocks, many water sources and rivers 'flow' below ground. Much of the water charges the deep Saharan aquifer that sits largely untapped below the depression. Locally, it rises to the surface creating the famous desert oases of the Sahara. Settlers to these lands recognised that accessing and directing these water flows could increase both the amount of water and the consistency of the flow, therefore making living and agriculture possible. This, in turn, enabled the locals to move from their historic nomadic lifestyle to permanently settling these arid lands. The main water management was the digging of khettaras, a network of subterranean irrigation canals (see text box on page 23). By the late 20th century, this traditional water management had largely been superseded by a number of large concrete dams and associated irrigation channels built to serve the burgeoning population of the region. Their impact on the local hydrology has resulted in the khettaras drying and being abandoned in many areas, particularly north of the High Atlas, around Marrakech and the Haouz plain.

Although wadis are normally dry, localised rain storms suddenly transform them into torrents that can make travelling a challenge.

LANDSCAPE

Climate

Heat dominates the Moroccan climate. The towns have tightly packed buildings and narrow streets to provide shade. In the fields, trees are planted to enable the crops beneath to escape the worst of the heat. Yet, to simply state that Southern Morocco is hot oversimplifies the complex relationship between the topography, the ocean and latitude.

As a broad brush, it gets hotter and drier the further south you go and the further you go from the sea. The mountains, both Anti-Atlas and High Atlas, provide relief as they are high enough for the temperatures to be appreciably lower at their summits than on the surrounding plains and they attract cloud formation and, in case of the High Atlas, precipitation. In addition, the shading provided by their bulk means the north facing slopes are much cooler than those facing south.

The Atlantic provides a cooling influence and more humidity and therefore the coast is cooler and wetter than the areas further inland. Seasonal differences are also marked with winters being wetter and cooler than summers. All of these general trends hold true, but the details of how they interact and the impact on localised climate ultimately drives the ecosystems and land use in each area.

The climate is a result of the battle between the continental weather systems, generally formed in the Saharan depression and moving north

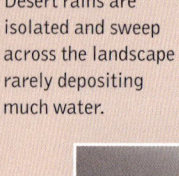

Desert rains are isolated and sweep across the landscape rarely depositing much water.

into the region, meeting the oceanic weather systems driven by the Atlantic currents from the west.
Southern Morocco is washed by the southern edge of the North Atlantic Conveyor (formerly known as the Gulf Stream), however this southern branch forms a cold offshore circulation of water, known as the Canaries Current. This north-south flow of water stalls the air movement above it. Therefore, throughout much of year the usual westerly Atlantic frontal weather is negligible and is replaced by a stationary high-pressure system that prevents the cool, rain-bearing winds from making landfall. This has a substantial impact on the local climate, both in respect of temperature and rainfall. In some years, the stationary high pressure never relinquishes its grip, resulting in prolonged drought and rising temperatures.

Temperature

As we have mentioned, Morocco is hot and in defining temperatures there is often confusion over the numbers mentioned. Most climate statistics are defined by average daily temperature or peak daily temperature. In low humidity areas such as the desert, the temperature range is often 20°C resulting in a large gap between the two figures. In addition, in common with convention, all quoted numbers are shade temperatures. As there is little shade in the desert, temperatures are at least 10°C hotter than quoted. Furthermore, temperatures in the desert rise and fall strongly over the day, obscuring a much higher peak temperature. Marrakech, for example, has peak summer temperatures of just over 40°C in summer and 15-20°C in winter. Here, the nights stay relatively warm due to the higher humidity of the northern Low Arid Steppes. Ouarzazate, although with very similar average figures, tends to be hotter on summer days and colder on summer nights due to the lower humidity and higher altitude. In the winter nights, the temperature will occasionally drop to zero just before dawn and even snow has been recorded.
This pattern is repeated close along the Saharan edge, where peak daytime temperatures are higher still. Night-time frosts are rare, but since there is little cloud to hold the temperature once the sun has gone down, it can still get very chilly at night.
Along the coastal strip, the summer heat is reduced by cool onshore breezes aided by the relatively cold waters just offshore. Normally, the mercury doesn't reach over 30°C. Fog is a feature of the coast and provides shading, so even then the effective temperature is not much more. The higher humidity along the coast also holds a higher night-time temperature. Frosts are very rare here.

CLIMATE AND WEATHER

As mentioned before, the stable and cool coastal system blocks the air circulation inland. In the summer, the Souss valley often becomes stuck in stationary weather systems, jammed between the mountains and the sea. The heat just builds, with little relief at night. This often becomes the hottest part of Southern Morocco with peak temperatures in the high 40s and even above.

In the High Atlas Mountains, the temperature decreases with altitude and can be 15°C cooler than nearby Marrakech, with freezing periods during the winter in the Alpine zones. Still summer peak temperatures of 30°C at 3,000m are not exceptional. Of course, here cloud cover is more prevalent, and precipitation can cool the land very quickly. This rainfall does not only impact the weather in the High Atlas Mountain, rain falling here generates winds immediately to the south, with a cooler northerly airflow blowing off the mountainsides onto the steppes and Sahara edge, especially in the afternoons.

Further south during late spring or summer, a hot, dusty wind from the Sahara frequently blows up with southerly, desiccating winds of over 40°C. These can whip up the sand and dust into a thick blanket that hampers visibility and makes being outside very uncomfortable.

Rainfall

The High Atlas Mountains receive some 760 mm of rainfall per year, the majority of it in winter (for comparison, the annual average for

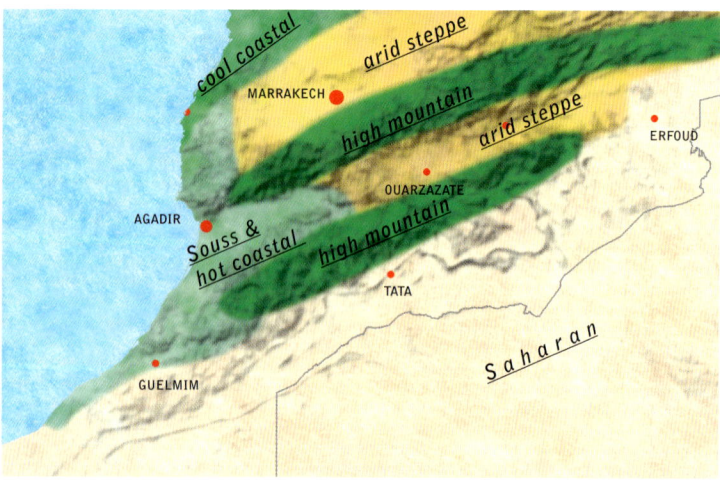

London is 615 mm). Snow is common down to approximately 2,000 metres and will occasionally block the roads and passes over the mountains. The snowpack lingers in the highest elevations until late spring or early summer but rarely lasts through the year, even on the highest of north facing slopes. The Anti-Atlas Mountains are substantially more arid than the High Atlas. Only the Atlantic facing slopes have more rain than the surrounding area which is limited to around 200mm per year. In addition, only in extreme circumstances will this fall as snow on the higher peaks.

Reservoirs have been constructed to capture rainfall, here at Ouarzazate.

Due to their height, the mountain ranges do create a significant rain shadow, meaning that to the east, the land is in the lee of the prevailing winds, and the rainfall is much lower. Therefore, the desert reaches much further north here than in the more westerly districts. Away from the mountains, the majority of Southern Morocco is officially classified as desert with less than 250mm of rainfall per year. The average precipitation decreases from north to south and from the coast to inland. For example, Essaouira on the coast north of the High Atlas has a mean annual rainfall approaching 300mm, but this mean is down to 250mm and less in the Souss Valley near Agadir and further south by Tiznit it is barely 200mm per year. Heading inland the mean rainfall on the High Arid Steppes around Ouarzazate is only 100mm per year and even this drops further as you approach the edge of the Sahara, for example, Rissani (the main town near the sand dunes of Erg Chebbi) is classed as having less than 70mm of rain per year.

However, quoting annual averages is only part of the story. Many areas have all of their rainfall during a single storm and it is not unusual for these storms not to happen on an annual cycle. Therefore, in any single year, there may be no rain or only patchy showers.

HABITATS

Habitats

"a plant on the edge of a desert is said to struggle for life against the drought, though more properly it should be said to be dependent upon the moisture."
Charles Darwin, On the Origin of Species

Habitat is defined as the intersection of flora and fauna with the geology, hydrology, climate, topography of any given place. This latter group is the landscape and by understanding the landscape a biologist can understand what species can thrive there.
Nearly all of Morocco's habitats are Mediterranean; in fact, this is considered the second most diverse country within the Mediterranean basin in terms of flora and fauna. This biodiversity is due to the wide variety of different habitats.
As Darwin alluded to,

Schematic cross-section of the habitats of Southern Morocco.

HABITATS

the key to understanding the biodiversity in this parched land is to follow the water. The relative scarcity of it defines what can, and cannot, survive. Climate, combined with the permeability of the underlying rock and the altitude creates a mosaic of micro-climates and with each comes a different mix of flora and fauna adapted to surviving the particular challenges of their environs.

In an attempt to categorise this diversity, scientists have recognised and categorised 29 different biological ecosystems within Morocco as a whole. Although this is the result of an attempt to more accurately guide the expert, it is confusing to the visitor. We have taken a simpler approach with seven areas that, although not necessarily totally honouring the scientific definitions and a little simplistic, does form a practical guide to the variety of landscapes and the species likely to be found in each habitat.

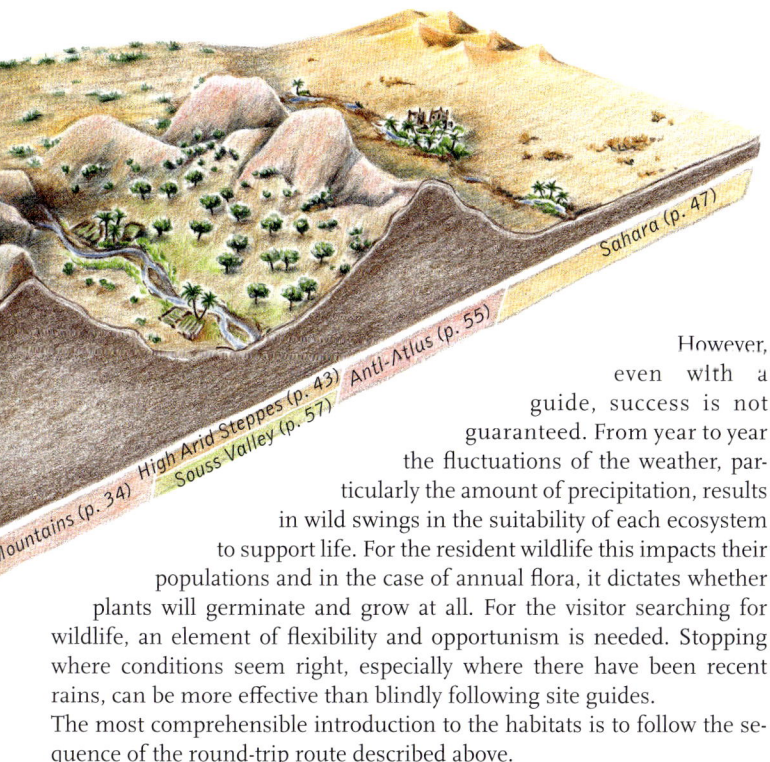

Mountains (p. 34) High Arid Steppes (p. 43) Anti-Atlas (p. 55) Souss Valley (p. 57) Sahara (p. 47)

However, even with a guide, success is not guaranteed. From year to year the fluctuations of the weather, particularly the amount of precipitation, results in wild swings in the suitability of each ecosystem to support life. For the resident wildlife this impacts their populations and in the case of annual flora, it dictates whether plants will germinate and grow at all. For the visitor searching for wildlife, an element of flexibility and opportunism is needed. Stopping where conditions seem right, especially where there have been recent rains, can be more effective than blindly following site guides.

The most comprehensible introduction to the habitats is to follow the sequence of the round-trip route described above.

LANDSCAPE

Low Arid Steppe

Most visitors arrive in Marrakech, which is the region's largest city and is well connected with Europe. The city now has grown to a population of around 1 million and it dominates the Haouz plain, the section of the Low Arid Steppe beyond the city walls, or what remains of it.
The area is flat with views to the south to the High Atlas Mountains.
As the name suggests, the Low Arid Steppe lies at a relatively low altitude compared to the steppes south of the High Atlas. It has an overall Mediterranean climate, meaning it is relatively wet in the winter period, although, with permeable soils and few rivers, the natural vegetation is still dry and scrubby. However, much of it is urban or converted to agriculture leaving little of the natural habitat remaining.
To the northern side of the city, the land is initially dominated by the formal gardens of the royal palaces and then the typical low intensity agriculture that covers nearly every part of the land not yet built upon. The trip out of the city is marked by a journey across the flat lands where houses, shops and other buildings stretch along most of the major routes. Only by going on the side roads do you escape the modern linear development and find the network of traditional small arable fields. For most of the year these seem rather scruffy, and it is not easy telling the difference between those that are abandoned, those that are fallow for that season and those that will be prepared for planting.
The natural vegetation consists of scattered bushes and isolated stands of Barbary Gum and Wild Pistachio. Remnants of it dot the landscape, but in most places, the wild trees have been supplemented by eucalyptus

Medina gardens with High Atlas behind – a place of tranquillity in the bustle of Marrakech.

LOW ARID STEPPE

and orchards of citrus and other commercially valuable trees.

Most of the area is heavily irrigated. The historic system of khetteras (see page 23) has been abandoned and concrete channels are now a familiar sight bringing water from the dams higher in the mountains or supplementing the flow of the River Tensift and its tributary the N'fis. The natural beds of the rivers are nearly always reduced to pools or even totally dry, except in the snow melt season. Nevertheless, the riverbeds are lined with dense vegetation.

The area is not generally of much interest to the visitor, but this is a distinct habitat and some Maghreb endemic species such as Barbary Partridge, and in winter, Moussier's Redstart are easy to find. One Mahgreb speciality easily found here is the Maghreb Magpie. Superficially it looks very like the familiar Eurasian Magpie from the rest of Europe, but is readily identified by the patch of blue skin around the eye. Since the environment in the Low Arid Steppes is less harsh than in the other parts of southern Morocco insects and reptiles are more numerous and can be easier to find, being active longer into the winter than in higher areas. Most are species that have a typical Mediterranean distribution and may not be the main target of visiting naturalists. Amphibians are typical of this group, being more plentiful than elsewhere. Two of them, the Moroccan Painted Frog and Moroccan Toad, can both be found around watercourses.

Plain Tiger (top) and the endemic Maghreb Magpie (bottom) are both common and showy species in the Low Arid Steppe.

Butterflies can be common around the field edges, with Plain Tiger and African Babel Blue being the most interesting species for the visitor. Find them by looking for the flowers and nectar sources that attract them.

Most visitors cross this area quickly and travel south to the High Atlas. Although mountain slopes rise abruptly from the plain, the underlying geology and land use does not immediately change. Only as the road climbs higher the true character of the mountains can be seen.

LANDSCAPE

The High Atlas Mountains

> Routes 1-5 and the sites on pages 156-159 visit the High Atlas Mountains.

The High Atlas is a formidable mountain range. With peaks over 4,000m it is almost as high as the peaks of the Alps. Ascending brings you past several distinct vegetation zones, which are very different on the northern slope from those on the southern slope due to the shadowing effect of the mountains themselves.

Heading south from Marrakech and leaving the steppe, the zone up to 1,800m is covered in natural woodland and areas of scrub of distinctly Mediterranean character. Above that lies the Sub-alpine zone, between 1,800m and approximately 2,400m. Here the woodland is more open, interspersed by meadows with cold-adapted species. The treeline lies at roughly 2,400m, which is, perhaps surprisingly, not much higher than the treeline in the central European mountains. In the High Atlas, it is not only the low temperature that sets the treeline. Rather it is the temperature in combination with drought that make tree growth impossible.

Snow regularly falls down to 2000m in the High Atlas Mountains.

The treeless areas above 2,400m are in the Alpine zone where the slopes are covered in scree, dry grasslands and, for much of the year, snow fields. Needless to say, each of these vegetation zones has its own particular flora and fauna.

After crossing the pass, the southern face of the mountains has a distinctly different flavour. Here the direct rays of the sun desiccate the soil and the vegetation is much reduced except in the river valleys. There are few trees and the scrubby maquis type vegetation survives only in a narrow band just below the snow line.

The low slopes (up to 1,800 metres)

The main roads up to the cols (tizis) that give access to the southern slopes each follow deeply carved river valleys. They thread between the houses of mountain villages keeping above the riverbeds that flood regularly. Nearly all of the valleys are inhabited and worked for a range of arable crops, meaning that finding undisturbed natural vegetation is very difficult.

The lower north facing slopes themselves are covered in coniferous woods (route 3), where the predominant tree is the Aleppo Pine. Although this is the native tree here, most of the forest is man-made to some extent, and planting continues today as part of the concerted effort to manage the water catchments. Within the natural stands, the pine is frequently accompanied by Barbary Thuja, a species endemic to the western Mediterranean basin. The iconic Atlas Cedar grows in isolated stands in the eastern High Atlas, but to find the full ecosystem associated with the majestic cedar forests you need to head further north out of our region into the Middle Atlas.

Yellow Bee Orchid (top) and Portuguese Squill (bottom) are two Mediterranean species that occur locally on the lower slopes.

The woods are a resource for the villages and are extensively grazed by herds of goats and sheep. These are so prolific that except in the fenced areas the natural understorey of herbs and shrubs is rarely visible. Where the grazing is controlled, there is a spring flush of wildflowers, including Yellow Bee and Mirror Orchids. Often more noticeable are the plants that can withstand the ravages of the livestock, especially the unpalatable white-flowered Branched Asphodels, which, together with a number of other species, have a second flowering season in the autumn when the first of the rains brings a 'second spring'.

Although the components of the ecosystem are familiar from the Mediterranean basin there is a twist. Many of the common species have evolved into distinct local forms. With birds, this includes the endemic

THE HIGH ATLAS MOUNTAINS

African Blue Tit and Levaillant's Woodpecker together with distinct local subspecies of Red Crossbill (ssp *poliogyna*), Coal Tit (ssp *atlas*), and Chaffinch (ssp *africana*).

There are no particular butterflies in this habitat, but widespread species can be found. Moroccan and Desert Orange-tips and Moroccan Hairstreaks are widespread and of interest. The African Knapweed Fritillary can also be sought here.

The valleys themselves are dominated by Poplars, including the more drought tolerant Desert Poplar* (*Populus euphratica*), which are an important source of building material and provide shade to the small arable fields. In addition, other fruiting trees are grown, notably Olives, Almonds, Pistachios, Pomegranates and Apples.

The near permanence of the streams means that amphibians can be found, such as Moroccan Painted Frog and Spiny Toad (or Southern Common Toad). The stream beds are also attractive to dragonflies, including species that are endemic to the Maghreb, including Barbary Featherleg and Atlas Goldenring. In the western High Atlas, the more Mediterranean type environment also supports species from that area (route 23). Of note is the Ringed Cascader, a large well-marked species, which likes the more Mediterranean-style habitat afforded here.

In addition, some of these valleys have been dammed for reservoirs that supply water to the surrounding area. Originally these were local schemes, but large-scale concrete dams were built more recently to secure water for the towns on the steppe below and fill the irrigation channels. The areas close to these reservoirs are taken out of production and now are the best places to look for the more natural vegetation. Cistuses, brooms, rockroses, lavenders and other groups familiar from the Mediterranean basin dominate these areas, although the species that represent these groups are often endemic to these mountains.

The valleys in the High Atlas Mountains are dominated by Poplars, beneath which crops are grown in their shade.

THE HIGH ATLAS MOUNTAINS

The Sub-alpine zone (1,800 to 2,400 metres)

Above 1,800m on the north-facing slopes the forest begins to open out and the dominant pines of the lower slopes give way to junipers. This marks the transition to the Sub-alpine zone. (route 2 and 4). Here the sharp ridges and incised valleys become clearer to see. The slopes are steeper and the friable rocks and the scree slopes become notable. Where vegetation can survive, which is normally where the substrate is volcanic rather than sedimentary, there is a mix of open low-density woodland, interspersed with open meadow of dwarf scrubs, grasses and other flora. During the coldest of winters, the Sub-alpine zone is covered in snow, however in most years there are shorter episodes of snow with only brief flurries. Together with the cold this is enough to inhibit growth and therefore the growing season is limited to the spring, and again in the autumn. During the summer plants aestivate (sleep through the summer) due to the high temperature and lack of rain.

Three species of junipers co-exist on these slopes, namely Thuriferous* (*Juniperus thurifera var africana*), Prickly and Phoenician Juniper. They are joined in some places by the Barbary Thuja that are also present on the lower slopes. Another special tree, the critically endangered endemic Moroccan Cyprus* (*Cupressus atlantica*) can be found in the upper reaches of the Oued N'Fis. The understory is much thinner as the trees provide little shading and the meadows dry out in summer. Drought tolerant dwarf shrubs and brooms cover the open parts of the slopes.

Where grazing pressure allows it, there are some spectacular wildflowers to be found. These include many asters and other annuals (often being endemic forms or species). More notable are the bulbous plants, like daffodils, irises, leeks (or *Alliums*) and other relatives of the lily family. They can put up a great show, especially in spring, but also in autumn. Their beauty is short-lived though, as these plants flower and wither in two to three weeks. Unfortunately, their flowering time is hard to predict accurately as the plants respond strongly to the local weather conditions and the extent of the previous winter's snow fall.

The slopes above Imlil show the transition to the Sub-alpine zone.

LANDSCAPE

THE HIGH ATLAS MOUNTAINS

From March well into summer the Sub-alpine slopes attract a good number of butterflies, many of which are endemic to the Maghreb countries. Of particular interest are the Vogel's Blue and Vaucher's Heath. Reptiles are also adapted to survive these areas. The endemic Vaucher's Wall Lizard is the most likely to be seen, especially in more rocky patches. The Moroccan Ocellated Lizard and the Common Chameleon can also be found as high as the Sub-alpine zone. Although much scarcer than the Vaucher's Wall Lizard, they can be easier to see here than lower down the slopes where the vegetation is thicker and the reptiles need less time to bask.

The valleys are steeper and the beds of the streams are strewn with boulders. Villages still cling to the mountain sides, but are less frequent and smaller. Surprisingly, small arable plots are still carved out from the valley floor and Almonds and Pistachios provide shade to the Barley and other low intensity arable crops. However, at this elevation the agricultural focus shifts to livestock. Sheep and goats are kept and move seasonally between the open forest here and the Alpine meadows higher on the slopes.

Vaucher's Heath (top) and Allard's Silver-line (bottom) are two Maghreb endemics limited to the sub-alpine zone of the High Atlas and Anti-Atlas.

The water management, including the digging of pools and cisterns has created good habitat for dragonflies and amphibians. A surprising number of species are able to find suitable habitat high into this zone. Dragonflies are largely those that can cope with the seasonal torrents and rocky streambeds such as the Atlas Goldenring and various pincertails. These streams also hold birds more typically thought of as being from Europe. Grey Wagtail and Dipper both occur, the latter of the Maghreb endemic subspecies minor. Along the banks the large trees are an attraction to the endemic Levaillant's Woodpecker. Its ringing call is a familiar sound in the High Atlas Mountains in the spring.

Opposite page: The heavily grazed slopes of the alpine zone at Oukaimeden.

Alpine zone (above 2,400 metres)

True Alpine habitat is treeless and covered in snow during the winter, which holds well into spring. The mountains are barren and stark with sharp eroded edges and with a heavily incised topography.

Accessing the Alpine zone is usually tricky and time consuming. There are only seasonal villages connected by rough tracks and even the highest roads only cross into the lowest hundred metres or so of this altitude zone. To go higher you need to walk from one of the mountain passes or walk upwards from one of the main trekking centres such as Imlil (route 2). Those interested in exploring the Alpine zone of the Toubkal Massif should hire a guide, who can ensure that both the route is safe and support is at hand (see page 259).

The easily accessible Ouikaïmeden (route 1) is by far the best way to explore the Alpine zone. A tarmacked road goes up to over 2,600m to Ouikaïmeden, which is just over an 80 km drive from

THE HIGH ATLAS MOUNTAINS

Marrakech. It is a stretch to call it a ski resort as four of the five simple ski lifts only operate when the snow is right. Still the road is kept open all through the winter.

At Oukaïmeden, the mountains surround a large Alpine meadow and all consist of sedimentary rocks, predominantly limestones. There are tracks from the upper car parks that can be followed on foot. The last section of the access road crosses good transitionary habitat from the Sub-alpine to the Alpine levels.

In the first few hundred metres above the tree line, grasses and scattered dwarf bushes survive in a similar but more extreme version of those species found in the Sub-alpine zone. It is this vegetation and the spring flush of growth for which goat and sheep herders bring their flocks up from the lower slopes. The mountain sides are dotted with the simple shelters that provide the homes for the shepherds and their families during the summer months.

Immediately following snow melt, flowers appear, the majority being either bulbs or annuals, that provide a focus for the visiting botanist. Getting the timing right for a visit is tricky, as the heavy grazing pressure can remove the flower heads and, especially on the south facing slopes, the ground dries very quickly, leaving only a very small window for both the plants and their admirers. Because of this very short flowering season, it is worth looking in places where there is shade and residual water, which prolong the flowering season somewhat.

As the summer progresses, it is only the vegetation adapted to drought and extreme temperature fluctuations that can survive. It is these

Choughs, of both species, are found in the alpine zone across the High Atlas.

THE HIGH ATLAS MOUNTAINS

extremes of conditions that triggered plants to evolve specific adaptions against drought, heat and cold.

The High Atlas Alpine zone forms an isolated ecosystem. The Middle Atlas and the Rif are both substantially lower, with very limited true Alpine habitat in the former and none in the latter, which means that the closest range with similar conditions is the Sierra Nevada in Southern Spain. Plants and insects in the High Atlas have evolved here in near-perfect isolation, hence the percentage of endemic species in the Alpine zone is the highest of all of the Southern Moroccan habitats. Even with the large grazing pressure, Alpine plants hang on, and the bulbs especially can be spectacular with several endemic fritillaries and narcissi.

For butterfly lovers, the Alpine zone as very attractive as well. The highest diversity of butterflies is lower down, but the true specialists are found up here. In summer, there is a wide range of endemic graylings on the wing. Of particular interest are the two Berberia species, Giant and Dark Giant Grayling that are found around the scree slopes (see page 130).

Naturally, the roof of the Atlas is the realm of the native Barbary Sheep. After years of absence these wild sheep have been reintroduced in the area (see page 100). They are not easy to find but look carefully when you are close to the tree line, as this is where they often are.

Among the birds, the iconic species of the Alpine zone is the African Crimson-winged Finch. It is probably resident along the whole of the range but easiest to see at Oukäimeden. Like many mountain birds, they are ambivalent to human contact and at times they can appear quite tame around the market areas and the ski pulls. However, they are really looking for seeds at the edge of melting snow patches and therefore are nomadic throughout the whole area, meaning even here they can be difficult to find. Once the snow has gone, they tend to go higher still, beyond the reach of the casual visitor. Other typical birds of these areas are Atlas Wheatear, Horned Lark (*ssp atlas*) and both Red-billed and Alpine Choughs.

Perhaps surprisingly, but with summer temperatures regularly over 20°C, it is warm enough even in the Alpine zone to support reptiles and many of them are unique to these high rocky slopes. Skinks, lizards and geckos all have endemic mountain forms that survive in this extreme environment.

The south-facing slope

Heading on south from the top, the journey down the mountains on the southern slopes is not a simple repeat of the journey up. The direct

THE HIGH ATLAS MOUNTAINS

The south-facing slope of the High Atlas, here near Tizi n'Tichka lacks the trees and scrub of the shaded north (top). The endemic Tristram's warbler is a feature of these dry slopes (bottom).

sun on the slopes has an enormous desiccating effect. The snow line is higher and the tree line lower. Only scrubby brooms and cistuses can survive in the south-facing Sub-alpine zone and they are stunted specimens in otherwise open scree slopes. Lower down, the trees reappear, but in a very different habitat from that on the north slope. The pine forests, so typical of the lower slopes to the north, are replaced by acacias and towards the western end of the range, the endemic Argan forests reach up onto the lower slopes of the mountains (see page 92). Elsewhere there is little permanent vegetation except in the few river valleys. The rivers are fewer and carry less water than on the northern slopes, but even here they have been adapted for agriculture and planted in a similar manner to that seen on the north side.

Wildlife on the south-facing slopes needs to be able to withstand the direct rays of the sun. The species found here are more typical of the High Arid Steppe than of the mountains themselves.

The higher elevations, where bushes and scrubby understorey is present, is the favoured breeding haunt of the endemic Tristram's Warbler and you should listen out for its scratchy song in the spring. It is often joined by Moussier's Redstart and Rock Sparrows.

High Arid Steppes

> Routes 6 to 9 and the sites on page 173-175 visit the High Arid Steppes.

The area to the south of the High Atlas has a very different character from the low steppe on the north side of the range. Here it looks like desert – open, flat and desolate, with few trees and little in the way of green vegetation. There are only scattered signs of human habitation. This is not surprising as the as the rainfall is similar to that in the desert, and as the altitude ranges between 1100-1500m above sea level, it is quite cold, particularly at night when frost and snow are not unheard of in winter. The lack of water is exacerbated by the predominance of permeable sedimentary rock. Surface water soon percolates into the rocks beneath.

There is a complete ecosystem attuned to this environment. The shrubs are mainly drought-resistant wormwoods (*Artemesia*). Underneath their shadows survives a rich insect life and upwards along the food chain is a surprising diversity of highly-adapted fauna that thrives under these harsh conditions. It is these specialists that make this area so exciting to the visiting naturalist.

As with elsewhere, the ability to 'read' the steppe is key to finding where the species are. Sandier areas tend to hold a higher diversity than those on rocky beds and this is where you should concentrate your efforts. Rain falls mainly in October and November, and two or three months on is when the majority of plants are in bloom, with a short-lived herb layer joining the shrubs and setting seed shortly after.

The High Arid Steppes are mainly gravel, with scattered low artemisia shrubs.

LANDSCAPE

HIGH ARID STEPPES

Because of the permeable bedrock, there are few permanent river valleys. Across most of the steppes, wadis congregate the season's rainfall, and then rather than forming flowing rivers into a catchment, the water 'washes out' into the flat areas lower down the course. This action accumulates seeds and vegetable matter and other detritus that attracts life. The few trees that survive are concentrated in these washout zones and the most likely are acacias and Date Palms. After any further rains these zones become suddenly alive with new growth as the seeds germinate and a new season's growth then attracts a web of life to take advantage of the sudden bounty of nectar, plants and seeds. Invertebrates will respond quickly to the new food sources and then vertebrates including birds, mammals and reptiles follow on. These are the places you should concentrate searches. Cape Hares will be present although the normal view is one shooting away after being flushed. In the softer sandier areas, Fat Sand Rats (see page 96) nest in colonial burrows and these engaging animals can often easily be seen going about their business.

The Fat Sand Rat (top) and Thick-billed Lark (bottom) are specialists adapted to the variable food supply and hard seeds of the local plants.

Not all of the burrows are inhabited by mammals. These are also used by Agamid lizards. The largest is the Moroccan Spiny-tailed Lizard, which can be seen basking and head nodding in the early mornings as they try to warm up.

If you've found such a good area, it is worth returning at dusk as many animals, such as small rodents and some reptiles are nocturnal. They do respond to the sudden abundance of life and vegetation just like the diurnal animals do. So, activity during the day is an indication that you might be successful with the nocturnal wildlife as well.

HIGH ARID STEPPES

The bird species are primarily a mix of open country species, dominated by larks and wheatears. These are all resident in Morocco, but are essentially nomadic across the steppe following suitable conditions that follow the patchy rain storms. Other dry country species that can be found in the steppes include sandgrouse, Cream-coloured Courser and Trumpeter Finch. These are all particular favourites with visiting birders. During migration, many species cross the High Arid Steppes on a broad front. They tend to congregate in the same places that hold the resident species and can be looked for at the same time. Birds that don't breed here such as Greater Short-toed Lark and Northern and Western Black-eared Wheatears all can be seen in large numbers.

The seemingly endless steppe still supports nomadic pastoralists.

River valleys

The main roads and most of the villages are concentrated along the lines of the two major rivers that rise in the High Atlas. In contrast to the many wadis we have just described, these carry water throughout the year. The Imini flows from west to east and the Dadès from east to west. Both meet at Ouarzazate and then head south as the Drâa. Both river valleys are heavily modified by arable farming. This is all low intensity agriculture, supported by irrigation from the river. Tamarisks and small trees are grown around the fields to supplement the shade. Along the Dadès, the fields are bordered by Damask roses, which flower in June and are cultivated for the rose water industry, a traditional product for cosmetics and food flavouring across the Arab world.

These rivers and some of their tributaries form deep gorges on the southern edge of the High Atlas, for example the Dades and Todra gorges

LANDSCAPE

HIGH ARID STEPPES

Date Palms grow in river valleys and are reliant upon both natural and man made water sources.

(route 7 and site E on page 167 respectively). As access is from the High Arid Steppe and the wildlife is more dominated by the arid country species, these are considered as part of this area rather than the mountains themselves.

Despite the altitude and the cold, palmeries have been established along some of the rivers, especially where khetteras supplement the water supply along the southern edge of High Atlas Mountains. The palmerie at Skoura (site C on page 166) is one of the largest and gives a good indication of the traditional lifestyle. The Date Palms are still underplanted with arable crops and the mud brick Kasbahs dot the landscape.

The low intensity agricultural areas, with a ready supply of water, are normally cleared of native plants although arable 'weeds' such as crucifers can be found around the tilled areas. These weedy areas can be good for the widespread butterfly species, particularly African Babel Blue, Spanish Festoon and Southern Scarce Swallowtails. Birds are attracted to the insects and Booted Eagles, although migratory, sometimes spend the winter here. Around the Kasbah's the fluting call of Blue Rock Thrush is often heard. House Bunting, Moussier's Redstart and wintering chats and warblers can all be found as well.

With increasing population pressure, new housing has recently appeared in other strategic locations along the main roads and there is increasing conversion of marginal land to agriculture by ploughing up the steppes away from the river valleys. How productive this will be remains to be seen but the damage to the habitat makes it unsuitable for the natural flora and fauna adapted to the local conditions. Fortunately, this appears to be a feature only of the main routes and by turning off on to side tracks pristine habitat can still be found.

CROSSBILL GUIDES • SOUTHERN MOROCCO

The Sahara

> Routes 10 to 14 and the sites on page 193-195 visit the Sahara.

"No man can live this life and emerge unchanged. He will carry, however faint, the imprint of the desert, the brand which marks the nomad; and he will have within him the yearning to return, weak or insistent according to his nature. For this cruel land can cast a spell which no temperate clime can match."
Quote by Wilfred Thesiger

The classic mental image of the Sahara is one of rolling sand dunes as far as the eye can see. This idealised vision is a feature of the southern boundary of the area covered in this book and can be satisfied at the 'dune seas' at Erg Chebbi, near Merzouga, and at M'hamid in the southern Drâa. Everywhere else it is the gravel plain that dominates this part of the Sahara – a rolling flat land of gravel and small stones. The plains are punctuated by isolated rocky outcrops and where there are depressions, sand can congregate, blown by the regular winds that cross the whole of Saharan depression. Very locally, gypsum deposits 'waterproof' bedrock where ephemeral lakes appear after the rains (e.g. route 11). Human habitation is infrequent and can only be found close to old oases or trading routes. Overall, this is a land of heat and wind.

Initially the Sahara is not visually distinct from the high steppes described in the previous chapter. Here you are greeted by the same dusty plains and small towns surrounded by Date Palms nestling wherever there is water. The few roads were built along the trading routes that served the

Halfa grass stabilises the dunes and is beloved of African Desert Warblers as a nest site.

LANDSCAPE

THE SAHARA

trans-Saharan camel trains to Mali. They follow the river valleys of the Drâa and the Ziz. Ecologically, the big difference from the High Arid Steppes is that the Sahara is, due to the lower elevation, both drier and hotter, and this becomes evident as you leave these valleys and head into the more remote areas beyond.

Despite the untouched appearance of the hinterland, humans have made a life here for many millennia. The original herding lifestyle developed as the desert expanded since the last African Humid Period (see page 81). Cattle and sheep were replaced by the Camel, a native of the Arabian peninsula, sometime around the 4th Century BCE. Although ideally adapted for these arid lands, the move to herding camels had a profound impact for the Berber nomads. Evolved to survive on desert vegetation, camels have an innate sense of where they have browsed, and will not return to a recently eaten area. The herdsmen are forced to move on continuously to keep pace with their charges.

Traditional Berber nomadic herdsmen are almost totally a thing of the past. Most have settled into the small desert towns, but you can still see their camels wandering in the landscape. These are all owned by someone, even if the herders are not immediately apparent.

Berber encampments at M'hamid.

Visiting the Sahara

Exploring the desert is different from nature watching elsewhere and a visit to the Sahara is for many the highlight to the trip to Southern Morocco. The immense space, the remoteness, the seeming indifference of the landscape to its visitors, the brutal heat and the total silence – the desert has a harsh beauty to it. One that easily leaves you in awe and feeling belittled by the scale of the emptiness. As the explorer Wilfred Thesiger noted, even a short trip can leave you changed forever.

The desert may appear lifeless, but it has a varied flora and fauna. The list of exciting species is long and diverse, but the densities are very low and finding wildlife is often a real (but pleasurable) challenge. To access all but the fringes of the Sahara demands specialist equipment and time

THE SAHARA

beyond the limits of a normal tourist visit. The more adventurous can try to go further off the beaten track but you need both preparation and expertise to do so. Even then the risks remain high as there is little chance of a rescue if you get it wrong. Rather than try to access it alone, it is simpler to hire a local 4x4 and nature guides and they will bring the best of areas within reach.

Gravel Plains

Large areas of gravel plain are completely devoid of plants, but where vegetation does occur, it consists – surprisingly – of trees. On the plains, Flat-topped Acacia (*Vachellia tortilis raddiana*) dot the landscape. Others, including the conspicuous rubbery-leaved Sodom's Apple Milkweed (*Calotropis procera*), primarily follow the wash out zones and depressions. The acacias flower in the autumn and their pollen and nectar provide valuable resource for insects, which in turn attract predators. It is not unusual to see these alive with birds, particularly warblers, chats and flycatchers, feasting on both insects and nectar. For these south-bound migrants in autumn it is one last opportunity to build up their fat reserves prior to attempting the perilous Saharan crossing.

Hoopoe Lark (top) and White-crowned Wheatear (bottom) are typical species of the gravel plains.

The other plentiful tree is the non-native Camel-thorn Acacia (*Vachellia erioloba*) which is a fodder plant. The leaves and especially the large bean pods provide sustenance for camels and goats. Initially only planted around palmeries, the Camel-thorn Acacia is now plentiful across the plains, probably spread widely by the domestic animals, which dropped the seeds with their dung.

Relatively few animals seek out these gravel plains as their permanent homes. The Agamas, which live in burrows are one such group, and most of the Desert Racers (a group of lizards) prefer these broken habitats. The most obvious bird is the White-crowned Wheatear that often appears to be the sole bird around, in part due to its habit of perching out in the open on whatever high spot it can find.

LANDSCAPE

THE SAHARA

When rain falls, the stony plain can be transformed remarkably quickly. Bulbs such as Broken Asphodel* (*Asphodelus refractus*) and White Asphodel* (*Asphodelus tenuifolius*) can respond very quickly. Ramad (*Euphorbia calyptrata*), Spider Flower (*Cleome africana*) and several grasses take longer to grow, but can form remarkably thick swathes of vegetation, especially in the depressions and wash out zones.

This brief flush of growth attracts insects and their predators. The birds are the quickest to take advantage and both seed eaters, such as Bar-tailed Lark, and insectivores such as Hoopoe and Maghreb Larks are found in such places. Both latter birds probe around the bases of plants looking for larva and other invertebrates.

Some species that are present in the High Arid Steppes are also found here. The Cream-colored Courser is one of them and the Thick-billed Lark will escape the colder winters by arriving here in autumn. Sandgrouse are also present. Three species – Spotted, Crowned and Lichtenstein's – can be found in the Sahara. They are most likely to be found at drinking pools. The special species of the desert is the Houbara Bustard (see page 110).

Outcrops of sedimentary rocks are a feature of the landscape. Most form isolated bluffs in the desert and are under perpetual assault from the wind and extreme temperature variations. The eroded scree at the base of these cliffs is often rich in fossils and it can be a simple matter of picking them off the ground. The rock faces are often full of holes and attract both mammals and birds for den and nesting sites respectively. This is where

Most of the desert is formed of gravel plains, and life tends to congregate along 'washout' lines.

THE SAHARA

Ruppell's Foxes are found, which often choose a den surprisingly high on the cliffs. Birds that depend on these cliffs include Brown-necked Ravens, Long-legged Buzzard, Lanner Falcon and Pharoah Eagle Owl. Most of them favour isolation and will not tolerate pairs of either their own kind or others anywhere close.

Sand Dunes

Despite the look of permanence, all the sand dunes are mobile, constantly being blown by the wind.

Almost all the dunes in Morocco are formed with sand blown up by wind over the gravel plain. They are mobile and vary in shape and height. At the one extreme are the ergs, large sand seas with high dunes, and at the other end are mobile crescent shaped dunes that are only a few centimetres high and can move from day to day.
The movement of every sand grain is the same regardless of the dune size. The grains are pushed up the windward slope and then deposited in the lee, slowly pushing and shaping the dune. The physical form of the dunes ranges enormously, each of which has its own terminology in both Berber and Arabic.
The mobile sands look almost totally devoid of life but even here highly adapted species make a life. The Sandfish is the quintessential dune creature. It is not a fish but a form of Skink that can 'swim' through the sand matrix. Side-winding snakes are also present and their distinctive trails can frequently be seen, much more often than the animals themselves, which hide in the sand during the day.
It is where these sandy areas are stabilised by vegetation that you find the richest habitats. Halfa Grass, a sturdy tussock-forming grass with a long network of roots, stabilises the dunes and provides an anchor into which other plants can grow, flower and set seed. These complexes of grassy mini-dunes are relatively rare and normally sit in the depressions of the plains. The permanent and often dense stems form the ideal habitat for sand dwelling reptiles and small rodents. The tussocks are also the favoured nesting location of African Desert Warbler.

LANDSCAPE

THE SAHARA

Finding species in the sand dunes is often even more tricky than elsewhere. Usually all that can be found are the tracks of the activity in the night before, and only until the wind wipes them from the sand again. With some patience and understanding, rodents, lizards, snakes and scorpions can be seen to make distinctive markings and you can make out the small pads of foxes and even the Sand Cat. Seeing the animals themselves means a nocturnal adventure. Dusk and the first hours of darkness are the best. Later in the night, the temperature falls too far for most animals to remain active.

The birdlife is richest along the line where the sand meets the gravel and along the lines of vegetation. Cream-coloured Coursers, Hoopoe, Dunn's, and Maghreb Larks are all particularly fond of these boundary areas. Fulvous Babblers join the African Desert Warblers in their preference for the grassy tussocks.

Palmeries

Palmeries are a distinctive part of the desert landscape, and although some have natural origin, they have been subject to human expansion and management for so long that the original oases have been lost. As the name suggests, these are dominated by palms, more specifically Date Palms (*Phoenix dactylifera*). The dates are the wonder-fuel for the crossing of the Sahara, being energy-rich and capable of being compressed into dense blocks that take little space in the caravans. The palms provide shade and the area beneath them is used to propagate a series of crops, including fodder for the animals and a range of food crops including grain, lentils and chickpeas. Other trees are often planted as a mid-canopy, including tamarisks as windbreaks and fruiting trees within the palmeries themselves. All of this is supported by irrigation from cisterns and khetteras.

The combination of water, greenery and flowering plants attracts a range of wildlife to the palmeries. Birds such as Desert Sparrow and Fulvous Babbler need the Palm trees to breed and the irrigation runnels even attract some damselflies and dragonflies, such as Sahara and Oasis Bluetails, Violet and Orange-winged Dropwings, and Epaulet and Yellow-veined Skimmers. African Green Toads find a home in the damp fields with well-tilled sand soils and their tadpoles can be seen in the irrigation channels.

During migration, the palmeries attract a mix of birds that rely on them as feeding stations to minimise the trauma of the Saharan crossing. In winter many birds find food around human habitations, livestock and foliage. In short, the palmeries are oases in the widest sense of the word.

THE SAHARA

Desert rivers

Desert rivers are rare and transitory, creating a line of irrigation rather than a permanent watercourse. However, there is an exception. The Drâa is the longest river in Morocco and for the majority of its length it flows in the Saharan zone. It rises in the High Atlas and after heading south it forms a large part of the border between Morocco and Algeria.

The main part of the course is across sand and sedimentary rocks, and after leaving the Anti-Atlas it crosses the flat plains which despite the proximity of water does not create much more than a narrow strip of vegetation, primarily Date Palm and Flat-topped Acacia. In their shade some herbs can survive, but they appear normally only after rain. Most of the southerly flowing part of the river follows the northern section of the trans-Saharan caravan route. The land has been adapted as palmeries and these stretch in a narrow band on both sides of the river as it heads south.

As the river swings westwards, the palmeries drop away and the sand pushes right to the edge of the watercourse. Tamarisks and palms provide shade that helps a number of water reliant species to survive. The

Palmeries provide home to a wide range of species including the Rufous-tailed Scrub Robin.

LANDSCAPE

THE SAHARA

When the acacias are in flower, their nectar provides for a whole web of life including this Plain Tiger.

palms themselves are valued as a nesting site for Desert Sparrow, and the rocky bluffs attract African Rock Martin and Blue-cheeked Bee-eaters to stay and nest. They are reliant on the insect life supported by the oases and can often been seen hawking for insects over the trees.

Butterflies are few in these arid lands, but the oases provide both food plants and respite from the sun. A number of whites hang on and have obviously followed the cultivated crops to these areas but some other butterflies are native to the desert edge. Plain Tigers are plentiful (as across most habitats), while Desert Swallowtail and Desert Babul Blue are Sahara specialists and should be sought out in these areas.

Ephemeral lakes

Before leaving this section, a final word needs to be said regarding the ephemeral lakes that can form in the desert. Where gypsum occurs, this can bind the sand and create an impermeable layer that can result in lakes forming after rain. These can be surprisingly large and long-lasting. The most famous is Dayet Srij, a few kilometres to the west of Erg Chebbi (route 11). It is often over 1km long and can hold water over many summers, being replenished by autumn rains, although it does dry out periodically. Its size and location attract a substantial range of water-dependent species that can opportunistically take advantage of this resource. Dragonflies can appear in enormous, numbers. Red-veined Darters and both Blue and Vagrant Emperors patrol the shallows and other species can be searched for. But it is the birds that dominate. Flocks of up to 5,000 Greater Flamingos and hundreds of Ruddy Shelduck feed on the lake, but anything can turn up. Migrant waders including Temminck's Stint and Grey Phalarope show that these 'coastal' species actually migrate on a broad front. American vagrants such as Franklin's Gull and Blue-winged Teal also indicate that wandering birds can arrive from almost anywhere.

THE ANTI-ATLAS MOUNTAINS

The Anti-Atlas Mountains

> Routes 19 to 21 the sites on pages 222-224 visit the Anti-Atlas.

Between the Moroccan Sahara and the coast lies the Anti-Atlas. When you travel from the desert to the coast you will likely cross this range, although as the chain is both shorter and fragmented it is possible to by-pass them entirely. At first glance, it does not seem radically different from the High Atlas. It rises up impressively from the plains and is deeply incised. Even in its geology it resembles its bigger brother, with a mix of volcanic and sedimentary rocks. The big difference is the vegetation, or lack thereof. The Anti-Atlas is more barren, lying between the Sahara to the south and the arid steppe to the north. The range is not high enough to create rain clouds, nor hold snow in winter. but at higher altitudes the colder temperatures and intense sunlight bring their own unique challenges.

As a result, the Anti-Atlas Mountains do host a surprisingly high level of endemic plants and animals. It is interesting to see how various plants must have common ancestors with the species in the High Atlas and show a progress of adaptation to increasing heat and aridity. In the Anti-Atlas Mountains some unique species evolved and the entire vegetation can be seen as a bridge from the dry Mediterranean flora of High Atlas the Saharan species of lowlands further south.

The stark landscape of the Anti-Atlas still provides a home to people and a wide range of species.

LANDSCAPE

THE ANTI-ATLAS MOUNTAINS

Most of the plants are either bulbs or annuals as they must survive periods of desiccation and drought. Drought-adapted scrub, (mainly wormwoods; Artemesia) is concentrated on the more shaded northern slopes and wadi beds and is stunted and able to be dormant during the scorching summer months. As with the higher mountains to the north, the underlying geology is important, again with the predominant sedimentary rocks leading to very dry surface conditions, but enable irrigation through the khettaras system (see page 23). The volcanic outcrops are less permeable, so water remains closer to the surface, but the range is too dry to feed rivers, except immediately after rain. With the unique flora comes a unique series of butterflies, including the Allard's Silver-line and Allard's Blue.

The section of the Anti-Atlas that is closest to the coast has its own special character. Here the humidity is higher due to the proximity of the ocean. Within sight of the Atlantic, Jebel Imzi is a high point that at first glance looks very similar to the deeply incised dry mountains inland. However, that slight increase in moisture brought in from the ocean has allowed a unique blend of mountain and coastal vegetation to evolve with several species that are found only here and on the Canary Islands. Within the cliffs and gorges, there are Dragon Trees, shrubby spurges and even laurels. Unfortunately, it is a remote region that is not easy to visit.

The Anti-Atlas mountains are known for their rich mammalian wildlife, which is the main target for the few naturalist travellers that make it all the way out to this remote region (see page 95).

Gorges indicate a wetter past, and provide some shelter from the dessicating rays of the sun.

The Souss Valley

Routes 15 to 18. and the sites on pages 208-211 visit the Souss valley.

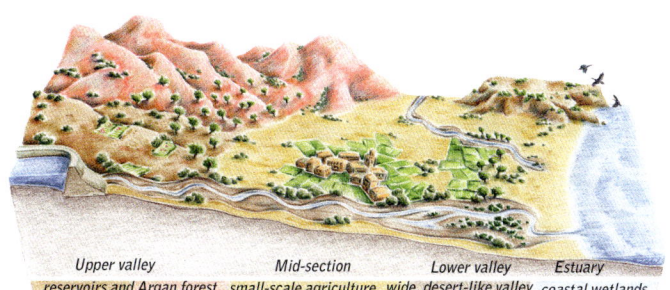

| Upper valley | Mid-section | Lower valley | Estuary |
| reservoirs and Argan forest | small-scale agriculture | wide, desert-like valley | coastal wetlands |

The different sections of the Souss Valley and their main attractions for naturalists.

North of the Anti-Atlas and west of the High Arid Steppe, the terrain drops into the Souss valley. Confusingly, the same name is given to the main river in this area as well as to the large depression between the High Atlas to the north, the Anti-Atlas to the south and the Atlantic to the west. The overall landscape is that of a flat-bottomed valley which is primarily formed from sedimentary rocks. This is a tectonically active zone and some areas are of volcanic origin. There are inselbergs of volcanic rock (see page 18) and the plateau inland of Sidi Ifni does not hide its volcanic origins.

Again, at first glance, there is nothing very different from the areas already described. The main exception is that there are more villages and there is more agricultural land. However, from an evolutionary perspective the Souss valley is radically different. It is an important and unique relict zone, a place where species found refuge from the last ice-age or reached during the last African Humid Period (see page 81) and have since been able to ride out the desertification and expansion of the Sahara.

The key relict species is the Argan Tree (see page 92). Originally a species from the Horn of Africa, it spread here during the African Humid Periods. The Argan forest is typically 25% of tree cover leaving an open park like habitat. It supports a wide range of flora and fauna that are either unique to this area or a relict from the other side of the continent.

The landscape style and use are typical of silvopasture – a dual land use of forestry and grazing. Historically, the understorey was used for low

THE SOUSS VALLEY

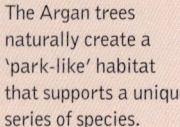

The Argan trees naturally create a 'park-like' habitat that supports a unique series of species.

intensity grazing by sheep and goats and the trees themselves were cut for animal fodder and firewood. Now the management is targeted to the health of the trees and their nuts.

Ecologically it is the shade and also the fruits of the tree that define this ecosystem. The canopies form the protective parasol under which an entire floral community can thrive. The historic enrichment of the soil from plant derived humus, supplemented by the dung of grazing animals, support a wide range of plants, which in turn feeds insects, rodents and reptiles. The latter are especially well represented including the iconic Egyptian Cobra and a number of skink species. In turn these populations support a large number of raptors, which can find plenty of nesting sites in the canopies of the trees. Short-toed Eagle, Bonelli's Eagle and Long-legged Buzzard are most frequent. Sadly, two species that were the hallmark of this ecosystem, have all but disappeared. The Tawny Eagle and Dark Chanting Goshawk, both species that are widespread south of the Sahara, had their only northern outposts here in the Argan forest.

This decline reflects the reality that this unique ecosystem is under threat. Probably as much as 50% of the forest has been cleared, especially in the areas closest to the coast. The fertility of the soil has made it attractive for conversion to agriculture. Crops are not only grown for the Moroccan markets but are increasingly exported to Europe. Only recently has the interest in the commercial value of the Argan nuts, or more specifically the oil from the nuts, been recognised. The locals have re-evaluated the forest and its management has changed for the better. Organic Argan oil is now

THE SOUSS VALLEY

a premium product, and this has not only stopped the loss of Argan trees but has encouraged more trees to be planted.

Just like the Argan tree itself, much of the flush of flowers and insects that live beneath it are relict species from sub-Saharan Africa. The same goes for some of the reptiles and mammals, such as African or Striped Ground Squirrel. Although first spotted in the 1940s, it was only recently fully realised that Morocco has two Ground Squirrels – the widespread Barbary Ground Squirrel that is found across the Maghreb, but also the African Ground Squirrel, which has been overlooked here by naturalists, both professional and amateur, until recently despite occurring 'in plain sight' in the Souss.

African House Snakes and Sahel Egg-Eater (also a snake) are other widespread African species that are north of the Sahara only present in the Souss.

Butterflies too are more plentiful here than in most other lowland areas, particularly where agriculture is more traditional. Within this group, as with the dragonflies, there are few species from sub-Saharan Africa. The majority however, are familiar from Southern Europe and include Spanish Festoon, Scarce Swallowtail and a mix of whites. In amongst these are some species typical of the Maghreb (e.g. scarce Green-striped White, False Mallow Skipper, and Moroccan Small Skipper). The most remarkable butterfly of the Souss is, paradoxically, one you know all too well: the Painted Lady, for which the valley is THE emergence site for the entire western population. (see box on page 128).

Widespread species, such as this Spotted Fritillary (top) and North African Water Frog (bottom) are very similar to, and need to be separated from the local endemics.

The Souss River

It is worth spending time on the Souss River itself. As with most lowland rivers south of the High Atlas its flow is naturally sporadic and this has been made worse with damming of the tributaries in the High Atlas and then extraction downstream for irrigation. What is truly remarkable of the Souss is that the riverbed is often

THE SOUSS VALLEY

over a kilometre wide and is comprised of many individual channels. For most of the year each of the many channels is dry and the flow is often below ground with only a few visible pools, or cisterns holding water. As elsewhere, the presence of water can attract fauna from the surrounding areas. The wide sandy riverbed is unexpectedly analogous to the more bird-rich habitats in the Sahara many kilometres to the south and attracts similar wildlife. Fulvous Babbler, Egyptian Nightjar and sand-loving lizards have all adopted this area as their home, but with one big difference for the visitor – in contrast to the real desert zone, the Souss valley is much closer to the region's major cities.

The Mediterranean Chameleon is widespread in the Souss Valley.

Where water can still be found, the stream bed is lined with vegetation that includes reeds and Tamarisk and can be dense. For toads and frogs, the Souss river is a hotspot. Here you can find Moroccan and Brongersma's Toad, and North African Water Frog. Spanish Terrapins can be very plentiful and the water is also home to Viperine Snakes, the only Natrix snake in Southern Morocco.

The river also holds the widest range of dragonfly species in Southern Morocco, including emperors, skimmers, chasers and darters. They are mainly of a Mediterranean origin and therefore already familiar to visitors from Europe. At the same time it is the most likely area to find a new incomer from remaining parts of Africa.

Wherever there is water, there are migrating birds. The Souss is a magnet to them. Herons, crakes and waders of a wide variety of species can all be found along the river on passage. Nightingales and Cetti's Warblers are common breeding birds in the river bank vegetation and therefore illustrate that this environment is still Mediterranean in its flavour, but one bird is a cryptic species of African origin. The African Reed Warbler is resident in the waterside vegetation. As the numbers of the migrating Eurasian Reed Warbler dwarf the small breeding population of the African, this bird was only recognised recently. Its discovery was not helped by the fact that it is effectively indistinguishable in the field (see also page 112).

The coast

> Routes 22 to 25 and the sites on pages 240-243 visit the coast.

The final distinct landscape on the circuit of Southern Morocco is the coast. Watching the sun set over the ocean in the west on a warm, but not uncomfortably hot evening is a wonderful experience. Realising that the sea here is unbroken to the west all the way to the Americas only adds to the experience.

The pleasant temperatures and the wide ocean make it easy to believe that the Atlantic has a great cooling effect on the climate of the South Moroccan coast, as it has in Europe. But it does not have as great an impact as you might expect. The cool Canary Current off the Southern Moroccan coast stabilises the weather systems and frequently blocks the flow of cool water-laden air from the ocean. This means that whilst the ocean's impact on the weather is directly on the coast, this effect quickly disappears further inland. Directly on the coast, the temperature is markedly cooler, and coastal fogs are frequent during the summer months. This creates a narrow climatic band that 'drags' the Mediterranean style ecosystems further south.

The mix of habitats both on land and beneath the waves makes this the richest ecosystem in the area, yet it is one that is disappearing fast.

The majority of estuaries are 'blind'; cut off from the sea by a sand bar as this one of the Asif N'Srou at Tamri.

LANDSCAPE

THE COAST

The main pressure is the expansion of the coastal tourist facilities. Resorts and their supporting infrastructure and the ever-growing demand for fresh water is drying the natural river systems. The squeeze is also occurring from the expanding cities of Agadir and Essaouira and the intensive agriculture zones inland pushing towards the coast. In addition, overfishing impacts the offshore ecosystem. Despite these pressures, this remains an interesting area and one that warrants investigation.

Most of the coastline is formed of low cliffs and sand dunes. Even at Cap Rhir, where the formidable High Atlas Mountains reach the sea, the cliffs are barely 20m high – incredible as just a kilometre inland the ground rises to 400m or so. By contrast, the Anti-Atlas does not reach the coast at all. Around Sidi-Ifni a plateau of pre-Cambrian volcanic rocks forms an elevated plateau that demarcates the Souss from the Saharan depression further south.

A habitat of transition

Although ecologically classified as Mediterranean along most of its length, the coastal habitat changes tremendously from north to south. Around Essaouira in the north, the habitat is a classic Mediterranean one – scrubland dotted with low, evergreen trees of Aleppo Pine, Holm Oak and in some places native Wild Olives. Further south, as the climate gets hotter and drier, the scrub becomes thinner, with fewer trees before finally becoming truly Saharan in character south of Sidi Ifni.

The 'cool' Mediterranean zone in the northern part has a classic maquis found further north and is dominated by cistus and rock roses. Between the bushes, there is a rich spring flora with orchids, snowdrops, narcissi and other bulbs, similar to that of the European Mediterranean coast. This more European-Mediterranean feel is also reinforced by seasonal pools that form the home of the only newt of the region, the Sharp-ribbed.

Offshore islands are few, but where they exist, they are protected and have a great value for wildlife. Just offshore to Essaouira lies Mogador Island, which has a nesting colony of Eleonora's Falcons

As you proceed south, the vegetation gradually changes. The scrubland remains, but the typical Mediterranean species make way for those that are even better adapted to the high temperatures and low rainfall. Succulents and 'xerophytes' (drought-plants with very small leathery or hairy leaves) take over. This hotter and drier habitat is more favourable to reptiles. Geckos, skinks and lizards become more plentiful together with a wider range of snakes.

The few rivers that reach the sea have distinctive estuaries with dune systems and are often 'blind' (i.e. they do not flow openly into the sea). Instead, sand bars block the estuary outlet, so their end point is a (series of) pool(s) on the landward side. These damp slacks offer a more humid version of the sand seas of the Sahara. It is therefore not surprising that versions of the same group of reptiles have found their home here. Skinks and fringe-fingered lizards are both present, but their isolation has meant that those here are now recognised as separate species.

The estuaries are rich wildlife sites. From north to south these are the river mouths of the Tensift, near Essaouira (site A on page 232), Asif N'Srou near Tamri (route 22), the Souss near Agadir (route 24) and the Massa near Tiznit (route 25). The Drâa reaches the sea beyond the southern edge of our area. These estuaries form extremely fragile habitats. Most have been squeezed by conversion to agriculture and their distinctiveness, at least in part, is under threat. However all but the Tensift are included in the Souss-Massa National Park, so at least some recognition of their value has been made and a certain level of protection is in place.

The coast south of Agadir shows influence of the Souss, Mediterranean, Canarian and Saharan in a unique blend.

The coastal zone is home to two isolated bird species that are again more typical of Sub-Saharan African. The Black-crowned Tchagra (ssp *cuculatus*) and Brown-throated Martin (ssp *mauritanica*) are represented by endemic races and are separated from the rest of their ranges in tropical Africa. However, the most important bird of the coast is the Northern Bald Ibis. Nearly all that remains of the original population of this species that was once widespread across Europe and Arabia is now limited to the coast south of Agadir (see page 114).

Travelling further south to the area around Sidi Ifni, the flora resembles the mix of species more typical of the Canary Islands, with more succulents and other dry country species. This is a beautiful region, where the odd, spherical bushes of spurges give the landscape their typical appearance. This scenery looks a bit like the drier south slopes of the

THE COAST

Canary Islands and indeed there are 18 floral endemics shared between Morocco and the Canaries, plus many more that obviously have common ancestors. Other species have colonised from the south and continuing research is showing more species are endemic to this zone and can give clues as to where their ancestors have come from.

The Ocean

Morocco has a large fishing fleet that profits from the richness of the cold-water currents just off the coast. The inshore fishing boats are a popular and picturesque backdrop to many tourist photos of Essaouira and coastal villages.

The offshore fleet based in Agadir is less photogenic, but both together reflect the bounty ready to be harvested from a short journey offshore. These waters are indeed very rich in marine life, due to the aforementioned Canary Current, which, through upwellings, brings the cooler and nutrient-rich deeper waters close to the surface. Fish benefit from this abundance of food and they in turn are joined by whales, dolphins and marine birds.

From a wildlife perspective, much remains to be learnt about the species and their movements. Certainly, any brief visit to any of the headlands will reward even a shortwhile staring offshore with sightings of pelagic species such as Cory's and Balearic Shearwaters or Northern Gannets and perhaps a Pilot Whale or a dolphin at almost any time of the year. Pioneering pelagic trips have found that migrants pass in the autumn from further afield and it is already clear that Great Shearwaters, Wilson's Petrels and some of the great whales can be found here.

The rich, cool waters of the Atlantic Ocean wash the beaches on the western shore.

CROSSBILL GUIDES • SOUTHERN MOROCCO

History

Morocco has been home to humans for at least 400,000 years. What little record remains, including in rock art (see page 140), shows that the main inhabitants were pastoralists reliant on the rich grazing on the edge of the Sahara in a time when the whole region was overall wetter, cooler and more productive (see page 81).

The area covered in this book was always on the borders of the recorded history. Phoenician traders are known to have utilised the Canary current and the coastal area, especially the natural harbour at Mogador (current day Essaouira). It was part of the network of influence that this trading nation established throughout the whole of the Mediterranean in the period 800-550 BCE. The Phoenicians didn't occupy the land in this part of Morocco, but their trading post at Carthage (modern-day Tunis) grew into a city-state and then an empire that spread throughout the Maghreb. Evidence of the landward Carthaginian occupation is found further north in Morocco. At Mogador again, archaeological excavations have found Roman-style villas and goods showing that either the Romans or Carthaginians were present after the annexation of the Carthaginian empire into Imperial Rome in 40 CE. The Roman province of Mauretania corresponds with the modern-day Morocco and Algeria as far south as the High Atlas Mountains, but the hinterland was always left in the control of the local Berber rulers.

To some extent the term 'Berber' for these indigenous peoples is disputed, especially as this group call themselves '*Amarzigh*'. Berber is originally a Greek term that refers to all non-Greek speakers. In Roman times, it became '*Barbarus*' and referred to any foreigners, particularly those that didn't speak Latin. Later the term was adopted specifically for North-west Africa in the form of the Barbary coast. Only in the 1830s, did the French use the term Berber to distinguish between the Tamazight speaking Amarzigh of inland North-West Africa from the remaining mainly Arabic speakers along the coast. It is this Amarzigh definition of Berber that we follow.

Reminders of the ancient relationship with Islam dot the landscape as here near Tissint.

LANDSCAPE

HISTORY

Middle Ages

The collapse of the Roman empire created a vacuum that was partially filled by the Vandals, and thereafter the Byzantine Empire in the 6th Century, although neither fully controlled the former Roman province of Mauretania. Islam reached Morocco in the 8th Century CE brought by Arabs from the east. This expansion of Islam led in 711CE to the invasion of Iberia, by a joint force of Arabs and Berbers under the Umayyad Caliphate, which was only checked in Western Europe by the Battle of Tours in 732CE. However, it resulted in over 750 years of Moorish occupation in Spain. In reality, these Moors were, as we will see, a succession of different Berber rulers.

Back in Morocco, the Berber Revolt of 740CE and the resultant formation of the Moroccan State in the late 8th Century meant that Southern Morocco remained a Berber area. The whole of the region was aligned to the Abbasid Caliphate that ruled either directly, or by overlordship, across the Muslim world from their base in Baghdad, an empire that spread from the Atlantic to India by 850CE.

In Morocco, it was the Almoravid dynasty that grew under this overlordship of the Abbasid Caliphate. In 1070, it was still a regional power with a capital in Marrakech, but by 1120, the Almoravid controlled an empire from Zaragoza in current day northern Spain to Aoudaghost in today's southern Mauritania.

The Almoravid's influence spread even further south into Mali, Ghana and Sudan. The importance of this southern part of the empire is that

Islamic geometric decoration and tile making were introduced from Morocco to Spain and Portugal in the Middle Ages.

it controlled the trans-Saharan trade that connected with the established trade network in the Niger basin. This helped to establish Timbuktu as a major centre and brought control over much overland trade in West Africa. It also brought gold and slaves from West Africa and salt from the Saharan depression itself.

The Almoravid dynasty was short lived. Lisbon was recovered by the Portuguese and Zaragoza by the Spanish with aid from the French. In 1147 the Almoravids we overthrown in Marrakech by the Almohads. The influence of Marrakech over the region declined and in Spain, city states were progressively recovered by the Spanish with Córdoba (1236) and Seville (1248) being conquered by the Christian alliance.

In the Maghreb, the north Moroccan tribes, the Marinids, increased their influence and by 1269 they had seized Marrakech. They moved the capital to Fez and so decreased the importance of Marrakech even further. The more eastern caravan routes therefore became more important as they more easily connected Fez with Timbuktu. By the mid fifteenth century, although the Marinids stayed in power, the expansion of Portuguese colonial aspirations meant that the coastal areas were effectively under foreign control. This led to tribal disputes in the hinterland and the Marinids were overthrown by the Wattasids, another northern Moroccan tribe. It is worth noting that in 1492, the Moorish occupation of Iberia ended with the capitulation of Granada to the forces of Ferdinand and Isabella, the Catholic monarchs of Aragon and Castille that completed the Reconquista, or reconquering of land from the 'Moors'. This ended over 750 years of Muslim rule in Iberia and the

The Portuguese fort at Essaouira is a reminder of the colonial past

HISTORY

exiled King Boabdil sought refuge in Morocco. The Alhambra Degree by the victorious Spanish exiled all Muslims and Jews from Spain, except for those who converted to Christianity. Many didn't and escaped to settle in Morocco instead.

The new relationship with Spain did nothing to prevent an increase in Portuguese influence on the coast and in 1506 the Portuguese built a fortress at Mogador (Essaouira) and another at the mouth of the Souss (Agadir) to control offshore trade. The Portuguese did not try to conquer the hinterland, but to influence it through treaty. However, the situation in Morocco as a whole was increasingly unstable. From 1509 onwards, the Saadi tribe, who were originally from the Drâa valley, became increasingly influential from their capital in Taroudant, bringing together the southern tribes, in opposition to the northern Wattasids. With little or no support from the latter, the Saadi led a revolt against the Portuguese in Southern Morocco and had immediate success in 1510 at Mogador. They subsequently drove the Portuguese out of Agadir in 1541. During this time, the Wattasids faced their own problems, being under enormous pressure from the expansionist Ottoman Empire that was challenging Morocco from their easternmost base in Algiers. The Wattasids even entered into a treaty with the Spanish to hold them at bay.

Marrakesh still holds a number of exquisitely decorated royal palaces in its ancient medina.

By 1554, the Saadis ousted the Wattasids and reunited the country, re-establishing the capital at Marrakech. The early years of this new, unified Morocco were marked by attempts by the Wattasids to reclaim the country. They even sought support from their former enemy the Ottomans. The Palace of El Badii-Ksibat Nhass in Marrakech was commissioned in 1578 by Saadi Sultan, Ahmad al-Mansur, the remains of which can be still be visited today. In 1591, the same Sultan pushed southwards and invaded modern-day Mali, seizing Timbuktu and reinforcing his control of the trade around the Niger and the trans-Saharan routes from his capital in Marrakech. However, after his death in 1603 the empire fragmented. Although Southern Morocco continued to be ruled from Marrakech, a

HISTORY

splinter group led by the sultan's brother controlled northern Morocco from its capital in Fez before being brought back under control of Marrakech by 1628.

As the country continued to fragment, a new group, the Alawi, began to grow in influence from its base in the eastern Oasis in wadi Ziz (around today's towns of Erfoud and Rissani). They took control of the eastern part of our region by 1631 and finally overthrew the Saadi by taking Marrakech in 1659. By 1670, the Alawi had united the whole of Morocco under a single ruler, with their capital in Rabat this time. It is this dynasty that remains in power today. However, after decades of effective civil war in Morocco, the area around Timbuktu was lost and the country approximated to the current-day borders.

Colonial Morocco

Even before the establishment of a unified Morocco in 1670, there was an interest from other world powers in the country, especially because of the strategically important coastal cities and harbours. The British were already present in Tangiers (from which they controlled the Straits of Gibraltar prior to taking Gibraltar itself in 1704). The Spanish had colonised nearby Larache. After the unification in 1670, the Alawi turned to these British and Spanish territories and drove them out in 1684 and 1689 respectively. Meanwhile, the Ottoman empire continued their efforts to annex the country from their westernmost outpost in Algeria up to 1696, but then gave up.

The Moroccan control of the western approaches to the Mediterranean, both alone and with France, has a turbulent history including the First and Second Barbary Wars between 1801 and 1815. These wars were launched by the fledgling United States and brought the British to bombard Algiers to control the local rulers. France annexed the whole of Algeria in 1830 further destabilising the Maghreb. By 1859 the Alawid Sultan of Morocco, Abd el Rahman, disputed the Spanish use of their enclave of Ceuta (inherited

The walls at Taroudant remind that this was once a capital of Morocco.

LANDSCAPE

HISTORY

from the Portuguese) on the southern coast of the Straits. However in the resultant war, he lost and ceded further land to the Spanish. By 1884, Spain unilaterally declared the whole of the northern coastal region of Morocco a Spanish protectorate, annexed the Western Sahara and established direct rule of the area around Sidi Ifni.

France sought to protect its colony in Algeria, and in the increasing geopolitical tension in the late 19th century, Morocco became a football between these global powers. France secretly agreed with Spain to take control of Morocco, whilst leaving Spanish interests intact. France then signed the 'entente cordiale' with Britain in 1904, and this effectively brought in the support of the British to this arrangement. Germany was upset with the situation and the Kaiser met with Abdul Aziz, the Moroccan Sultan in 1905, which was seen by the French as interference in their relationship with Morocco's ruling dynasty. Finally, in a conference in Algeciras in 1906 France's control of Morocco was officially agreed – all the European powers and the United States of America were present there, but not Morocco itself.

After accusations of collaboration, Abdul Aziz was deposed by his brother Abd al Hafid, and further internal tribal fragmentation made Morocco unable to stop France's colonial expansion. Despite the Algeciras agreement, by 1911 France's military build-up yielded further reaction from Germany. In a move seen as destabilising an already fraught Europe, the Germans sent a gunboat to Agadir. In support of the existing treaties, Britain responded by sending a battleship to chase the German navy from the scene.

In the end the dispute was resolved diplomatically with Germany gaining control of a part of the Congo in return for supporting French interests in Morocco. Now that the quarrels between the European superpowers had come to an end, the Treaty of Fez could be signed in March 1912 between France and the cowed Sultan of Morocco, which reinforced that all of the hinterland beyond the northern Spanish Protectorate was surrendered and came under French colonial control. Abd al Hafid abdicated in shame having not being included in the plans for governing the country and his brother Yusef assumed the title of Sultan of Morocco with the support of the French.

The French poured into Morocco, building new infrastructure (roads, rail and irrigation schemes) and claiming title to the best of the land. They adopted Rabat as their administrative capital. The native tribes diminished in influence and uprisings were ruthlessly put down. This reduced the wealth and influence of Marrakech and the rest of Southern Morocco

HISTORY

and it effectively became a forgotten part of the country. The increased militarisation was characterised by the formation of the French Foreign Legion in Marrakech in 1920 (strictly 4th Foreign Infantry Regiment; 4ème REI). This base, together with outlying forts, effectively brought the remaining trans-Saharan trade under French military control.

Moroccan independence

When Yusef died in 1927, Mohammed V succeeded as Sultan and his role continued unchanged under the colonial protectorate of France until WWII. In common with Algeria, Morocco was then under indirect German influence, as it was administered by the occupied French Vichy government, although it did not see any fighting in the early stages of the war. The Sultan was not happy with this change of power and his disaffection reached a peak when the authorities requested a handing over of all Jews. He refused as in his words "he only had Moroccans".

The status of the Vichy Government was made untenable when in November 1942, in America's first action in the western theatre, the allied forces landed in North Africa near Casablanca under 'Operation Torch'. The action at Casablanca largely destroyed Vichy France's naval presence in Morocco and not only resulted in Allied and Free French control but also initiated the formation in 1943 of a local independence movement, with tacit American support.

It soon became clear that at the end of the war in 1945, the French expected things to return to the pre-war status quo, with Mohammed V being France's puppet. However, in 1947, Mohammed V made what became known as the Tangier speech in which, in a departure from the agreed text,

Islam is an important part of daily life (top). The minaret of the 12th Century Koutoubia mosque dominates Marrakesh's skyline (bottom).

LANDSCAPE

HISTORY

he demanded independence. France responded by inciting opposition to his rule and placing Mohammed V in exile in Madagascar in 1953. This predictably prompted a period of unprecedented civil unrest and attacks were made on Europeans in the protectorate areas of both France and Spain. The Pasha of Marrakech, Thami el Glaoui had been a supporter of French rule and as one of the richest men in Morocco (his family had controlled the trade over the Tizi n'Tichka pass for generations) had substantial influence both across Morocco and in Paris. Despite being a major architect of the deposing and exile of Mohammed V, he realised the damage the exile was doing to his country and petitioned the French to allow Mohammed V's return. This was successful and Mohammed returned in 1955. Morocco gained independence from both France and Spain on 2nd March 1956, although the enclaves of Cueta and Mellila still remain in Spanish hands. The following year he was officially made King of the newly independent state.

Hassan II succeeded in 1961, reigning until his death in 1999. During this time the country lagged behind in economic development and large numbers of Moroccans migrated to both France and Spain to start a new life. Economic migrants settled in a wide range of European countries as migration expanded beyond the limits of post-colonial relationships. In addition, Israel initiated Operation Yachim in which 97,000 Moroccan Jews were secretly shipped or flown to Israel, mainly via France and Italy between 1961-64. Together with the initial emigration on the formation of the State of Israel, this meant that nearly all of the previously vibrant Moroccan Jewish community had left.

In 1975 Spain relinquished its role of colonial power over the Western Sahara following a United Nations resolution in 1965, and although this was initially administered jointly by Morocco and Mauritania, Mauritania withdrew its claims in 1979. The attempt by the Polisario front to pursue self-determination led to a conflict with Morocco, which continues today, despite a brokered ceasefire in 1991. The Polisario's activities are limited to Algerian territory and all borders between Morocco and Algeria are closed, a source of continuing tension in Southern Morocco.

Developments in the 21st century

The current King Mohammed VI came to the throne at the age of 36 in 1999 and has been seen as a moderniser. He has developed the country as a clear bridge between Arab and African countries. He has promoted human rights, particularly women's rights and his reign is seen as a stable and progressive government. Education is now mandated for both sexes

to 16 and is seen by many of the population as the route to escape from poverty.
Access to higher education has increased. The local culture was celebrated again. In the south this led to the formalisation of the Tamazight alphabet in 2002 and the official recognition of the language for public buildings and education soon afterwards.
Economic progress has also been made. Since the millennium GDP has risen by 300%, 10 years were added to the average life expectancy, and the overall wealth of the population has increased markedly. The push to earn foreign exchange led to the investment in tourist infrastructure. In 2019 more than 13 million visitors were recorded, compared with just 4 million in 1999. More than the headline numbers is the broadening appeal. Where previously visitors were almost exclusively from the old colonial powers Morocco now attracts people from all over the world.
Farming, particularly for supplying the European market, is the other major change. This has allowed a doubling of the income per worker in the sector and a move to commercial agriculture rather than the subsistence agriculture of the past.
Of course, this is not without its challenges. The growth in the population from 27.9 million at the dawn of the new millennium to 36.7 million in 2019 has put a strain on all of the public services, most importantly the provision of housing and meaningful jobs for the increasingly educated population. Even in the south the cities have grown enormously. Marrakech and Agadir both now have populations of close to 1 million. The towns south of the High Atlas Mountains remain much smaller with Ouarzazate and Taroudant both having populations of around 75,000. Migration to Europe is still a major feature. Many leave temporarily to earn money before settling back in their home towns, but more join the substantial diaspora around Europe.
Despite these strains, Morocco has been seen as a stable and relatively liberal member of the wider Arab World. The explosive 2011 'Arab Spring' that impacted most Mediterranean Arab states, left Morocco largely unaffected. The changes in the constitution and the modernisations already enacted in Morocco were seen by their neighbours as aspirations that needed to be fought for in their own country.
The consequence for the natural world is not so clear. The population increase since the millennium has put pressure on land use. New housing can be seen everywhere, and pristine steppes are marked out for ownership and ploughed for new agriculture. The biggest issue is the increasing demand for water. Agriculture of non-traditional export crops including

NATURE CONSERVATION

citrus, banana, blueberries and tomatoes demands enormous amounts of water. In addition, the growth of tourist complexes with swimming pools and first world expectation of showers and other water-consuming commodities has come at a time that rain is less frequent. The increased demand for water is pushing water tables lower in the steppes and drying the remaining khetterras, in turn impacting the palmeries and what little remains of the natural vegetation.

Nature Conservation

A trip around Southern Morocco shows little in the way of visible conservation in line with the typical European model. However, there are a number of initiatives lead by both government and other organisations that promote tree planting, protecting water catchment and taking action against desertification.

The Moroccan Birdlife's partner is the *Groupe de Recherche pour le Protection des Oiseaux au Maroc* (GREPROM). It works with both the government and local schools to promote the protection of habitats and birds as a valuable part of Moroccan culture. These activities are concentrated in the cities, mostly in the north. They are slower at making a difference in the sparsely populated, poorer and more traditional deep south.

National Parks and protected areas

Although Morocco has splendid habitats and a rich wildlife, there are few areas that are actually protected solely for wildlife. The premier designation of those lucky few is the Biosphere Reserve. These are part of the UNESCO global network of reserves and are focused upon being 'learning places for sustainable development'. In common with the global model, each has three defined areas, namely a core area, a buffer area around this core, and then a transition area around this buffer. The Biosphere Reserves are focused on the continuation of traditional land use rather than the protection of flora and fauna. Two out of the four Moroccan Biosphere reserves are in the south, namely Arganeraie, in the Souss valley (2,560,000 ha), and Oasis du sud Marocain, in the High Arid Steppes and Sahara from the High Atlas south to the Algerian border (7,185,371 ha). Together these two cover nearly all the area in this book south of the High Atlas Mountains and include towns and villages as well as areas of natural importance.

The core areas are often demarcated as being the best for flora and fauna,

NATURE CONSERVATION

or for research into the ecosystems. Unfortunately, even there traditional grazing and other historic land uses are promoted over conservation. This means that overgrazing to the point that damage to the habitats is still a concern especially in years of drought, and one that doesn't seem to be effectively managed. In any event, these core areas are a small proportion of the overall areas and are insufficient to prevent the deterioration of habitat in general.

If the Biosphere Reserves define the overall umbrella of landscape protection, the next level would be the *Parc National*. There are 11 National Parks in Morocco of which three are in our area. A fourth, in the Eastern High Atlas Mountains, is proposed.

Toubkal is the oldest National Park, formed in 1942. It covers the high peaks of the massif and 38,000 ha of sub-Alpine and Alpine zone mountains around them. The second is Iriqui on the Algerian border, covering 123,000 ha north from the Drâa valley. Both of these parks are beyond the limits of roads and therefore access is tricky. In contrast, the third, Parc National de Sous-Massa, is close to Agadir and easy to visit. It covers 33,800 ha, plus another 30,000 ha of buffer zone to the south.

Park visitor centres and notice boards have increased the infrastructure to support local eco-tourism, here at Souss-Massa.

Although tourism is a reason for the formation of these parks, there is little in the way of infrastructure to aid the visitor. Protection of habitat and species is far from complete, the only exception being the breeding areas of the Bald Ibis in the Souss-Massa National Park (see page 110). As with the Biosphere reserves, traditional life is still allowed to continue as before. The designation protects the landscape from modification through infrastructure or other large construction projects, but again not from more traditional environmental pressures like over-grazing. In some

NATURE CONSERVATION

places it is even failing to prevent conversion to less sustainable forms of agriculture. In the case of the Parc National de Souss-Massa, the expansion of the city of Agadir has put substantial pressure on the protected areas, although the presence of the Royal Palace on the southern boundary of the city protects it from encroachment.

Species protection and reintroduction programs
In addition to the land protection, Morocco does have a considerable number of projects focussing on the preservation of individual species, including programs to actively reintroduce iconic species.

The Northern Bald Ibis is seen as a key Moroccan success story and a source of local pride. The conservation effort is aimed at protecting the breeding sites and the feeding areas of what is now the last surviving native population of Northern Bald Ibises in the world.

Other programmes concentrate on the reintroduction of large ungulates that had previously been extirpated from Southern Morocco, particularly Scimitar-horned Oryx, Cuvier's Gazelle and Barbary Sheep. Hunting decimated the populations of these species, and reintroduction in combination with a ban on hunting should allow a successful recovery. There are a number of large-scale pens where this native fauna has been reintroduced, such as in the Parc National de Souss-Massa (site C on page 234) near the Tizi n-Test pass in the High Atlas Mountains (site E on page 151) and in more remote locations in the Saharan zone . Those at Souss-Massa are certainly the simplest to access and will guarantee sightings, even if the setting is more akin to a safari park or zoo.

These programmes are a welcome first step in the preservation of these species, but they do not enhance the protection of the wider habitat that is threatened by the increase in population, intensification, the increased conversion of fragile habitats to agriculture and the intensification of that agriculture. In addition, climate change and desertification put the remaining habitat under severe pressure.

Other conservation issues
Regardless of where you go, any trip will be marked by large amounts of rubbish and fly tipping, especially close to roads. This plague of plastic is common around Africa and is as much a problem in Morocco as it is in the rest of the continent. Fortunately, efforts to both reduce the waste and deal with disposal of it have increased enormously in recent years.

The desert itself is particularly sensitive to damage, not only from rubbish but especially by wheeled vehicles, and the growth of adventure trips

NATURE CONSERVATION

in the edge of the Sahara threatens the species there. The number of 4x4 trips, quad-biking and 'desert raid' motor sport events have increased enormously. When these stick to existing tracks, there is probably little additional damage, but they have become more free-ranging and this threatens ground-nesting birds and other vertebrates. The demand for dawn and dusk visits to the sand dunes has also grown and has led to an increase in temporary camps and the development of more hotels.

The problem this poses is not often recognised. The general sentiment that the desert is so immense that whatever damage is done is so local that it can't pose any real, overall threat. This line of thinking misses the point that the entire desert ecosystem and all of its wildlife depends on very specific areas that are for some reason richer in water and nutrients. And it is precisely these areas where desert tourism is concentrated.

In addition, the demand for water and the generation of waste stresses this fragile environment further. There is, as yet, little understanding of the tipping point for development. At some point the increase in visitor numbers will actually destroy the sights and solitude that people seek to find in the first place. It is arguable that in the most popular places this point has already been passed.

Tourism, despite its negative impacts on the environment, can also do good. For one it can spark interest in the environment, both for intrinsic and econoffers omic reasons. More visitors looking for the special places that Morocco will encourage locals to look after the places around them. This can start at a low level, such as paying locals to show you iconic species, through to making sure that local hotel and restaurant owners know that you are here because of the landscape and wildlife. If not properly cared for, their business disappears as well. Although the nature tourism market isn't a very large one, the local communities are rather small as well, and nature tourism on a scale like this can really make a positive impact.

Organised visits, especially to the Sahara, bring rare and exciting species within reach.

LANDSCAPE

FLORA AND FAUNA

Southern Morocco has a surprisingly high diversity of flora and an even richer fauna. Many naturalists come here for the birds, which form an attractive mix of Mediterranean and desert species. In addition, the reptiles, the butterflies and even the dragonflies are also excellent. Many, however, are not so easy to track down.

Many species moved into Morocco and subsequently became isolated from their original population, either due to the growth of the Saharan desert or as a result of a warming climate in Europe (see page 81 for details). This isolation has been a driver for speciation. DNA-led research, especially since the millennium, has had a profound effect on our understanding of local evolution and in some instances has created no less than a landslide in the taxonomy of species groups. So much in fact, that the current list of species is unrecognisable compared with guidebooks published even as recently as just before the millennium. That is not to say that the dust has settled in the taxonomy of various groups. No doubt there will be further analysis that is likely to result in even more different species being recognised. Although further changes are to be expected what will not change is that every habitat zone has its own specialities, often restricted to just a few square kilometres, to which conditions it is optimally adapted.

The key issue for any visiting naturalist is to understand the habitat requirements of the local flora and fauna; in other words, how to 'read' the habitat in order to understand for which range of species it may be suitable. In Southern Morocco this 'reading the landscape' is not just about the 'where', but just as much about the 'when'. Seasonality is key in the distribution of plants and animals, but it is something very different from the seasonality you know from Europe. For many South Moroccan species, the habitat suitability very much depends on the weather, or more precisely, on the weather in the days, weeks or months prior to your arrival. To complicate things even more, this is relative to places elsewhere, especially for mobile species. Did it rain recently? Then a certain site can be great. But did it rain more, or earlier, somewhere else, then even great-looking sites can be deserted. In short, searching for flora and fauna can be super-rewarding, but sometimes also frustrating.

The species that inhabit Southern Morocco are not evenly spread.

Northern Bald Ibis at Souss-Mass National Park, where the last remaining wild population still thrives.

INTRO

In general terms, the dry and hot zones have a low diversity, which increases as you move to the more humid zones. But of course, it is not only about the overall numbers of species, but the nature of them. Pride of place goes to the endemics – species that are found nowhere but in this specific spot – and also to the more exotic species of the desert and of African origin. The desert may have a lower biodiversity, but it still is the habitat with the highest number of sought-after wildlife, especially for those interested in birds and reptiles.

There are some species that can be described as geographic endemics, meaning that they are limited geographically, but are widespread within their region. Moussier's Redstart serves as an example. It can be found almost anywhere in the region. However, most endemics are limited by specific climatic and habitat requirements, and these specific needs – their niches – have to be recognised to find them.

There are two broad habitat areas that are important in Southern Morocco. The mountains, both High Atlas and Anti-Atlas, have a myriad of differing niches driven by humidity and altitude. Such spots can be tiny, less than a kilometre square, but have the ideal conditions for one of the localised endemics. Finding them is also complicated by seasonal timing, especially in the High Atlas Mountains where the season is triggered by snowmelt. This timing is different between the north and south slopes of the mountains and, in addition, it varies by a few weeks from year to year.

In the flatter desert lands to the south, suitable terrain covers much larger areas. The landscape seems simpler, even uniform. Be aware though that the habitat complexity comes from the variation in rainfall. If the rains fail, the flora and smaller animals remain dormant and the larger animals move away. Following rains, life suddenly bursts into the landscape and the flush of new plant growth attracts firstly invertebrates and then the birds, mammals and reptiles follow. These become 'hotspots' of life. The following year, the hotspots are likely to be elsewhere.

The result, of course, is that it is unlikely that you are going to find everything on any single trip. The result is also that the spots described in the route section (page 137 and onwards) can fail to produce the attractions that are listed there.

As a travelling naturalist, flexibility is key when searching for flora and fauna. Being able to respond to localised rains can bring a once in a lifetime experience of a 'green' desert and an explosion of life. In the mountains, a shift in altitude can aid finding your targets, going higher when spring is early or lower when it is late. It is best to access a range of elevations to discover where the optimal conditions can be found at that particular time.

Climate History and Speciation

Morocco is jammed between two climatic cycles that have a profound influence on the habitats and species found today. To the north, the European continent is formed by the series of ice ages and inter-glacials, while to the south, there is a cyclical change between dry and wet periods known as the African Humid Periods.

Both cycles have had a massive impact on the Moroccan climate. Interestingly, both northern and southern species found refuge in Morocco to survive uninhabitable periods 'at home' or take advantage of newly created habitats and expand their ranges. In Southern Morocco you can find refugee species that fled the northern cold during the ice ages alongside species that migrated into Morocco during one of the African Humid Periods and subsequently formed an isolated population during the following dry period.

The migration of the Eastern Olivaceous Warbler still echoes the wetter history of the Sahara, following the Rift Valley north and then crossing directly west to Southern Morocco.

The Last Ice Age

The last Ice Age created a 'permanent' ice sheet that covered Eurasia to the southern edge of today's Baltic Sea. It ended nearly 12,000 years ago, having lasted around 100,000 years, during which it pressured Eurasian species to spread south and find refuge from increasingly cold weather in the north. In addition, increased glaciers in the mountains meant that many highlands were uninhabitable, and the increased ice sheets in the Alps and Pyrenees cut off routes on which flora and fauna could spread south. This isolated the Iberian flora and fauna. In Morocco, permanent glaciers formed in the High Atlas Mountains and these had the double impact of making some land uninhabitable yet

The Alpine Chough is a relict of the ice ages.

CLIMATE HISTORY AND SPECIATION

also providing a reliable water source to the lowlands below. Large amounts of water were locked in the ice sheets and glaciers, which caused the sea levels to drop to, at the driest period, 120m lower than today. This reduced the sea barriers to Eurasia and the Canaries. Flora was pushed from the Maghreb to the ice-free islands offshore, finding refuge in the milder sea climate before returning to the mountains after the icesheet retreated.

There is evidence to suggest that during this time the Straits of Gibraltar were 'permeable' to migration and with pressure from the north, species were driven south to find more hospitable areas in the Maghreb. In the south, the Sahara was still as desolate as today, even if the northern edge was more verdant, being fed from the glaciers in the Atlas Mountains.

The majority of the dragonflies and butterflies in Morocco are of European origin, probably because in this period they migrated south to seek refuge in Morocco where many have then stayed. Recent analysis has shown that even land mammals crossed the Straits, and populations were interchanged, resulting in common ecosystems on both sides of the Mediterranean and along the Atlantic coast of the region.

The Maghreb during the last Ice Age. The Atlas Mountains were partially glaciated, however the climate was mild. European species migrated southwards and settled in North Africa.

African Humid Period

The Sahara, the world's largest desert, grows and shrinks under a cyclical climate change of a period of around twenty thousand years. This cycle has its impacts across the whole of northern Africa and the Arabian Peninsula. The part of the cycle, in which the weather systems are fed by Monsoon rains and is therefore wetter than today is known as the African Humid Period (AHP). The peak of the AHP, that is the wettest part of the cycle, last occurred around 9 thousand years ago, so not long after the last northern ice age ended, and temperatures rose again in Europe. The diversion of Monsoon rains turned the Middle-Eastern and North African landscape into a savannah and removed the arid barrier of the Sahara Desert.

This resulted in a climate and ecosystem that is typical of the area known today as the Sahel and many species of this region and the savannah further south migrated into the Mahgreb. Giraffes, Elephants and a mix of grazing animals reached Morocco and predators such as Lion, Leopard, Serval and Caracal followed them.
Not only did this connect Morocco to the tropical areas of West Africa directly to the south, it also cleared the way for species to move all the way from the Horn of Africa to move up the Rift Valley and across to the west. Today, you can find west African species in southern Morocco, like African House Snake, Sahel Egg-Eater (also a snake) and the plant Spiderwort (*Commelina rupicola*) in the local ecosystem. The Argan tree is known to originate from an ancestor from the Rift Valley and Horn of Africa. This species is likely to have 'migrated' here through a series of humid periods to Morocco. It is likely that the other components of the Souss Valley ecosystem arrived by a similar route.

The Maghreb during the last African Humid Period. The Sahara desert was much reduced. Species from savannahs of tropical Africa were able to move northwards from the Sahel and from the Rift Valley.

This Rift Valley route is still used by some migrating birds today. Eastern Olivaceous Warblers still move north along the Rift valley in spring before turning to the west to Morocco and then reverse the route in the autumn.

The desert returns

By five thousand years ago, the influence of the monsoons had passed and the desert had returned to the Saharan basin. The species that 'migrated' into the Maghreb to take advantage of the benign conditions, soon found that their return route was cut off. The southern edge of Morocco became the home of desert-edge species such as

The Ostrich is a sub-Saharan species that went extinct in the wild in southern Morocco.

CLIMATE HISTORY AND SPECIATION

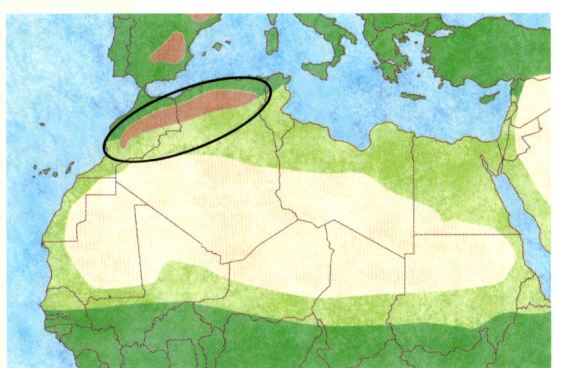

Addax, Scimitar-horned Oryx and Gazelles.
The herbivores that arrived during the AHP, either adapted by heading to the mountains and coast, such as the gazelles, or died out as climate became too extreme such as Elephant and Giraffe. Some of the predators disappeared as well, but populations of Lion and the smaller cats hung on in the mountains.

The Maghreb after the last African Humid period. It is cut-off from Europe and the rest of Africa. Species already in place are isolated and evolve to suit their new environment

The Maghreb today. Ongoing desertification is threatening the survival of Mediterranean and steppe species.

The continuing drying of the climate and isolation, both to the north and now the south, created ideal conditions for the formation of distinct sub-species that with time became fully distinct species. Barbary Ground Squirrel and Barbary Sheep are examples of animals that became isolated and in the former case are now distinct from the African Ground Squirrel ancestor. Other relict species can be found, including snakes and lizards, some that have developed to new species and others are well on the way. You can recognise this process also in the local birds, where the African Crimson-winged Finch and Atlas Wheatear are recognised as full species, whilst most authorities are yet to consider the local form of Horned Lark as sufficiently distinct. As DNA analysis has progressed other localised species have been recognised, where in the past they were simply ascribed to more widely ranging species or groups.

Today, the extent of desertification is believed to be at an all-time high,

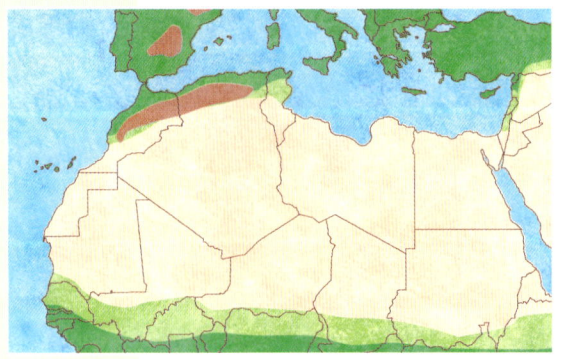

and human impact, especially goat herding, is considered the main reason for this. The Sahara reaches the Mediterranean Sea in Libya and Egypt and is only prevented in doing so in the Maghreb by the Atlas Mountains. The persecution by man extinguished populations of the larger fauna that were already pressured by the increasing aridity of the landscape.

CROSSBILL GUIDES • SOUTHERN MOROCCO

Flora

> High Mountain flora is best on route 1 and 3 and to a lesser extent also on route 2 and site E on page 151. The desert flora is hard to pin-point as it very much depends on the rains (see text). Routes 10 and 11 can be rewarding in good years. The special Souss flora is best seen on route 17. The Mediterranean coastal flora can be tracked down on sites A and B on pages 232-233, while the 'Canary' flora is seen on sites D and E on pages 234-235.

With over 4,200 species, Morocco as a whole has the richest flora of all of the North African countries. This is obviously due to the many different climates and microclimates, ranging from Atlantic to the Mediterranean, and from high mountains to the desert. What further diversifies the flora is that it has a mix of influences related to the evolutionary pathways that meet here from Africa, Europe and the Canaries. With tectonic and climatic shifts, Morocco was 'invaded' with plants not only from Europe and the desert but also from tropical and southern Africa and the more humid Canary Islands.

The majority of plant species are limited to the relatively humid zone of the north of Morocco. The southerly area covered in this book has a comparatively poor diversity, but it has a comparatively high

Two plants of sandy areas found most often at the coast: *Malcolmia triloba* (top) and *Androcymbium gramineum* (bottom).

FLORA

number of specialities. Over 50% of the 879 or so plant species endemic to Morocco are present here, and nearly 300 species are truly endemic to Southern Morocco. As with other faunal groups, further research is showing increasingly that the local populations are in fact so different from their relatives further north that they are considered to be separate, endemic species. This list of local specialities continues to grow, especially with relicts from the ice age and/or from the African Humid Period and are now remote from the normal range of their antecedents.

The vegetation makes up the main structural feature of the habitat. The dominant trees and shrubs (where they exist) are described in the habitat sections of this book. In this chapter, we focus mostly on the wildflowers that can be looked for across the region.

Many wildflowers spend much of their time with little evidence of them being present at all. Many lie dormant as a bulb or seed, or are reduced to a desiccated wad that is barely recognisable. They wait for the rains and since these are infrequent and unreliable, plants can wait for years. But when the desert blooms, it does so rapidly. For a brief period, the dull brown sand and rock become covered in new growth and a mix of crucifers, peas, asters and asphodels burst into flower.

The majority of the flora, however, consists of perennial species. They are mostly woody and belong to the xerophytes – plants with special adaptations to withstand the drought. They generally have reduced flowers and leaves, and succulent stems. Although they are superb champions of survival, the majority are not very showy to our eyes. In the mountains, most plants are closely related to similar-looking species from Europe, meaning identification of the local forms can be difficult. To complicate things further, there are few resources to call on to assist.

Even where the climatic conditions are good, most flowering plants come under intense pressure from domestic animals. Many species contain discouraging chemicals or rely on spines to discourage browsers, however the normal combination of sheep and goats seems to ignore most of these. Flowering plants are relatively palatable compared to the normal feed, so these tend to disappear very quickly.

Despite the issues raised above, there are many species that catch the eye and those are the subject of this chapter.

Mountain Flora

The elevation and humidity create a series of micro-ecosystems that make of the high mountains the most plant-rich habitat in Southern Morocco. This is particularly true of the High Atlas Mountains. These mountains

FLORA

have a very different character between the northward facing slopes and those to the south. The north-facing slopes are often humid enough to have two flowering seasons in the year, with a second 'spring' in September/October if conditions are right.

Overall, the flora of the High Atlas Mountains is similar to that of the Mediterranean regions, but due the isolation from other high mountain ranges many endemic species have evolved. Most species are either widespread in the Mediterranean basin or are local species related to more widespread Mediterranean species. Although it is the trees that define the main structure, the understorey comprises a mix of cistus, brooms and lavenders. These include endemic lavenders, such as *Lavandula maroccana* and *L. tenuisecta*, which can provide a profusion of purplish-blue flowers in spring.

The herb layer is also rich in endemics. Most are relatively subdued asters, peas and crucifers, which have grown to adapt to the particular conditions found. An endemic yellow foxglove (*Digitalis transiens*) is both large and relatively showy in the Sub-alpine zone. Another large group worthy of note is the Mints (*Lamiaceae*). Not only are there many endemics to be found in this group, but also Mint is significant culturally as drinking Mint Tea is a national pastime and a significant part of any display of hospitality, particularly in the more conservative south where alcohol is frowned upon. Here this national drink goes under the nickname of 'Berber Whisky'.

Some of the most eye-catching plants are the bulbous species. These include asphodels, narcissi and fritillaries. The most widespread is the small, pale blue iris-like Barbary Nut (*Moraea sisyrinchium*), which is not limited to the Barbary coast and actually part of a family of flowers that has its evolutionary roots in southern Africa. The asphodels are a dominant

Broad-leaved Marsh Orchid of the local endemic form *sesquipedalis* can be found in the Alpine zone of the High Atlas.

FLORA

Barbary Nut is a widespread spring bulb.

feature in many areas, often with their sword-shaped leaves and flower spike lasting well beyond the last flowers have died away. The main species here is Branched Asphodel, which is also common in the Mediterranean. There is a large variety of narcissi, both yellow and white. The Hoop-petticoat Daffodil, familiar to visitors of Spain, forms yellow drifts in late winter on dry meadows. In autumn there is the Moroccan endemic *Narcissus broussonetii*, a beautiful, white-flowering species that is relatively widespread including in lowland areas. *Narcissus watieri* is a small, white-flowered daffodil, which is limited to the Alpine zone and flowers in spring.

Fritillaries are another group of the Alpine zone, where *Fritillaria macrocarpa* should be looked for, especially as it is now regarded as distinct from the Spanish Fritillary (itself a scarce species in Morocco found further north in the Rif and in a single site on Jebel Lkest in the Anti-Atlas (site A on page 222).

Orchids are the most popular sought-for group of wildflowers, but if you are an orchid lover, Southern Morocco is not the best region to visit. Most of the terrestrial species evolved in Eurasia and don't grow well in arid regions. Most Moroccan orchids don't reach all the way to the south, and those that do are at the very limit of their range here.

In Southern Morocco, most orchid species are better searched for on the coast (e.g. site A on page 240), but in the mountain pine woods on limestone soils, you can come across Mirror and Yellow Bee Orchids, flowering from February to April, depending on the altitude. High in the Alpine zone grows the only mountain species of this group, a local form of the Broad-leaved Marsh Orchid, *Dactylorhiza majalis ssp. sesquipedalis*. It grows in wet spots and riverbanks (e.g. on route 1).

The Anti-Atlas Mountains are more extreme than even the southern slope of the High Atlas Mountains. The Anti-Atlas contains a large number of endemics, most of which are short-lived and relatively small-flowered. Much of the flora have their equivalent to the High Atlas species. For example, of the lavenders, the form *Lavandula rejdalii* found in the Anti-Atlas is unique, and the endemic white-flowered *Narcissus peroccidentalis* shows

FLORA

structural similarities to the Hoop-petticoat Daffodil mentioned earlier. Most visits to the Anti-Atlas will be notable for the lack of plant cover, but as always, visiting shortly after rains makes an enormous difference.

Steppes and Desert Flora

The flora of steppes and deserts is completely attuned to dealing with extreme temperature differences and lack of water. This is a habitat that is hostile to plants, and only few species have found a way to survive here. The species diversity is therefore low. Conversely, almost all plants that do manage to grow here, have a special significance for the ecosystem, the fauna and the people that live here.

Below the scarce trees and scrub layer of xerophytes (drought-resistant plants), the majority of species are annuals and they are dependent on the infrequent and unpredictable rains to survive. Most of them are asters, crucifers, spurges (euphorbias), goosefoots and from the pea family and generally have insignificant flowers.

Under normal conditions (that is during the dry period) plant life congregates in runnels, wadi beds and on the edge of sandy zones, where there is a bit more water and where nutrients are gathered by the flow after rain. In both the desert and the steppes the main rain season is between Octo-

Desert Melon (top) and Sodom's Apple Milkweed (bottom) are desert plants that appear to have welcoming fruits. Both deceive as every part of them is unpalatable.

FLORA

ber and December. Following any rain perennial bulbs and annuals will bloom, often providing a burst of seeds in February and March. The local form of Bladder Dock, *Rumex simpliciflorus*, is often common and the asphodels *Asphodelus tenuifolius* and *Asphodelus refractus* can form great drifts following the line of the wash out, often mixed with other desert species such as Sodom Apple Milkweed, the spurge *Euphorbia calyptera* and *Cleome africana*, the latter being a member of the caper family. Halfa Grasses (*Desmostachya bipinnata*) form tussocks that not only stabilise the movement of sand but provide burrows and nesting places for the animals and birds that make this extreme environment their home.

One plant that is impossible to ignore is the Desert (or Bitter) Melon (*Citrullus colocynthis*). It is its fruit that makes it so conspicuous – a football-sized 'melon' that lies on the desert floor. The fruit is incredibly bitter and is ignored by most animals, although it is supposedly useful in traditional medicine as a laxative and the seeds are eaten or carefully turned into a flour.

Of the flowers, the most dramatic are arguably the cistanches, a group of parasitic plants related to broomrapes. The Yellow Cistanche (*Cistanche phelypaea*) is the commonest, being widespread in the sandy habitats throughout and the flowers are a feature around most oases. The Violet Cistanche (*Cistanche violacea*) is arguably more dramatic and flowers in March in saline areas in the desert and arid steppes. It parasitises *Hammada*, *Zygophyllum* and *Limoniastrum* species but is nowhere common and the flowers are comparatively short-lived.

River Valley flora

In most places, the river valleys have been adopted for agriculture and the native flora is scarce, the area being dominated by the introduced and planted species except where 'weeds' have been allowed to grow.

One key exception is the Souss Valley, a wedge of low-lying land bounded by the High Atlas and Anti-Atlas Mountains and open to the coast to the west (see page 57). This area has a unique climate that is more humid and often hotter than the Mediterranean zones. It is in places almost tropical – a unique condition that is not to be found elsewhere in North Africa. Its isolation means that it is an endemic hotspot. The main attraction here is the Argan tree, which shapes the local ecosystem (see box).

Argan trees grow as an open woodland. Beneath the canopies, plants find a (slightly) cooler and damper habitat than in the desert and steppes. This more benign climate supports a scrub and herb layer that is rich in endemic species. As the Argan zone extends from near sea level to over 1000m,

there are differences of the actual species present across the range. As with the Argan itself, most species can also have their ancestors traced back to the Horn of Africa. Over 1000 plant species have been found here, of which 140 are endemic to Morocco, making this one of the most important ecosystems in Morocco. Some of the attractions that grow here are *Genista ifniensis, Euphorbia echinus, Teline segonnier, Lavandula pedunculata atlantica, Warionia saharae, Hesperolaburnum platycarpum* and *Micromeria arganietorum*.

Both Yellow (top) and Violet Cistanche (bottom) are parasitic plants with highly visible flower heads.

Coastal Flora

The Mediterranean zone is not limited to the High Atlas Mountains but also is represented in the northern coastal area around Essaouira. This area is actually richer in some groups than the corresponding floral zone in the High Atlas Mountains. This is particularly the case with the Bee Orchids (*Ophrys sp.*) where Sawfly, Woodcock, Dull Bee and Spanish Omega Orchids* (*O. dyris*), can be found in the maquis habitat. Also here are endemic bulbs. The Sand-crocus, *Romulea engleri* is found on the calcareous sands around Essaouira and the leek *Allium paniculatum ssp antiatlanticum* was found near Cap Rhir. It is worth noting that the

FLORA

The Argan Tree

Argan (*Argania spinosa*) is an endemic tree of Southern Morocco and one that is found only in the Souss valley, especially between Taroudant and Agadir. It is related to species in Southern Africa and arrived here during the African Humid Period. It is adapted to survive in hot and semi-arid places.

The Argan forest was adopted for a classic silvopasture land use, combining forestry with husbandry. The fruiting trees are grazed beneath by livestock, and both have an agricultural value.

Argan Trees are now prized for the fruit, the Argan Nut, which contains one, or rarely two or three, oil-rich seeds which are very high in unsaturated fats. The nuts take over a year to mature on the tree. The oil has been known for its healthy properties for many hundreds of years, however, it is only really since the millennium that demand has soared. It is likely that this was kick-started by the availability of micro-finance to women's collectives, and today it is a major income generator selling not only locally but across the world. The oil is used in foodstuffs, cosmetics and in alternative medicines.

Historically, the silvopasture in these forests was low intensity, lightly stocked with sheep and particularly goats. Foliage was cut to feed camels, cattle and other livestock. During the 20th century, the then low economic value of the trees led to over 50% of the forest being cut down and converted to arable crops. The remainder was overstocked with goats to the extent that the remaining trees were often damaged through direct browsing and cutting for animal feed.

Argan nuts take over a year to mature and both flowers and nuts can be found on the same branch.

Recently, since the growth of the Argan oil industry, there are signs of replanting of previously cleared areas. A specific group 'Argan Care' has been established to support and co-ordinate the socio-economic benefits of the Argan and May 10th is now officially Argan Tree day. Additionally, the goats are managed to reduce the competition for the nuts and to limit grazing to the understorey alone. The nutcake leftover from oil extraction has started being used as an animal feed, again reducing the need to prune the trees.

timing of spring flowering is different for the same habitat between the coast and the mountains, as the latter is driven by snow melt rather than the more predictable seasonal change on the coast, where flowering starts in December and normally runs through to early March.

As you travel south along the coast the overall flora changes, reflecting the increasingly dry climate. The true Mediterranean species decrease and the more drought-resistant species increase, especially stem succulents, such as the spurge *Euphorbia officinarum* and the aster *Kleinia anteuphorbium*. Of particular note are the five species of small, but exotic-flowered, succulents that were previously attributed to the genus *Caralluma*. These members of the dogbane family are more reminiscent of cacti and include two endemics *Apteranthes burchardii subsp. maura* and *Orbea decaisneana var. hesperidum*.

The sandy estuaries also provide a home to halophytes (salt-loving plants) such as *Traganum moquinii, Arthrocnemum indicum* and *Atriplex ifniensis* and species that are familiar in the true desert. Yellow Cistanche (*Cistanche phelipaea*) can be commonly found and the bizarre-looking Desert Thumb (*Cynomorium coccineum*) is much commoner in the coastal dunes than inland.

The area around the town of Sidi Ifni has become a renowned floral hotspot in its own right. Although geographically part of the Souss Valley, it is geologically unique as a coastal plateau of pre-Cambrian rocks rising to 900m above sea level and cutting the Souss from the Saharan depression further south. Here, the mix of species has been called Canarian flora (in literature usually referred to as 'Macaronesian'). After all the Canary Islands are only 100km off the Moroccan coast and the

Desert Thumb is a strange parasitic plant which although widespread is simplest to find on the coast (top). The Shrubby Pimpernel is a spring flower of coastal areas (bottom).

FLORA

climatic conditions (a desert-like climate tempered by cool and moist sea winds) are very similar. This area does share a good number of species with the Canary Islands, but in addition, also has many species in common with (or has close relatives in) the Rift Valley in East Africa. It is even the home to some truly tropical species from directly south of the Sahara. Here, the coastal cliffs hold species like the blue winter-flowering squill, *Autonoë* (or *Scilla*) *latifolia* and the Canary Rock-rose (*Helianthemum canariense*). More widespread in this area are the bush forming King Juba Spurge *Euphorbia regis-jubae* and Fringed Lavender (*Lavandula dentata*). Additionally, this is the only place where you can find the Spiderwort (*Commelina rupicola*), the sole representative of a tropical African group of plants that has its only outpost north of the Sahara.

A bit further east, where the elevation increases towards the western end of the Anti-Atlas Mountain, in the Oumaghouz massif, there is a different mix of plants. Within the gorges, especially around Jebel Imzi, there are rich populations of the dramatic Dragon Trees (*Dracaena draco ssp. ajgal*), another plant known from the Canary Islands, but here a different subspecies is found. Close to this site there are petroglyphs (ancient rock art) made with the tree's red sap, which shows that this is a truly ancient population. Other species found only here including Canary Island Laurel (*Laurus azorica*), the Bitumen Trefoil *Bituminaria antiatlantica*, Hare's-foot fern (*Davallia canariensis*) and African Spleenwort (*Asplenium aethiopicum*) reward the adventurous plant hunter (see site A on page 222).

The succulent spurge *Euphorbia officinarum* is an obvious plant that marks the transition from Mediterranean to Saharan climate.

Mammals

> The majority of the mammals in Morocco are very hard to find and are best searched for in the company of a local guide during a dusk or night excursion (best at Erg Chebbi; route 11 and M'Hamid; route 13). Some of the more exotic species, can also be found at the Gazelle Reserve (site C on page 234). Cuvier's Gazelle and Sengi make route 19 a hotspot. Egyptian Mongoose is frequent on the coast (route 25), Look for Barbary Sheep on route 7 and sites A and B on pages 214-215 and E on page 151 (the latter also for Cuvier's Gazelle). Barbary Ground Squirrel is common throughout and particularly easy to see on route 7.

Even the briefest of looks at a list of Moroccan mammals shows how different the country's wildlife is from the European. A plethora of exotic genera is suddenly added. Serval, Caracal, Honey Badger, jirds, jerboas, gazelles, Sengi; even Lion and Leopard feature on the surprisingly long list, which makes for exciting reading. Some you may know from African safaris or wildlife programmes, yet many Moroccan mammals are species that do not occur south of the Sahara. When it comes to mammals, Morocco is truly something else.

The reality is, unfortunately, that the vast majority of these animals are hard if not almost impossible to find. They are nocturnal in their habits and with the exception of the smaller mammals, they are also very scarce or, in the case of Lion and Leopard, went extinct in recent years.

For the normal visitor, mammal experiences are likely to be limited to the ubiquitous Barbary Ground Squirrel and perhaps some of the larger reintroduced ungulates (hooved animals). Some of the gazelles and antelopes can be seen in, or close to, their large release pens. It is the mammals, more than any other group, that have been impacted by the growth in the human population, the pressures of grazing and increased desertification. Those that remain are almost invariably in the most remote areas, in particular in the deserts and semi-deserts, where human population densities are very low. However, with effort, a number of species can be found. Perhaps you may even 'luck' into one of the more iconic species.

Rodents

The most numerous, widespread and diverse group of mammals are the rodents. There are fourteen or so species of jerboa, jird and gerbil that inhabit the desert areas, predominantly on the Sahara edge. All of these are

MAMMALS

Jerboas are strictly nocturnal and have kangaroo-like legs.

small mouse-like animals that feature long hind legs and comparatively short forelegs. This is most extreme in the jerboas, which have such large hind legs that they hop in a manner akin to mini-kangaroos. Jirds are the most mouse-like, and gerbils are somewhat intermediate between jerboas and jirds. All of them are nocturnal and although their numerous tracks in sandy areas suggest that they are common, it is difficult to actually see them unless a specific trip out is made after dark.

True mice, in contrast, are represented by relatively few species and are limited to the more humid area of the coast, the Souss and High Atlas. The Barbary Striped Grass Mouse is one of them. It is the sole representative north of the Sahara of a widespread African genus.

Three species of mouse-like rodents are both larger and, since they are active during the day, they are more likely to be encountered. All three are relatively large and slow moving, spending a large proportion of their time out of their burrows and often basking in full view. Two of them are gundis –large almost tail-less rodents, endemic to this area and the other countries of the Maghreb. The Common (or Atlas) Gundi is present in the eastern area of region on the edge of the High Atlas Mountains. The closely related Val's Gundi is a desert specialist found in the rocky area close to the Algerian border in the far east of the country. The third day-active rodent goes by the unflattering name of Fat Sand Rat, which is a literal translation of its scientific name *Psammomys obesus*. This is not a true rat, but a charming colonial rodent that looks superficially like an enormous jird, to which it is more closely related than to rats. It is an inhabitant of the High Arid Steppes and can be common in the sandy wash out zones on the edges of gravel plains where it feeds almost exclusively on Goosefoot plants. It lives in an extensive social burrow system and uses its long black-tipped tail as a signalling flag to communicate amongst the colony and warn of danger. It is specifically adapted to alternating periods of famine and then plenty. It can pile on fat reserves that carry it through the next famine. This adaptation has brought it to the attention of medical researchers as the species is susceptible to diabetes, but is somehow able to withstand the impact of the disease.

There are no arboreal squirrels in Morocco, but there are two species of ground squirrel. The Barbary Ground Squirrel is the most common one and easy to find as it is diurnal and tolerant of people. They are found along the coast, in the steppes and lower reaches of the High Atlas Mountains, preferring rocky areas where they feed on seeds and other vegetable matter. You will typically find them hanging around car parks and stealing food in some tourist hotspots. In the Souss Valley, it was only recently realised that the ground squirrels in the Argan forest are actually of a different species, the African Ground Squirrel, which is widespread south of the Sahara. This is an isolated population and, no doubt, one that followed the Argan trees on their evolutionary route to the area (see page 81). Two further large species can also be sought, both being almost exclusively nocturnal. The Crested Porcupine is associated with the edge of cultivations and needs the more humid ecosystems north of the High Atlas Mountains and the Souss Valley. The Cape Hare prefers the high Arid Steppes and edge of the Sahara, especially where there is good scrub cover. It may be flushed from its daytime resting places.

Insectivores

One surprising insectivorous animal of Morocco is the Sengi, sometimes called Elephant-Shrew. Sengis are a widespread group of sub-Saharan species that are not closely related to shrews, although superficially they look like a large version of one. They have long legs and a long mobile snout that has led to them being dubbed 'elephant'. This is the only member of the family north of the Sahara and like many other Moroccan species got isolated by the expansion of the desert (see page 83). Sengis are crepuscular and best searched for in the early morning in the rocky hillsides around the Anti-Atlas (see route 19). They are very active hunters and incredibly quick, often quoted as being the fastest small mammal in the world.

There are around 20 species of bat to be found in this part of Morocco, yet there is very little information regarding them. Some are very difficult

MAMMALS

The insectivorous North African Sengi or Elephant-shrew is a strange creature that is considered the fastest-running small mammal in the world.

to identify even with specialised equipment like bat detectors, as their sonogram signatures are not well understood.
The towns in the desert areas can show strong flights of bats in the evenings. The commonest species on the edge of the Sahara appears to be Kuhl's Pipestrelle. It roosts and hunts around hotels on the edge of the palmeries. It has a very similar sonic call to Common Pipestrelle, but the habitat is different. With more people using advanced bat detectors nowadays, we can hope that a better understanding of all the species will be available in the future. But there are more observations needed to build a pattern of occurrence. The same can be said of the five species of shrew.
Larger insectivores include two species of Hedgehog. The Algerian Hedgehog favours the more humid Mediterranean habits of the coastal fringes and the mountains. In the desert areas, it is replaced by the more drought-tolerant Desert Hedgehog. Both species are widespread and can be found anywhere here, but again are strictly nocturnal.

Carnivores

Morocco's list of carnivores is large, but as said, most of them are scarce and occur in remote areas. Sightings are very few, and it is presumed that all carnivorous species occur in very low numbers. Their stealthy and nocturnal habits plus the general remoteness and inaccessibility of much of Southern Morocco, make their presence somewhat mysterious.
Your best chances are of finding Egyptian Mongoose, which prefers to be out at dawn and dusk and is most common in the Souss Valley and coastal areas. The same area is home to the Spotted Genet, but as this animal is only active at night, it less likely to be seen.

MAMMALS

Night drives are the only opportunites to see the nocturnal mammals such as this Fennec Fox.

Two small cat species are listed for the region, namely the Sand Cat and African Wildcat. They are rarely reported, although recently Sand Cats have been found around Merzouga (route 11). This gives hope that the population hangs on.

The larger cat species are Caracal and Serval, both of which are said to still occur, particularly in the more remote parts of the eastern High Atlas Mountains. Nevertheless, there are so few sightings that it is almost impossible to say anything about their behaviour and occurrence in the region. Wild Leopards and Lions, represented by the endemic form the 'Atlas Lion' are definitely a thing of the past, although the Atlas Lion still exists in captivity.

Among the canids (dog family), the familiar Red Fox will be the most likely to be encountered. As in Europe, it is widely distributed and even occurs around desert towns, where it is reliant upon human activity to be able to survive. Its two local relatives are true Sahara specialists: the Rüppell's Fox and the Fennec Fox. They shun the towns and are adapted to live in these arid lands. Neither of them needs water to drink, surviving on the moisture from their prey alone. The Fennec is primarily a species of the sandy areas and the Rüppell's of the rocky bluffs, but there can be overlap in some areas. If footprints are any indication, there appears to be a healthy population around several routes in this guide (e.g. routes 11, 12, 14, 20 and 21). Again, both species are wholly nocturnal and only seen if you are (very) lucky. The best chance is if you find a guide who knows a denning site, although care must always be taken not to disturb them.

FLORA AND FAUNA

MAMMALS

Ungulates

Most ungulate species (hooved animals) were extinct in the wild in Morocco – the result of heavy persecution. The only exception is the Dorcas Gazelle, of which wild populations remain, albeit rare, on the edge of the Sahara and Cuvier's Gazelle that is found further north to the southern edge of Anti-Atlas Mountains (route 19). Fortunately, this grim situation can still be reversed. All of the species that until recently roamed the region are the subject of captive breeding programs with the aim to release them into the wild across their historic range. The main species are Barbary Sheep, Addax and Scimitar Oryx, together with Cuvier's Gazelles which are all held in large scale fenced pens with an intention to return them to their past range (see site C on page 234). Re-introduced Cuvier's Gazelles and Barbary Sheep have already recovered sufficiently to be considered semi-feral.

Now, Barbary Sheep can be found well away from the release sites. This species is indigenous to North Africa from Egypt to Morocco and as far south as Mali and Niger. It is very well adapted to drought, never needing to come to drink as it can get all the water it needs from the vegetation. The Barbary Sheep grows to one metre tall at the shoulder and weighs up to 140kg. Historically it was the favoured prey of Atlas Lion and Leopard, but now its only persecution comes from people. The sheep can be found on the slopes and in the gorges of the High Atlas and are not welcomed by goat herders as they are seen to be in direct competition. They are best looked for at higher altitudes than the goat herders' flocks or on the crest of gorges.

the endemic Barbary Sheep can now be seen on arid slopes after a successful re-introduction scheme.

The Cuvier's Gazelle is also doing well, but does not appear to have spread very far from the release pens. It is still best looked for around the Tiz-n-Test pass across the High Atlas Mountains or around Tafraoute in the Anti-Atlas Mountains where, in this latter case, it is thought that some at least are descendants of truly wild animals. Although they are the same height as the Barbary sheep, this is a typical gazelle, very slight, with a maximum weight of only 35kg. They are best searched for at dawn or dusk.

CROSSBILL GUIDES • SOUTHERN MOROCCO

Birds

> Routes 1 to 5, site A on page 148 and E on page 151 are good for finding the birds of the High Atlas Mountains. Routes 6 to 9 and sites A to E on pages 165 to 167 are excellent for tracking down the birds specialised in surviving on the high arid plains. For desert birds, try routes 10 to 14 and any place where plants are growing due to recent rains. Sites A, C and D on pages 185-186 are also good for finding desert birds, as are the Anti Atlas routes 19, 20 and 21. The Argan forest avifauna is best explored on routes 15-18, site A on page 200 and C to E on pages 202-203. On the coast, visit the estuaries, routes 22, 24 and 25, plus site A and B on pages 232-233.

Morocco has long been a focus for many European birders as it brings together the perfect mix of desert, mountain and Mediterranean species. Large numbers of migrants pass through the area as part of their journey to or from Eurasia. There is relatively easy access to Saharan habitat with its specialities and there is a good number of North-African endemic and near-endemic birds. To make it tangible – it is here and only here, that you can see a Wryneck, having a break from its travel north, sitting under a bush in which a Desert Wheatear is perched and a Tristram's Warbler (one of the local endemics) is hiding. If you are lucky, all in a single view. The migrants include both sub-Saharan winterers and a number of species that go no further south than the northern fringes of the Sahara. These can be found widely spread across the region but funnel along the coast and across the passes in the High Atlas Mountains. In the desert areas, they stick to whatever vegetation they can find and concentrate in oases and around human habitation. At peak season, both the number and the diversity can be mind-boggling. At times, there seems to be more bird than there is bush for them to sit in.

The arid regions, both the Sahara edge and the High Arid Steppes are home to a series of birds that are not found further north and are adapted to survive in these unforgiving environments. By definition, they do not need the oases to survive (although many, such as Desert Sparrow and Fulvous Babbler use the oases as nest sites). Some even shun them, such as various larks and sandgrouse. Even though these birds are tricky to track down, Morocco is undoubtedly currently the best place in the world to find them. Although they are widespread along the northern edge of the Sahara and into the Middle East, access to the right habitat is nowhere easier than here.

BIRDS

The last group of birds is arguably the most exciting – the species that are only found in Morocco and the other Maghreb countries (Algeria, Tunisia). Before the millennium, only two such species were recognised (Barbary Partridge and Moussier's Redstart), with a third being limited to Algeria (Algerian Nuthatch). Now, depending on which taxonomy you follow there are up to 30 endemic species in the Maghreb, and proposals to adopt more. This in turn has increased the interest and with that a greater understanding of the behaviour and distribution of these birds. It is likely that with this greater interest and research further species will be recognised.

The assembly of species differs strongly from place to place, as can be expected in such a large area with an enormous diversity of habitats. Here we describe the birdlife for each of the main habitat zones of Southern Morocco.

African Blue Tit is plentiful in the forest and river valleys up to the Subalpine zone.

Mountain birds

As the High Atlas Mountains have long been isolated from the other Alpine areas, there are species that have evolved to be found here and nowhere else, which naturally became the target for any visiting birder. Each elevation has its own special birds.

Perhaps the best example of such an endemic is the African Crimson-winged Finch – a fairly large, seed-eating bird of the open mountain slopes above the tree line. It is present in the Alpine zone throughout the year and will move high up in the most inaccessible areas of the mountains, especially in the summer. The most reliable place to find it is at Oukaïmeden (route 1), but even here it can be difficult once the snow has gone. It is a classic example of an altitudinal migrant that is mostly found at the snow limit. Only at times of extreme snowfall it is found outside the mountains.

Above the tree line, another special species can be found in the summer months. The Atlas (or Seebohm's) Wheatear has recently been elevated to species level and is found here and as far north as the Middle Atlas. There is still mystery over where it actually winters as all that is recorded is that it migrates south, destination unknown, away from the region between November and March. Due to its isolation the 'Atlas' Horned Lark and local forms of both the Alpine Accentor and Eurasian Wren are coming under scrutiny as potentially separate species. Other high-altitude birds include Red-billed Chough, Alpine Chough and Northern Raven that are present year-round, whilst White-rumped Swift only arrive in late May to nest in the high cliffs. Above these cliffs, raptors can be found soaring. Bonelli's Eagles breed widely but in low numbers and a few pairs of Bearded Vultures still exist, particularly around the more remote parts of the Toubkal Massif.

It is not only the high massifs that hold special birds. The Sub-alpine zone with its Juniper woods and open meadows is also attractive. These are the preferred breeding areas for two of the local endemics, namely Tristram's Warbler and Moussier's Redstart. Both are only summer visitors to this area that spend the winter at lower altitudes and on the surrounding steppes, in the case of Tristram's Warbler right down to the Saharan edge. Moussier's can also be found much lower even as a breeding species and occurs in scrub all the way to the coast. In winter, the Sub-alpine zone holds Ring Ouzels that migrate from Eurasia to winter here, joining the resident local race of Mistle Thrush.

Lower still, and particularly in the wooded valleys on the northern slopes, Levaillant's Woodpecker nests. It is closely related to the Green Woodpecker, and like that species, it feeds mainly on ants.

The lower slopes are clad in pine forests. These are less valued by visiting birders as they appear to contain mostly birds that are familiar from Northern Europe. However, a closer look should reveal African Blue Tit, together with a selection of subtly different sub-species of more familiar birds such as Coal Tit (ssp *atlas*), Chaffinch (ssp *africana*) and Crossbill (ssp *poliogyna*), each of which is currently being proposed to be treated as a full species. A recent split from the Tawny Owl, the Maghreb Owl, is more common here than elsewhere, although it can also be found in town parks on both sides of the High Atlas Mountains and into the Souss Valley. In the few areas where the Atlas Cedar remains, the Atlas Flycatcher can be sought. Although certainly most common and easier to find in the Middle Atlas Mountains (outside the scope of this book) there are still a few remaining here.

Of course, the slopes of the mountains, at all elevations but especially where they connect with the Tizis (mountain passes) and other migration bottlenecks are good for grounded migrants. Almost anything can turn up but the flocks of Black Kites, Booted Eagles and Bee-eaters are difficult to

BIRDS

miss especially during migration after a period of bad weather when their passage is delayed.

Arid Steppe Birds

Although the stony steppe north of the Atlas is the first bird habitat encountered by most visitors to southern Morocco, this area is much changed in character and has been adapted for intensive agriculture by the burgeoning human population. Nevertheless, these steppes are not devoid of birds. Typical species of the farmlands are similar to the Mediterranean countries, with Corn and Cirl Buntings, Spotless Starlings and Spanish Sparrows frequenting the orchards and hedgerows. In the fields, Crested and Thekla's Larks are common and in winter these can be joined by flocks of Skylark and Calandra Lark from further north. Dotterel used to be a familiar winter bird of these steppes, but recent declines suggest that they have moved on, but it is not yet known where to (this is one of these avian puzzles that makes the Moroccan birdlife so fascinating).

It is not solely these familiar species that are present. Maghreb Magpies, recently split from the Eurasian form, are plentiful. Around towns and villages both Laughing Doves and House Buntings are resident and Little Swift joins Pallid and Common Swifts to breed. Other endemics such as Barbary Partridge and Moussier's Redstart can also be present, the latter mainly in winter as it breeds higher up in the local mountains.

The higher steppes to the south of the High Atlas Mountains offer much better birdwatching than those to the north. The southern steppes have been spared the wholesale conversion to agriculture, in the main due to the greater extremes in temperature and the lack of water. This is an area for larks, wheatears and sandgrouse. Note, however, that different species occur here from those on the edge of the Sahara.

The majority of the steppe is comprised of dark gravel plains covered with drought-adapted scrub. The landscape is interspersed with rocky bluffs and cut by dry wadis, which only flow immediately after rain. The species that inhabit the steppes are each focused on a particular habitat and these include Trumpeter Finch and a range of larks, each with very different feeding strategies. The Thick-billed Lark has developed an enormous hawfinch-like bill that can crack open the hardest of desert seeds, which it finds on the gravel plains. This bird is highly nomadic as it follows the rainfall and the flowering of the desert plants. The Greater Hoopoe-lark likes sandy edges and wash out zones, having a long down-curved bill with which it digs for grubs in the root balls of desert plants. Both species have large white flashes in their wings, more so in the Hoopoe Lark which has

a dramatic tumbling display flight launched from the top of a bush (see photo on page page 181). The Thick-billed Lark sings softly from the top of a pebble, even if that only lifts him a centimetre or two from the ground.
Desert, Temminck's, Crested, Thekla's and both Short-toed Larks can all be found in the same rocky habitat. All species are nomadic and can occur anywhere. The tried and tested 'hotspots' such as the Tagdilt track (route 8) are good places to start. One species that is substantially more enigmatic than most is the Dupont's Lark. Most of the Moroccan population has traditionally been found just outside the area covered by this book near Midelt, but a small population is known to exist near Ighri, in a very limited area around the Tizi n'Taratine (site A on page 200). It is an incredibly hard species to see, as it rarely flies and only quickly dashes from one patch of vegetation to the next. Most often it is located through its song, which is only sung around dawn and in spring.

One group of insectivorous birds stands out above all others, namely the wheatears. These characteristic birds normally sit up on the top of bushes, rock piles and even road signs – basically anything that sticks up and can serve as a lookout perch. In the arid steppes, the most often seen is the White-crowned Wheatear. This is a relatively large wheatear, which

Maghreb Wheatear (top) and Temminck's Lark (left) are two birds best looked for in the High Arid Steppes.

BIRDS

often occurs without its white crown, making it easy to confuse with Black Wheatear, which occurs around cliffs. In open areas with some scrub, the White-crowns are joined by Desert and Red-rumped Wheatears, but it is the Maghreb Wheatear (formerly considered to be the western population of the Mourning Wheatear), that is the main target in this habitat. It has become scarce in recent years and usually needs a special effort to find. During migration these are joined by Northern, Atlas (Seebohm's) and Western Black-eared Wheatears, however, these are not tied to the steppes and can occur anywhere as they migrate.

The steppes are also the haunt of sandgrouse. Of the five species that occur in Morocco, four can be found in the high steppes. Sandgrouse are notoriously difficult to spot on the ground as they are so well camouflaged. However, they have a habit of flying long distances to drinking pools. All sandgrouse have specially adapted breast feathers that function like a pouch, which they use to take water to their chicks. Black-bellied, the commonest here, Pin-tailed and Crowned Sandgrouse are all morning drinkers and the easiest way to find them is on their drinking flights to find water – a flight that they typically make 1-2 hours after dawn, when their distinctive typical flight calls can aid identification. The fourth species of Sandgrouse occurring in the high steppes is the Lichtenstein's Sandgrouse. This beautifully painted bird is much scarcer and only appears around the rocky hillsides where the southern edge of the steppe meets the Anti-Atlas Mountains (see route 20). Unlike the other sandgrouse, this species is an evening drinker, turning up just as the light fails.

'Atlas' Long-legged Buzzard is the only Buzzard present.

Other species found regularly on the steppes, but not tied to here, include Cream-coloured Courser, Great Grey Shrike, Tawny Pipit and Atlas Long-legged Buzzard. One further species worthy of mention is the Streaked (Saharan) Scrub Warbler, which can also be found where the steppes meet the mountains. They favour scree and barely vegetated slopes in the driest of areas and have a highly irregular distribution. There are only a few places where it occurs more frequently and where you stand a chance of finding them (e.g. route 21). They head to the desert edge in winter, however, these movements are not well understood.

Saharan Birds

In the Sahara, there are two major natural bird habitats: the gravel/rocky zones, and the sand desert. Each has a different mix of species, but both support some very special ones. The further bird habitat in the desert is formed by the oases that dot the landscape and have been supported and extended by the khetteras irrigation system (see page 23).

The sand desert of the northern fringes of the Sahara is fragile but also holds the most iconic birds. This is the area to find African Desert Warbler, Fulvous Babbler, Egyptian Nightjar, Desert Sparrow and a mix of larks that include Bar-tailed, Maghreb and, more rarely, Dunn's. Nearly all of the birds in this zone are irruptive, moving to and breeding where any rainfall results in the right conditions.

Cream-colored Courser is a bird of the steppes and Sahara.

There are subtle differences in the nature of the sand, which further differentiate the bird communities. African Desert Warbler likes the low dunes that are covered in clumps of Halfa grasses. This is the foraging area of Maghreb Lark, Fulvous Babbler and Desert Sparrow, but the last two are both dependent on the palmeries to nest in. The flat sandy plains and wadi washouts are preferred by Bar-tailed Larks and Dunn's Larks. Such areas with scattered bushes form the classic places to find roosting Egyptian Nightjars.

BIRDS

Crest to the test

If you have been birdwatching on the Iberian Peninsula, you may have faced a classic identification challenge – the separation of Thekla's and Crested Larks. Here in Morocco this challenge is brought to the next level, with a third species with a pointy crest, the Maghreb Lark. To confuse things further, across our region there are five subspecies of Thekla's Lark and a minimum of two differing Crested Larks, that means that physical features need to be considered with care. Habitat is often cited as a key feature, and to an extent this can help, but care is needed as this is rarely diagnostic.

Maghreb Lark is a species of the Saharan edge. Its longer bill is a feature evolved to probe deeper into sandy roots. However, Maghreb Lark has been found in the High Arid Steppes which hold the other two species as well. With care you can identify the birds with the mix of features that aligns to each of the species, but it is the song that makes this simpler. Crested Lark has a song that drops at the end, making it sound mournful. Thekla's tone rises at the end and therefore is a happy song. Maghreb is neither happy nor sad and is intermediate to the other two species.

The three 'crested larks' are not easy to tell apart. This is the Maghreb Lark.

The high sand dunes are almost birdless, only a Brown-necked Raven or two being present.

Where sand and gravel meet, a different mix of species is found, which includes Cream-colored Courser and Hoopoe Larks. Both use their long, curved beaks to dig in the bases of grass and bushes.

In the stony plains the premier prize for any visitor is the Houbara Bustard. This large and beautiful bird is extremely rare and its demise has been driven by both habitat loss and hunting. (see box on page 110).

Two species of sandgrouse occur in the desert – the aforementioned Crowned Sandgrouse and the Spotted Sandgrouse. These rarely form mixed flocks but can be seen in large numbers together when they come to drink as long as there is not much choice in drinking places. Both species like to collect water around two hours after dawn and will often congregate close to the water hole before heading to the drinking spot en-masse.

Spotted Sandgrouse (top) and Trumpeter Finch (bottom) are adapted to life in arid regions.

In winter, the stony desert also attracts species from the High Arid Steppe to the north, and flocks of larks can be found. It is interesting to note that the Maghreb Lark seems to move the other way, and in winter can be found spread more widely, including moving north to the higher stony plains.

The rocky bluffs should not be ignored. These are important nesting and roosting sites for African Rock Martin, Lanner Falcon, Pharaoh Eagle Owl and Brown-necked Raven, but with the exception of the last, it is unlikely that you will find one without assistance. Desert Larks can be found at the foot of the bluffs and in winter it is possible to find Scrub Warblers here.

The oases are generally close to towns and can be extensive. They are dominated by palms that are grown for shade, and often surrounded by Tamarisks that provide shelter from both wind and sand storms. Irrigation of the fields means that these are often full of insects and are attractive as re-fuelling places for migrants. Flycatchers, warblers, bee-eaters, chats and other species can be found finding shelter. A few hours of birding can bring a wide range of species especially in March-April and September-October.

The tamarisks are also popular wintering areas for the Tristram's Warblers, and they can be easier to find here than in the more natural habitat of acacias in the wadi edges. In summer, the palmeries provide the main

BIRDS

habitat for Blue-cheeked Bee-eater. This beautiful bird nests particularly in the large palmeries around Erfoud and in the Drâa valley. The Tamarisks are a favoured breeding habitat for Eastern Olivaceous Warblers of the subspecies *reiseri*, also dubbed the Desert Olivaceous Warbler and another favourite for being recognised as a full species in the future.

Typical desert species include the Crowned Sandgrouse of the gravel plains, whilst Bar-tailed Larks prefer the sandy areas.

Coastal Birds

The network of estuaries along the coast provides an important habitat for the 'East Atlantic flyway' – one of world's great migratory routes for birds. The East Atlantic Flyway is part of the Eurasian-African flyway, which is used by birds that breed in the western and central part of Europe as far north as the polar tundra between Greenland and Siberia. Although many species continue southwards to sub-Saharan Africa, a fair number spend the winter in Morocco.

Although the migration is most visible along the coast, many species of wildfowl and wader can be found many hundreds of kilometres inland. It is clear that much remains to be understood about the routes taken to the Gulf of Guinea and the Southern Cape.

Flamingos, Spoonbills, Glossy Ibis and a mix of herons that are familiar from the Mediterranean are all present in Southern Morocco although few stay to breed. Yellow-legged Gull and Lesser Black-backed Gulls are plentiful. In addition scarcer Mediterranean species including Slender-billed and

BIRDS

The plight of the Houbara

The Houbara is one of two large bustards that were once present in the stony steppes on the northern edge of the Sahara. The other, namely the Arabian Bustard, is now extinct in the country. The Houbara is critically endangered and is represented by the North African endemic subspecies undulata. Morocco holds an important population, however little is known of the movements of the birds in the remaining habitat, except that they are non-migratory and are assumed to move based upon the rains and local availability of food.

The Houbara is endangered due to a combination of disturbance, habitat loss and hunting with falcons. UNESCO has recognised Arabian falconry as an Intangible Cultural Heritage of Humanity. This has not only led to efforts to preserve the art, but also the traditional prey – Stone Curlews and bustards.

The modern version of this tradition has attracted wealthy Arabs to Morocco in their ongoing attempts to secure continuing traditional prey for their pastime. This came with enormous local prestige and funds – paradoxically, the interests of the hunters and conservation groups aligned.

Conservation action was started in the last millennium, with the rearing of birds in captivity, using the expertise developed by Sheik bin Zayed from the UAE. His group gained its experience from a captive breeding programme for the closely related McQueen's Bustard in Abu Dhabi. The Moroccan breeding centre for the Houbara lies north of our area. It was run firstly by Saudi Arabians and now Qatari groups. It is estimated that over 18,000 birds were released in the first 10 years and increasingly more since. Although many stay close to the release site, some wander widely.

Much of the Houbara population now resides close to the Algerian border, which is relatively untouched as it is mainly a 'no-go zone' given the tensions between both countries. For the Houbara this is a plus, as it means that there are few people around and they are not disturbed. However, even here, they are very scarce and rarely seen except by seeking the assistance of a local guide.

an important proportion of the world's Audouin's Gulls winter in Southern Morocco, especially around Agadir. Sandwich, Common, Arctic, Little and Caspian Terns are often seen, and Lesser Crested Terns are relatively widespread in the autumn. They are believed to originate from Mediterranean breeding colonies in Libya, and they pause on their migration to their winter sites in West Africa. In addition, immature birds can be found at any season during their first year, as they wander the coasts without need to reach their breeding grounds. A few West African Crested Terns (until recently considered to be the western population of the Royal Tern) have

BIRDS

started to join them. These come from the opposite direction to the Lesser Cresteds, being drift migrants from further south.

For various duck species that breed in Europe, the south Moroccan coast forms the southernmost wintering ground. Tufted Duck, Pochard, Pintail, Wigeon and Shoveler are all familiar in season. Among them is the Marbled Duck, a rare and threatened Mediterranean bird, of which relatively high numbers are present. It is most common in Southern Morocco in the winter months, but some do stay to breed. Ruddy Shelduck is commonplace, but relatively scarce further north.

Waders are plentiful, and whilst the numbers and diversity are often bewildering, the species found should be familiar to visitors from Europe. Big flocks of Oystercatcher, both Black-tailed and Bar-tailed Godwit, Red Knot, Dunlin, Redshank and Greenshank are all present along the coast. Many of them can also be found on waterways across the breadth of the area. Little Ringed Plovers, Curlew Sandpiper, Little Stint and Temminck's Stint do not appear to be tied to the coastal route and have been found around Merzouga and Ouarzazate. Perhaps more surprisingly, Grey Phalarope can also be found in these desert settings.

The coastal estuaries spread inland and these well-vegetated marshes attract Snipe of three species, Great, Common and Jack, along the muddy edges. These are also the best places to look for crakes during migration and again three species are possible, namely Little, Baillon's and Spotted. The bushes to the edge of the marshes are often the best place to look for migrants and it certainly appears that Iberian Chiffchaff and Western Olivaceous Warbler are more readily found here than elsewhere.

Besides this overwhelming diversity of migrants, there are also a number of breeding birds, which for visiting birders, are perhaps of most interest. Three species are often the target – African Reed Warbler, Brown-throated Martin and Black-crowned Tchagra. All three are widespread south of the Sahara, but have isolated populations along the Moroccan coast. The African Reed Warbler is perhaps the most contentious as it has only recently been proposed that the well-known population of local reed warblers is actually of the African species rather than the very similar looking Eurasian Reed Warbler. The African Reed Warbler is resident, but during migration it is difficult to tell the 'Africans' from the plentiful 'Eurasians' that pass through.

The Brown-throated Martin is found mainly in the estuaries and is a smaller and duller version of its relative the Sand Martin. Like the Sand Martin, it breeds in loose colonies along sandy banks of the estuaries. The Black-crowned Tchagra is by the far the most attractive of the three target birds. It

is the sole representative of the Bush-shrikes (a group from tropical Africa) to be found north of the Sahara. It is not closely related to the shrikes and does not, like shrikes, perch in the open. Rather, it is a skulking bird that moves about in the thickest of vegetation. It is more often heard than seen and the fluty calls are not uncommon along riverine vegetation. Every now and then it briefly comes out of the shrubs and shows its striking plumage.

Turning away from the land, the Atlantic Ocean itself has some attractive birds as well. One of the few colonies of Eleonora's Falcons outside the Mediterranean is on the island off Essaouira. Its presence demonstrates the abundance of the offshore migration of land birds, as Eleonora's Falcons specialise in hunting migrants and even breed in autumn when their prey is most easily caught.

Further offshore, the cool Canary Current provides nutrient-rich waters that form rich fishing grounds for birds. Pelagic birds are best seen from headlands or by chartering a boat from one of the coastal fishing centres. The two most frequently encountered species are Gannets and Cory's Shearwater but skuas, both Arctic and Pomarine are also often seen. They chase terns to rob them of their food and are mostly seen when flocks of terns pass through.

Adouin's Gull (top) and Marbled Duck (bottom) both occur in the estuaries of Southern Morocco.

BIRDS

The recent increase in focused pelagic trips has begun to show that Great, Sooty and Balearic Shearwaters are also regular along the South Moroccan coast, and that Wilson's Storm Petrel and Sabine's Gull both join them. More exciting species are sometimes found including White-faced Storm Petrels, and it is likely with more people looking the list will get longer. In addition, satellite tagging has thrown up some surprises including that Cape Verde Shearwaters enter these waters to feed, but as yet very few visual sightings can be added to these tracking records. With the increase in pelagic trips from Agadir and Essaouira there appears to be plenty to be added to our understanding.

The Bald Ibis

For many birdwatchers, the highlight of the coast is the Northern Bald Ibis. This unique bird breeds in colonies on the coast. The Bald Ibis was once widespread across Morocco but is now limited to the Souss-Massa National Park and these represent the last truly wild birds left in the world. Several centuries ago, the Ibis was widespread across a large part of Europe. The Moroccan birds were resident, but the northern and eastern populations were migratory, and this no doubt exacerbated the decline of the European population. The last wild birds outside of Morocco bred in Turkey and wintered in Yemen, but these were taken into care after a precipitous decline. A tiny, isolated population was found in Syria in 2002, but they are unlikely to have survived the war there. In recent years, the Bald Ibis has been reintroduced in Spain, Switzerland, Germany and Austria – places that were formerly part of its range.

The Moroccan birds are divided into two populations on either side of Agadir. Both groups inhabit the coastal scrub between the Souss and Massa estuaries. These populations have responded well to protection and the formation of the National Park. Numbers are currently at an all-time high. However, there is growing evidence that the current population is reaching the carrying capacity of the habitat and breeding success rates are reducing.

Birding during migration

Spring migration is the most popular time for birders to visit. The mix of resident specialities, (now displaying and most easy to see) and the literally millions of birds heading north to Eurasia to breed means that this is a fabulous time to come. For land birds, the African-Eurasia flyway is not uniform across the whole of the continent, but largely concentrates on two routes. First there is the Eastern flyway which concentrates around the Rift valley, and second the western route which is important to Morocco as it uses the the Straits of Gibraltar to minimise the sea crossings. The shorebirds and seabirds also follow the Moroccan coast and winter along the North African shoreline, including in Morocco.

Shorebirds that winter south of the equator are not limited to the coastal zones. Many winter on inland waters across the continent and even those that are primarily coastal will migrate overland, shortcutting the longer coastal migration route around the Gulf of Guinea.

Combined this means a large number and a wide diversity of species head through this zone twice a year. Unlike the local birds, they are not adapted to the deprivations of this arid land, and therefore they take advantage of any vegetation and water they can find, often creating wonderful mixes of species that seem strange, as they are composed of birds that have wildly different breeding habitat and breeding ranges. For example, I had the pleasure once of seeing a mixed flock of passerines, including Western Orphean, Western and Eastern Olivaceous, Sub-alpine and Moltoni's Warblers, Pied and Spotted Flycatchers and Black-eared Wheatears, whilst listening to flyover European and Blue-cheeked Bee-eaters, and following a family party of Fulvous Babblers through a wadi of Acacia.

Of course, not all species use the same migration strategy. In spring, birds hurry to chase north to secure the best breeding territories in competition with others of the same species. Many birds fly very long legs of their journey north, minimising travel time. The majority of them are forced to pause just south of the High Atlas Mountains though, which makes the area so good for finding migrants.

The call of the European Bee-eater is an indication that migrants are on the move.

There are two reasons most birds make a stop before crossing the mountains. First is the sheer size of the Sahara, which means that even the strongest birds are exhausted after crossing the desert and need to stop and rest after the Sahara crossing. Second, the High Atlas Mountains form a physical

barrier, made worse by the northerly winds that often flow off the peaks at this time of year.

Even in the Autumn, when the need to travel quickly is reduced, topography plays its part. The Saharan crossing is as bad as any ocean crossing, and the southerly driven sand storms are more plentiful in the late season. The benefit for insectivorous species is that the Acacia trees on the desert edge are in bloom and provide protein-rich pollen, nectar and insects in profusion, just as the birds arrive needing that final boost before crossing the desert.

Migrating Eurasian breeding species, such as Wryneck (top) and Western Black-eared Wheatear (bottom), regularly turn up in 'odd' habitats.

Of course, migration is not a happening but a process that covers many months. Each species times its move from the wintering grounds by a mechanism we still don't fully understand. Each individual species tends to move through during a 3-4 week window. In spring migration as a whole starts in February and ends in May. The return is even more drawn out, as birds that didn't breed or whose nests failed, may start drifting southwards already in June. Such birds are not in a hurry to move south as there are no territories to occupy and defend. The last individuals pass through southern Morocco in November.

There are also differences in migration strategies. Some species will travel in family groups, whilst in others adults and this year's young take a different timing (sometimes even a different route).

The strategy for birdwatchers who want to experience migration to the full, is to diversify. Try a mix of locations at different times. Spend time on the coast, watching not only the waders on the sandflats, but also searching the estuary side vegetation for any passerines. Perhaps invest some hours on a sea-watch from Cap Rhir or even a boat trip offshore. Inland, focus on the patches of water or the islands of vegetation. Stay close to a desert oasis, where early morning can be dramatic for passerines and even the surrounding areas can be full of migrant species. Finally, try one of the primary mountain passes over the High Atlas Mountains, especially when contrary winds are in play. Raptor migration and other visible migration can be spectacular and the riverine scrub can be full of birds.

Birding during the winter months

Whilst most birders visit Morocco during migration, winter certainly has its charm as well. Many of the most attractive birds – the species that people travel to Morocco for – are resident, so also present in the colder season. In addition, there are some species that find their winter home in Morocco. The winter is often a more comfortable time to visit, as the temperatures are lower and birding in the desert areas is not confined to the early and late hours, because birds remain active during the day and there is little or no heat haze.

African Crimson-winged Finch – a localised endemic – often raids nut stalls in the winter at Oukaimeden (route 1).

Visiting after the rains in October/November can show the desert in bloom, or at least greener than later in Spring and Summer, and this again can help find the more nomadic species. When visiting in winter, it is important to recognise that although resident in Morocco, some species migrate down from the mountains and are found in different areas. The most notable of these is Tristram's Warbler, which breeds in the High Atlas Mountains, but winters at lower altitudes on the edge of the Sahara. It can be easier to find in the tamarisks around Erg Chebbi (see route 11) in winter than almost anywhere else. Likewise, the birds of

BIRDS

the Alpine zone are pushed down with the dropping snow limit. This can mean that they are much easier to find, and interestingly, they can be remarkably tolerant of people at this time. Crimson-winged Finches, for example, will raid nut stalls around the ski-lift at Oukaïmeden and both species of chough plus Atlas Horned Larks will not be far away.

Being released from the breeding territories, many birds will form flocks and wander in response to the rain and food availability. This often makes them trickier to locate as, rather than be spread out thinly over suitable habitat, birdwatching becomes more of an all-or-nothing experience.

Ducks and waders that nest in Northern Europe and the Arctic spend their winters on the estuaries at the coast. The scale of these waterways is relatively modest, so numbers are not high, but the range of species is diverse and can be attractive, especially when more southerly species such as Marbled Duck get mixed in. These estuaries are also popular with wintering flocks of terns, and searching should produce some Lesser Crested Tern and perhaps even a West African Tern.

Two Eurasian mountain species make their winter home in the region. The Ring Ouzel becomes a familiar bird of the Sub-alpine zone in the High Atlas. The open meadows are rarely snowbound and the juniper forest provides a habitat akin to their breeding areas further north. The Dotterel is much more enigmatic and is a subject of concern. This wader breeds mainly in Scandinavia, with a relict population in Scotland. The population of Dotterel is decreasing and threatened by climate change and the bird's behaviour in winter is not really well understood. Ringing recoveries in the last century showed that the Haouz plain was an important wintering area, yet the increase in agriculture has meant that the birds largely disappeared here since the beginning of the millennium. However, there are few birdwatchers scouring the plains during the winter, so this species possibly remains. A report of a flock of about 70 birds in the Souss-Massa National Park gives some hope that Dotterels still remain somewhere in Southern Morocco.

Of course, not all species stay for the winter. Egyptian Nightjar are only a short distance migrant and will leave for Mauritania in October to return again in late February. Other species are part of the group that only migrates to the Sahel or Western Africa and therefore also tend to leave late and return early. Atlas Wheatears are believed to migrate to the Southern edge of the Sahel and are gone for the whole winter. Blue-cheeked Bee-eaters and Eastern Olivaceous Warblers are both solely summer migrants and will not be present until later in the spring.

Reptiles and Amphibians

All routes offer possibilities of finding reptiles, but for many species, it is hard to say exactly where to look. You need to acquaint yourself with the habitat preference and ranges to assist in the identification of 80 or so species found here.
The better routes for finding reptiles and amphibians are routes 1, 2, 4, 5, 6, 7, 8 11, 14, 15, 17, 19, 20, 21 22, 24 and 25.

Morocco is a herpetological hotspot and provides a home for many species that are unknown to the European visitor. The climate and habitats of Morocco are attractive to reptiles, both in the lowlands and in the mountains. As we have seen before there are species that are relicts from sub-Saharan Africa as well as Mediterranean species, creating an attractive blend.
The understanding of the taxonomy of these animals is still in its infancy. Currently eighty or so species are recognised – many more than those in guidebooks published before the millennium. Here is a group where isolation is resulting in speciation before your eyes, and this will lead to even more different species being recognised. At the moment, even to the interested amateur, there are several surprises. For example, the local population of Southern Smooth Snake is considered a relict population of a widespread Mediterranean snake, however in Morocco it has evolved to predate solely on Vaucher's Wall Lizard, which is an Atlas endemic. This relationship is considered unique, however the snake has yet to be recognised as a full species.

The Golden Fringe-fingered lizard, here eating a Striped Hawkmoth, is limited to the southern coast.

REPTILES AND AMPHIBIANS

As we have seen with the other groups, every habitat zone has its own special reptiles, often restricted to just a small region with conditions to which it is optimally adapted. It is not only the hot land and desert edges that are attractive. Perhaps surprisingly, species can be found up to at least 4000m in the High Atlas Mountains, well into the snow zone. In fact, many are limited to the Alpine zone itself. If finding many different reptiles is your aim, you should seek a wide breadth of locations to search.

Amphibians

The amphibian life cycle is strongly tied to the presence of at least temporary freshwater so it is no surprise that Southern Morocco is not the ideal place for amphibians. Therefore, it is remarkable that there is still a good diversity of amphibians, scattered over the limited number of locations that suit amphibian life.

Southern Morocco has one newt and eight frog and toad species. All are adapted to some extent to survive in ephemeral watercourses, but their ranges match their inability to cope with prolonged drought. Some of them are limited to the more humid Mediterranean climate zones of the north and along the coast.

Frogs and toads are most likely to be seen when the conditions are right for breeding. Then they return to the water to mate and lay eggs. The species that make their home in the mountains follow a typical 'European' annual cycle, emerging in spring when the temperature and day length triggers the breeding season. They remain active in summer and are dormant in winter. At higher elevations, activity is triggered by the snow melt.

The coastal amphibians tend to follow a different seasonal plan, being most active in the winter and early spring. The northern, relatively cool Mediterranean zone is the only place where you can still find the Sharp-ribbed Newt – a large species that occurs on the Iberian Peninsula and the Maghreb. The desert species are – like most desert life – dependent upon the pattern of rainfall, rather than being driven by the calendar. However, local irrigation provides reliable and predictable conditions to breed and species have adapted to take advantage of these artificial watercourses typical of small cultivations and palmeries.

Of the frogs and toads, the North African Water Frog is perhaps the most obvious of all, taking advantage of water wherever it can be found. This relatively plain, medium-sized species is closely related to the widespread Marsh Frogs of Europe.

There are two painted frogs, both with a light triangular mark on the head in front of the eyes. They are found in different areas, the Moroccan

REPTILES AND AMPHIBIANS

Painted Frog being widely distributed along the High Atlas Mountains and the northern steppes while the Painted Frog is a relict Mediterranean species limited to a few sites in the Eastern High Atlas Mountains.

The Stripeless Tree Frog usually occurs in permanently wet and well-vegetated areas. It seems to have adapted well to man-made water tanks and can be found in some remarkably barren habitats. Also surprisingly, it can be found all the way up to the cold Alpine zone, being even present at Oukaïmeden in the High Atlas Mountains (route 1).

African Green Toad is a familiar species in palmeries.

Of the four toads, the Spiny Toad (or Southern Common Toad) is a relict of the Mediterranean and limited here to the High Atlas Mountains. It is a large and relatively plain toad, whilst the remaining three species are heavily patterned and can be therefore easily told from the Spiny Toad. African Green, Moroccan and Brongersma's Toads are each representative of a different genus, yet appear superficially similar with 'camouflage' blotches of green or reddish-brown. The Moroccan Toad is widespread across a variety of habitats and needs careful separation from African Green Toad which is equally widespread, but is most often seen in palmeries and agricultural areas in the steppes and the Sahara. Brongersma's Toad is a relatively small species, less than half the length of the other two. Its pointier snout makes it superficially more frog-like, however the prominent parotid glands (the blotches behind the eyes) should avoid confusion. It is found in the historic range of the Argan Tree and along the coast, being the sole global representative of the genus *Barbarophryne*.

Reptiles

Reptiles are popularly called 'cold-blooded', but that is not accurate. They are not able to regulate their own temperature, which in Europe usually means that they need the sun to become warm and active. In Morocco, however, the heat can be too much and the animals need to find the relative cool of shady areas or burrows to hide out the hottest part of the day. Hence, reptilian activity is driven by the local temperatures (neither too hot nor too

REPTILES AND AMPHIBIANS

cold). In the lowlands the daytime temperatures are too high and therefore most species are active in the evening and even in the night. In winter and at higher elevations, the temperature can drop to freezing by dawn, meaning it is the dusk and early hours of the night that are the best to look for them. The dawn has the advantage that the reptiles are sluggish and often will be basking for a short time to get their body temperature up to the requisite level. However, it can be difficult to spot these inactive reptiles and in any event this 'window of opportunity' is pretty short.

A number of species have adapted to survive the challenges of the Alpine zone in the High Atlas Mountains. Reptiles have been found up to an astonishing 4,000m, way above the tree line and in areas where snow is often found for half the year or so. Atlas Dwarf Lizard, High Atlas Day Gecko and Moroccan Rock Lizard have all evolved to survive at these high altitudes. Another, the Vaucher's Wall Lizard is interesting not only in its own abilities to survive here but also, as mentioned previously, that a relict population of the Southern Smooth Snake has evolved to almost exclusively predate on the lizard here in the High Atlas. The Lataste's Viper is another Mediterranean relict species that has adapted to life in the high mountains.

It is the steppes and the Sahara which are the centres of diversity for the reptiles. The majority of species belong to four groups of closely related lizards. The *Mesalina* (desert racers) and *Acanthodactylus* (fringe-fingered) lizards are specifically adapted to life in the sandy soils around the tussock grasses and in the dunes. A visit during the day will show their plentiful tracks. There are five species of desert racer and eight species of fringe-fingered lizard in southern Morocco and they are each subtly different in size, appearance and habitat preference.

Moroccan Spiny-tailed Lizard is a species of the High Arid Steppes.

REPTILES AND AMPHIBIANS

Even more diverse is the group of skinks, which can be found in all the habitat zones. No less than 10 species of these shiny, smooth-bodied lizards occur. Many of them have reduced limbs and slither rather than walk. The most highly evolved is the Western Sandfish, which is an almost limbless skink that 'swims' through the sand of the Saharan dunes (hence the name fish). It is probably not a rare species but since it is mostly buried deep in the sand, it is hard to find.

Twelve species of gecko are present, the majority of which are nocturnal. Two of these are sand geckos, namely Moorish and Petrie's, that occur in the same habitat as the Desert Fringe-fingered Lizards, but are active later in the night, after the lizards have sought shelter. The remainder of the geckos are found in rocky habitat, and in the case of the Moorish Gecko they have adapted to live in and around houses. Most geckos are able to to climb vertical walls and even ceilings due highly adapted pads on the ends of the toes – a feature that reaches its zenith with Oudri's Fan-footed Gecko. However, there are a number of geckos that have normal toes. One such species, South Morocco Lizard-fingered Gecko, has some spectacular colour morphs in the Anti-Atlas, with bright spots and stripes and bright orangey tails (see photo on this page).

These rockier areas are also home to the robust agamid lizards. There are three species in the area, the largest being the Moroccan Spiny-tailed Lizard which can grow to a length of over 40 cms. Spiny-tailed Lizards vary enormously in appearance, but many specimens are strongly coloured with sometimes spectacularly bright and unnatural looking yellows, oranges, blues and greens. They live socially in burrows in the rocky steppes, both on flat areas and on slopes, and can be seen warming themselves on cooler mornings. Although ultimately harmless, they will hiss and try to bite if you get too close. Unfortunately, they are also caught by locals and used to attract curious tourists to photograph them (and part with a few Dirhams). In comparison, both Boheme's and Bibron's Agama are relatively

South Morocco lizard-fingered Gecko comes in variety of different colour morphs, some highly patterned.

FLORA AND FAUNA

REPTILES AND AMPHIBIANS

Amphibian and Reptile species of Southern Morocco

Widespread species North African Water Frog (*Pelophylax saharicus*), Moroccan Painted Frog (*Discoglossus scovazzi*), Moroccan Toad (*Sclerophrys mauritanica*), Spanish Terrapin (*Maurenys saharica*), Moorish Gecko (*Tarentola mauritanica*), Common Chameleon (*Chamaeleo chamaeleon*), Forskal's Sand Snake (*Psammophis schokari*)
Coastal species Sharp-ribbed Newt (*Pleurodeles waltl*), Helmethead Gecko (*Tarentola chazaliae*), Coastal Skink (*Chalcides mionecton*), Golden Fringe-fingered lizard (*Acanthodactylus aureus*), Sahel Egg Eater (*Dasypeltis sahelensis*)
Souss Valley species Brongerma's Toad (*Barbarophryne brongersmai*), Senegal Sand Skink (*Chalcides sphenopsiformis*), Margarita's Fringe-fingered Lizard (*Acanthodactylus margaritae*), Olivier's Desert Racer (*Mesalina olivieri*), Puff Adder (*Bitis arietans*), African House Snake (*Boaedon fuliginosus*), Egyptian cobra (*Naja haje*)
Arid Steppe species Algerian Dwarf Gecko (*Tropiocolotes algericus*), Böhme's Gecko (*Tarentola boehmei*), Bosk's Fringe-fingered Lizard (*Acanthodactylus boskianus*), Spotted Fringe-fingered Lizard (*Acanthodactylus maculatus*), Small-spotted Desert Racer (*Mesalina guttulate*), Moroccan Ocellated lizard (*Timon tangitanus*), Boehme's Agama (*Trapelus boehmei*), Moroccan Spiny-tailed Lizard (*Uromastyx nigriventris*), Moorish Viper (*Daboia mauritanica*)
Anti-Atlas and High Atlas species Moroccan Painted Frog (*Discoglossus scovazzi*), Moroccan Day Gecko (*Quedenfeldtia moerens*), High Atlas Day Gecko (*Quedenfeldtia trachyblepharus*), Mountain Skink (*Chalcides montanus*), Simon's Small Lizard (*Mesalina simonii*), Vaucher's Wall Lizard (*Podarcis vaucheri*), Atlas Dwarf Lizard (*Atlantolacerta andreanskyi*), Southern Smooth Snake (*Coronella girondica*), Lataste's Viper (*Vipera latasteri*)
Sahara species Moorish Sand Gecko (*Stenodactylus mauritamicus*), Desert Monitor (*Varanus griseus*), Western Sandfish (*Scincus albifasciatus*), Dumeril's Fringe-fingered lizard (*Acanthodactylus dumerilii*), Long-footed Fringe-fingered Lizard (*Acanthodactylus longipes*), Pasteur's Small Lizard (*Mesalina pasteuri*) Moorish Diadem Snake (*Spalerosophis dolichospilus*), Horned Viper (*Cerastes cerastes*), Sand Viper (*Cerastes vipera*)

dull, camouflage-patterned species of the High Arid Steppes that are both active during the day. As with the Spiny-tailed Lizard, the males of Bibron's Agama will develop breeding colours of blue, orange and yellow which are more intense the further south you travel.
The largest and undoubtedly most spectacular lizard is the Desert Monitor. It can reach 1.5m in length and it is limited to the edges of dunes and flat sandy deserts in the far south and along the valley of the Drâa near the

REPTILES AND AMPHIBIANS

Algerian border. It is never particularly numerous and also rather timid, which means that it is rarely seen, even though it is active during the day. It preys on beetles, small mammals (jirds, jerboas and the like) and also reptiles including snakes, both by ambushing them and actively digging them from their burrows.

There are no less than 21 species of snakes in the region, of which around eight, the cobras and vipers, are venomous and should be treated with care. It is extremely unlikely you will find anything other than tracks unless you specifically search for them. The Egyptian Cobra may be familiar only from the snake-charmers in the Jemma el-Faa in Marrakech, but is still plentiful in the Haouz plain and particularly in the Argan woodland of the Souss valley, a habitat it shares with less well known, endemic Moorish Viper. The Egyptian Cobra is rightly a poisonous snake of legend, although its hooded threat display means that it often gives plenty of warning before a strike. Without rapid treatment, the cobra's poison can be fatal.

A number of vipers can be found in the Saharan areas and sand seas of the south. Different from the European vipers, these are 'sidewinders', pushing themselves sideways as they snake through the sand. Their typical tracks can be seen on dunes and open sandy areas, but actually catching sight of either a Horned or a Sand Viper is much more difficult. During the day, they bury themselves in the loose sand and are almost impossible to spot.

The Horned Viper is a specialist of sandy desert areas.

The more humid areas of the Souss Valley and the coastal plain have a number of interesting species including a couple that are again relict populations from further south. The Sahel Egg-Eater feeds on birds' eggs and can dislocate its jaw as it swallows them whole and later crushes the shell when inside its body. The Common African House Snake lives, as the name suggests, in close proximity to humans across sub-Saharan Africa, but in Morocco, it is only found in coastal dunes and Argan forests.

INSECTS AND OTHER INVERTEBRATES

Insects and other Invertebrates

> Routes 1, 2, 3, 4, 5 and 7 are best for finding butterflies of the high mountains, as are sites B, C, D and E on pages 157-159. Desert species have been found on routes 10, 11, 12, 16 and 19. For dragonflies, focus on routes 6, 11, 13, 15, 18, 20 and 23, as well as on sites C and E on pages 174-175, C on page 194, B on page 208 and D on page 224.

There has been an increasing interest in the showier invertebrates of the Maghreb, especially butterflies and dragonflies. This is in part due to the list of endemic species and in part due to the feeling that something new can be discovered. After all, this is a large area where endemism is frequent and insect experts are scarce, so new or unexpected finds are within reach of everyone with an interest in these groups.

The recent new finds and insights show a similar pattern to that within the flora – South Morocco has a blend of species originating from all four points of the compass, plus a number of endemics that are the result of periods of isolation (see page 80).

The endemic *Berberia* graylings consist of two alpine species that fly over the higher scree slopes of the High Atlas in summer – this is *Berberia Lambessanus*.

Butterflies

Over 100 species of butterflies have been reported in Southern Morocco. Among them are a number of local forms that although not accepted as yet, are likely to be raised to species level once analysis is completed. Numerous butterflies in Morocco belong to widespread species in (Mediterranean) Europe. The groups that are not present there include *Azanus* Blues, Silver-lines (*Cigaritis*) and *Berberia* Graylings, the latter being a Mahgreb endemic genus. Relatively few are endemic purely to this part of southern Morocco, however this list seems to be increasing and includes Vogel Blue, Moroccan High Brown Fritillary, Moroccan Rock Grayling, Moroccan Grayling and Vaucher's Heath. Despite these attractions, most visitors are disappointed by the low numbers of butterflies encountered on their trip. Research carried out in similar habitat around the Mediterranean has shown

INSECTS AND OTHER INVERTEBRATES

that temperature is the main driver against both species diversity and numbers. Southern Morocco is very hot indeed, hence the scarcity. Butterflies that can be found across the region include the large and showy ones such as Swallowtail, Southern Scarce Swallowtail, Spanish Festoon, Plain Tiger, Spotted Fritillary and Moroccan Orange Tip. Some interesting Maghreb specialities are widespread as well, such as Moroccan Small Skipper and False Mallow Skipper. African Grass and African Babel Blues are African species that extend widely into Southern Morocco.

The most rewarding areas to explore for butterflies are the Souss Valley and especially the mountains. Most species here are very specific in their choice of habitat and larval food plant and occur very locally. But there is more. Most butterflies have relatively short flying seasons. To complicate matters further, the precise season depends on temperature and rain so it is hard to pinpoint on the calendar when they fly in any particular year. Therefore, it is unlikely that you will bump into many of the species through luck. A careful targeted effort across the various habitats and stopping where plants are still flowering should offer a good mix of species.

The Souss valley is a hotspot because widespread irrigation and low intensity agriculture produce the flowering plants that attract plenty of butterflies. The same unique mix of flora supported in and around the Argan forests provides the home for the butterflies. These include African Knapweed Fritillary, Two-tailed Pasha, Large Tortoiseshell, Tree Grayling and a range of hairstreaks, such as Moroccan, Provencal and False Ilex. Both the African Grass and African Babel Blues are easier to find here although they can also be found in the arid steppes. One species for which this area is particularly important is the Painted Lady as this is the source of the whole western population of this familiar

Moroccan Hairstreak (top) and African Babul Blue (bottom) are two of the special local species.

INSECTS AND OTHER INVERTEBRATES

butterfly, which is now recognised as having the longest return migration of any butterfly (see text box).
The mountains are the centre of interest. These areas have the majority of endemics and near-endemics. The timing of hatching is dependent upon the increasing temperature in the spring and in the High Atlas Mountains the specific timing of the snow melt. Below the Alpine zone, the season starts in the beginning of March. This is the realm of both Donzell's and Allard's Silver-line. These are often found with coppers (including the endemic Moroccan Copper) and a mix of orange tips, including Sooty, Desert and Moroccan Orange Tips. Early flying Blues include False Baton, Black-eyed and Lorquin's.

Painted Lady – portrait of a nomad

The Painted Lady is a familiar migrant species across the whole of Europe. For a long time, people knew that these butterflies came from somewhere in Africa and that during eruption years they spread widely across Europe. Only more recently is it realised that at the end of the season they fly back to Africa. More precisely to a few small areas, where the Painted Ladies spawn and initiate the whole process anew.

In eruption years, two arms of migrants reach Europe from both sides of Africa, the western source being from Morocco, specifically the area of the Souss Valley and Anti-Atlas. The butterflies all emerge in a very short period normally in March.

The scale of this phenomenon is breath-taking. In March 2009, 155,000 individuals were counted over a few days in an area of just 1.8 ha. There can easily be millions of individuals from across the whole of the Souss and nearby Anti-Atlas Mountains. The clouds of adults trigger a strong desire to migrate and they head north and into Europe, where they lay eggs that emerge a little later. The new generation then pushes further on north. In some years, the Painted Lady has 2-3 generations and reach as far north as into the Arctic Circle. At the end of the season, the remaining adults will fly south again. They normally migrate south at extreme altitudes, up to 10,000m. and arrive (by now tatty and worn) in Morocco in late September through October.

Painted Lady

Target butterfly species of Southern Morocco

Widespread species Swallowtail (*Papilio machaon*), Southern Scarce Swallowtail (*Iphiclides feisthamelii*), Spanish Festoon (*Zerynthia rumina*), Cleopatra (*Gonepteryx cleopatra*), Moroccan Orange Tip (*Anthochris belia*), Western Dappled White (*Euchloe crameri*), Green-striped White (*Euchloe belemia*), Cleopatra (*Gonepteryx cleopatra*), Plain Tiger (*Danaus chrysippus*), Painted Lady (*Vanessa cardui*), Long-tailed Blue (*Lampides boeticus*), Southern Brown Argus (*Aricia cramera*), Southern Blue (*Polyommatus celina*), Spotted Fritillary (*Melitaea didyma*), False Mallow Skipper (*Carcharodus tripolinus*), Moroccan Small Skipper (*Thymelieus hamza*), Mediterranean Skipper (*Gegenes nostrodamus*)

Souss Valley Species Scarce Green-striped White (*Euchloe fallouï*), Brimstone (*Geonpteryx rhamni*), False Ilex Haristreak (*Satyrium esculi*), Provencal Hairstreak (*Tomares balius*), Moroccan Hairstreak (*Tomares maurentanicus*), African Babel Blue (*Azanus jesous*), African Grass Blue (*Zizeeria knysa*), Common Tiger Blue (*Tarucus theophrastus*), Two-tailed Pasha (*Charaxes jasius*), Large Tortoiseshell (*Nymphalis polychloros*), African Knapweed Fritillary (*Melitaea punica*), Tree Grayling (*Neohipperchia statilinus*)

Mountain Species Sooty Orange Tip (*Zegris eupheme*), Desert Orange Tip (*Colotis evagore*), Donzel's Silver-line (*Cigaritis zohra*), Allard's Silver-line (*Cigaritis allardi*), Purple-shot Copper (*Lycaena alciphron*), Moroccan Copper (*Lycaena phoebus*), Atlas Blue (*Plebicula atlantica*), Spotted Adonis Blue (*Lysandra punctifera*), Lorquin's Blue (*Cupido lorquinii*), Black-eyed Blue (*Glaucopsyche melanops*), Vogel Blue (*Maurus vogelii*), False Baton Blue (*Pseudophilotes abencerragus*), Allard's Blue (*Plebejus allardi*), Amanda's Blue (*Agrodiaetus amanda*), Moroccan High Brown Fritillary (*Argynnis auresinna*), Aetherie Fritillary (*Melitaea aetherie*), Southern Grayling (*Hipparchia aristaeus*), Austaut's Grayling (*Hipparchia hansii*), Striped Grayling (*Hipparchia fidia*), Southern Hermit (*Chazara prieuri*), Moroccan Grayling (*Pseudochazara atlantis*), Moroccan Sooty Satyr (*Satyrus atlantea*), Giant Grayling (*Berberia abdelkader*), Dark Giant Grayling (*Berberia lambessanus*), False Grayling (*Arethusana arethusa*), Moroccan Meadow Brown (*Hyponephele moroccana*), Moroccan Dusky Heath (*Coenonympha fettigii*), Vaucher's Heath (*Coenonympha vaucher*), Moroccan Wall Brown (*Lasiommata meadewaldoi*), Large Grizzled Skipper (*Pyrgus alveus*), Moroccan Red Underwing Skipper (*Spialia ali*), Aden Skipper (*Spialia doris*)

Sahara and Steppes Species Desert Swallowtail (*Papilio saharae*), Greenish Black-tip (*Elphinstonia charlonia*), Mediterranean Tiger Blue (*Tarucus rosaceus*), Desert Babel Blue (*Azanus ubaldus*), Cardinal (*Argynnis pandora*), Desert Fritillary (*Melitaea deserticola*)

INSECTS AND OTHER INVERTEBRATES

Striped Hawkmoth is a migrant, that in some years occurs in its thousands as part of its journey north.

As the season progresses, a wider range of species emerges in the Sub-alpine zone and subsequently in the Alpine zone. For the latter, the main season is from late May onwards. Moroccan High Brown, Moroccan Dusky Heath, Vaucher's Heath, Moroccan Meadow Brown, Spotted Adonis, Atlas and Vogel Blues are all species that are best looked for in the Sub-alpine zone later in the spring. In the Alpine zone, and especially in the Toubkal massif species such as Aetherie's Fritillary, Moroccan Wall Brown, Moroccan Sooty Satyr, False Grayling and Amanda's Blue can be searched for. The most challenging group is undoubtedly that of the Graylings, which are both hard to find and hard to identify once found. In the High Atlas there are ten or so species and include the endemic Moroccan Grayling and Moroccan Rock Grayling. Furthermore, the Giant Grayling and Dark Giant Grayling are especially important as they are the sole representatives of the genus *Berberia* that is unique to this High Atlas range. They occur only on the Sub-alpine and Alpine scree and are most easily seen where access is possible around the Toubkal massif. All the Graylings are species of arid, rocky terrain. In late summer Austaut's Grayling is the often the commonest butterfly on the wing across the desiccated slopes.

The Anti-Atlas are more difficult to hunt for butterflies, as the habitat is more extreme. Most of the High Atlas species have outposts in the Anti-Atlas, where they are difficult to find once the food plants have desiccated, which they do all too quickly in this arid land. Only Aden and Moroccan Red Underwing Skipper are perhaps easier to see here than elsewhere. Allard's Blue is limited to the central part of the range.

The high steppes and desert edge have few nectar sources and therefore it is not surprising that butterflies are relatively few. Around palmeries, some of the less specialised species can survive, but it is of course the handful of true desert butterflies that make the journey worthwhile. The most likely butterfly to be found is Greenish Black-tip, but with searching, Desert Swallowtail, Desert Fritillary and Desert Babel Blue can also be found.

INSECTS AND OTHER INVERTEBRATES

Dragonflies

As can be expected of a group of species that are dependent upon water for part of their life-cycle, dragonflies are at a premium in this the driest part of the country. However, wherever there is water, they can be plentiful. Up to 50 species have been found in the region. Most have specific flying seasons, although there are some that are present throughout the year.

The majority of the dragonflies are of European origin and therefore perhaps not as exciting as could be expected from a first trip to the African mainland. However, in common with all other groups, there are a few endemic species and some of African origin that add a touch of the exotic to the dragonfly fauna.

The most widespread of the Moroccan dragonflies is the Vagrant Emperor. It is often seen a long way from water and is particularly common on the Haouz plain and the Saharan edge. Close to water they are often joined by the Lesser Emperor and this latter species appears to have adapted to the reservoirs and other irrigation dams across the region. Where there are small pools or irrigation ditches, Violet and Orange-winged Dropwings are invariably present, both impressively coloured with intense purple and orange colours respectively. If your hotel has a swimming pool or some ornamental water, these dragonflies are often present and they may be joined by the Epaulet Skimmer, another widespread species.

Most other species and especially the endemics are a little more specific in their habitat requirements. This is where the difficulty in finding them arises. Their presence depends on the state of the watercourses, both in terms of water flow and river-side vegetation – two conditions that are highly variable from year to year and also subject to disturbance. Even at well-known sites, the numbers of dragonflies fluctuate wildly.

The Oued al Maleh near Tissent (route 20) is a good site for dragonflies such as Faded Pincertail.

INSECTS AND OTHER INVERTEBRATES

The key species for an ardent enthusiast are two small, mainly blue damselflies that are each North African specialists. The Oasis and Sahara Bluetails are found south of High Atlas Mountains, the first being, as the name implies, a species of oases with some standing water, while the second prefers the irrigation channels. By contrast, the endemic Desert Bluet is barely found at all in desert habitat and nearly exclusively north of the High Atlas Mountains. It is easily confused with Common Bluet. The Barbary Featherleg is mostly found in the western High Atlas Mountains and likes areas where there is more verdant vegetation. The Cherry-eyed Sprite is a bit of an enigma. There are few confirmed locations on both sides of the High Atlas Mountains, which form a remote population of a widespread African species. However, these reported sites do not appear to match the habitat of this species in other parts of Africa.

The most attractive endemic is perhaps the Atlas Goldenring, which evolved from a European ancestor. This large dramatically coloured species occurs only in the High Atlas and is especially fond of the high river valleys on the northern slope. It can be found as high as the Sub-alpine zone.

A similarly sized species found in more westerly river valleys is the Ringed Cascader (see route 22). In contrast to the Goldenring, this is one of a group that is typical of Africa, south of the Sahara.

In the last ten years, many of the Maghreb species have expanded their range into Iberia and Southern Italy, but with the Sahara to the south there is little opportunity for new species to move into Southern Morocco in response to climate change. One other species of interest that has been recorded is the Wandering Glider. This pan-African species is familiar across a range of arid habitats and a prodigious drift migrant that is not tied to watercourses. Although a few have been sighted in Southern Morocco, there is no evidence, as yet, that this species is increasing. Also the Black Pennant seems to have spread to the area in recent years. Two other new discoveries, the Desert and Slender Skimmer, were probably always present.

Vagrant Emperor is a widespread species both north and south of the High Atlas.

INSECTS AND OTHER INVERTEBRATES

Target dragonfly and damselfly species of Southern Morocco

Coast/Valley species Barbary Featherleg (*Platycnemis subdilatata*), Desert Bluet (*Enallagma deserti*), Violet Dropwing (*Trithemis annulata*), Red-veined Dropwing (*Trithemis arteriosa*), Orange-winged Dropwing (*Trithemis kirbyi*), Northern Banded Groundling (*Brachythemis impartita*), Large Pincertail (*Oychogomphus uncatus*)
Saharan species Sahara Bluetail (*Ischnura saharensis*), Oasis Bluetail (*Ischnura fountaineae*), Desert Skimmer (*Orthetrum ransonnetii*), Slender Skimmer (*Orthetrum sabina*), Black Pennant (*Selysiothemis nigra*), Wandering Glider (*Pantala flavescens*)
High Atlas species Copper Demoiselle (*Calopteryx haemorrhoidalis*), Faded Pincertail (*Oychogomphus costae*), Western Spectre (*Boyeria irene*), Atlas Goldenring (*Cordulegaster princeps*), Ringed Cascader (*Zygonyx torridus*)

Other Invertebrates

When people think of the desert, the most often thought of invertebrate is the scorpion. This nocturnal animal has a fascination for many. THE scorpion doesn't exist though. There are around sixty (!) species of them in Morocco as a whole. They are not limited to the desert. In fact, as with the reptiles, there are species that happily survive in the Alpine zone where snow covers the land for many months of the year.

Although it is rare for scorpions to sting, there are still many accidents annually, some of which are fatal. Scorpions are common around towns and villages, and children playing and people wandering at night accidentally tread on them, which forms the usual cause of an incident. Generally, the size of their claws is a good indication for the potency of their sting. Large clawed scorpions have low toxicity and small clawed scorpions have high toxicity as a general rule. However, there are a couple of large-clawed species that buck this trend. Certainly, if camping in any part of the country, take care with bags and especially shoes. Scorpions like dark, dry holes to hold up in during the day, so shaking out shoes, boots and other containers should become second nature when spending the night outdoors.

Crickets and Grasshoppers are another interesting group. There are many species but the one that captures the imagination is the Moroccan Locust. This grasshopper normally lives a solitary life and is relatively common especially in agricultural areas. In Arabic it is called djerad-el-adami ('man's locust') because it is concentrated around farms and human habitation. The vast majority of the time it isn't a particularly impressive grasshopper, but periodically, in response to stimuli that are not really understood, the

MARINE LIFE

Pitted Beetles (*Adesmia moroccana*) and mantises (such as this Thistle Mantis; *Blepharopsis mendica*) are just two of the impressive invertebrates that can be found in Southern Morocco.

population explodes. All of a sudden, they become highly gregarious, forming swarms that devour any vegetation in their path.

Another intriguing group of invertebrates is the mantids. These have been called praying mantis due to the modified front legs and their distinctive posture, but their rapacious habits are far from pious. It is alleged that in Morocco, shepherds believe that mantids point their forelegs north, therefore acting as a way-finder whilst their English name, mantis, comes from the Greek for soothsayer. There are several species across the country, and with many of the invertebrates, a little effort is likely to find much in the way of new information. For example, a recent short research project found two species of mantid that had not been seen for over sixty years in Morocco.

Marine Life

The Canary current washes the Atlantic coast along the whole of Northwest Africa. It is a cold and nutrient-rich stream, which means that the offshore ecosystem has a high biodiversity, including a large number of fish. In southern Morocco, a large proportion of the fishing is artisanal and the small blue-painted wooden boats are a familiar sight offshore from most coastal towns. A short visit when these boats come ashore gives an idea of what is being found and caught. Most hauls include a myriad of colours and shapes of the fishes, some familiar and some are certainly not. Agadir itself hosts a sizable fleet of much larger boats that are capable of fishing further offshore.

This Canaries current also attracts cetaceans (whales and dolphins), but due to the very low level of survey work done in these waters little is known about their numbers. Harbour Porpoise, Common, Bottle-nosed and Risso Dolphins have all been recorded. Pilot Whales are also frequently reported but there is confusion on whether these are the Short or the Long-finned species. Certainly, sea-watches for bird migration from Cap Rhir and other promontories occasionally have included sightings of cetaceans in the autumn, but little is known from the remainder of the year.

Larger whales, including Humpback, Bryde's and Minke travel relatively close to shore and are sometimes seen both from shore and from small boats. Further south around Dakhla bay, just outside of our region, there used to be a wintering and calving ground for Northern Right Whales and they would have also used the offshore area to migrate through to the Northern Atlantic in spring and autumn. The population numbers are so low that it is not known from any recent sightings. Fin, Blue and Sperm Whales are truly pelagic. They do occur in the Canary Current, but are too far from the coast for land-based observation.

Six species of Marine Turtles are known to use the Canary Current for foraging but don't breed along the coast here. Most records are associated with by-catch from the fishing industry. Most records relate to Loggerheads although both Leatherbacks and Green Turtles have also been found and even some specimens of the critically endangered Kemp's Ridley Sea Turtle. Most are immatures that have probably wandered from breeding grounds further south.

The richness of the seas can be seen by beachcombing to find washed up sea life, such as this Portuguese Man O'War.

PRACTICAL PART

Morocco has long been the start of birdwatchers' forays into a more exotic avifauna after a grounding in mainland Europe. The mix of culture, habitats and species has resulted in a steady stream of visitors over the last 50 years or so, and, to some extent, the adoption of a set itinerary. Most visits take place in spring and word of mouth has created the draw for many to follow in their footsteps.

In the last ten years, tourism has exploded with regular cheap flights available from many European cities, primarily to Marrakech. This has increased the number of visitors in all months of the year, driving an increase in understanding that there are things of interest in all months. Agadir and Marrakech are large, busy cities and the roads may be congested. But away from these cities and especially away from the coast, the roads are pleasantly quiet. Visitors are still scarce in villages, whose inhabitants are welcoming to travellers. There has been an enormous programme of road building and improvement and even small, remote villages are connected by tarmac roads.

The routes included here are largely ones that are known and popular. They are based around habitats and follow a sequence that is familiar if one left Marrakech and continued on a clockwise circuit, firstly southeast via the High Atlas Mountains over to the High Arid Steppes and down to the Sahara edge, before turning west to the Souss Valley and Anti Atlas to the coast, which is followed up north, back to Marrakech.

Navigation is straightforward as there are very few main roads, and the road numbers are an important guide to finding a site. In each case, care has been taken to name places as they appear in Google Maps and GPS points are provided as well. However, note that spelling, and often even naming in Latin text is not fixed and you can see various spellings of the same place on signs in the same area. Also similarly named places are often hundreds of kilometres apart. There are many stories, no doubt some apocryphal, of travellers ending up in the wrong one!

In spite of the above, much remains to be discovered in this part of Morocco. Relatively few areas have been explored by naturalists. The following routes give access to areas where flora and fauna are known to be found, but there are likely to be other equally exciting areas elsewhere. Be prepared to stop and look whenever and wherever anything looks interesting!

In the High Atlas, the mud brick built villages merge into the hillsides above the fertile river valleys.

ROUTES IN THE HIGH ATLAS MOUNTAINS

Routes in the High Atlas Mountains

Since most travellers start their journey in Marrakech at the base of the High Atlas, the mountains are the first logical destination. Many of the better-known sites can be visited on day trips from Marrakech.
The scenery and wildlife of the High Atlas are stunning, but much of the range is hard to explore. There are few roads and little in the way of tourist infrastructure except around particular hotspots. The north face is more accessible than the southern side. From Marrakech there are several roads up from the city that take you directly to the highest part of the range, which is the area around the Toubkal massif. This means that it is possible to explore all habitat zones including, most importantly, to go all the way up into the Alpine zone.
As most travellers will see the mountains not solely as a destination but also as the gateway to the Sahara beyond, the routes here are concentrated loosely around the main trans-mountain road, the N9, which is the road to Ouarzazate. Not surprisingly, some of the best areas are a bit off this main route and there is no alternative but to embark on the adventure of the small roads.
In the winter, snow can make travel treacherous. Away from the N9 snow ploughing is not usually done and roads can be blocked. With the rock faces being very friable, mud and rock falls are commonplace, so be prepared for slower journeys.
With forests, scrublands, scree, Alpine meadows, juniper stands, streams and even bogs, the diversity of the ecosystems of the High Atlas Mountains is unmatched anywhere else in this region. The ecosystems break down into numerous smaller habitat types, due to the series of microclimates that form here, primarily on the northern slopes. This means that a number of stops is needed to see the range of species on offer. As the season's advancement changes with altitude, you need to be prepared to cross between the north and south slopes and in elevation to find the optimum conditions for your targets. It is worth it as all the flora and fauna groups have a number of fully and regional endemic species that can be found only here.

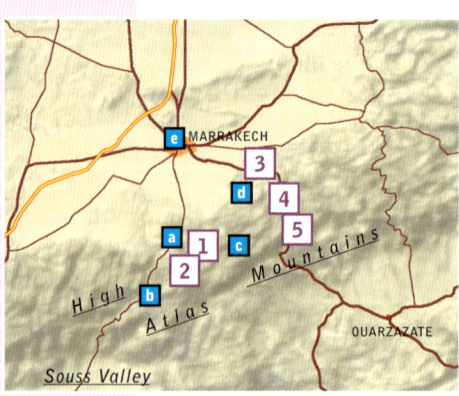

CROSSBILL GUIDES • SOUTHERN MOROCCO

Route 1: Oukaïmeden

3-5 HOURS, 5-8 KM
MODERATE-STRENUOUS

Simplest place to access the Alpine zone, even in the depths of winter.
Rich birdlife in winter and early spring.
Attractive flora, butterflies and reptiles in May-June.

Habitats: Alpine grassland, scree and high mountains
Selected species: *Fritillaria macrocarpa*, *Narcissus watieri*, Broad-leaved Marsh Orchid, African Crimson winged Finch, Horned Lark, Atlas Wheatear, Alpine Chough, Red-billed Chough, Vaucher's Wall Lizard, Atlas Dwarf Lizard, Atlas Blue, *Berberia* Graylings, Vaucher's Heath

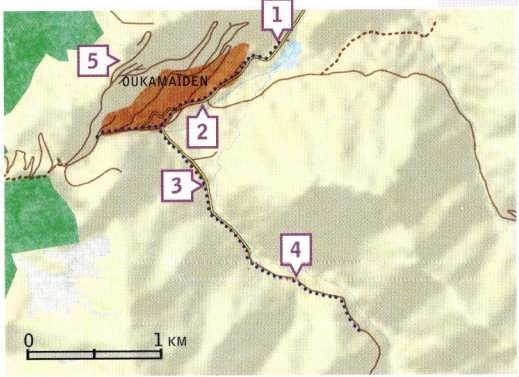

Much of the High Atlas is a daunting place to visit. There are only few roads that get you as high as the Alpine zone. Oukaïmeden is one exception, and a visit is therefore highly recommended even if it is not as pristine as the remoter parts of the mountains. Oukaïmeden was developed as a ski station in the 1950s, but increasingly suffers from a lack of snow. The ski-runs still function when there is sufficient snow cover, and a few cafes operate when there are visitors about, but the hotels and apartments have a distinctly run-down feel.

This is long regarded as the place to find high altitude species like African Crimson-winged Finch and various plants, reptiles and butterflies are readily found in season. Oukaïmeden is a hub of the grazing of the alpine meadows by sheep and goats, and herders' summer huts are dotted around the hillside. Cattle also graze the meadow in the main valley to the south of the main lake.

ROUTE 1: OUKAÏMEDEN

Lac d'Oukaïmeden marks your arrival in the Alpine zone.

Starting point Layby at Lac d'Oukaïmeden by the barrage. (GPS: 31.2086, -7.8526)

Getting there Most visitors reach this area either by self-drive car or by Grand Taxi from Marrakech (see page 247). The direct route is to Ourika, and then it is signposted from there.

1 Just across the road from the layby to the north-west are petroglyphs (rock carvings) dating from the mid-3rd millennium BC. The rock strata are horizontal and the images of animals and people were hammered into the surface. These come from a time when the Sahara was becoming drier and therefore mountain grazing was becoming more important. Although there is an interpretive board it is likely that a local 'guide' will appear to show you the details of these images in return for a few Dirhams.

Take a moment to look back down the road from where you have come. This is often the best place to look for Crag Martin, Grey Wagtail and Black Redstart. It is also worth looking across the lake itself as it can attract some species dependent on the season.

The way forward is along the valley to the main ski-lift car park at point 2 about 1 km away. If visiting in winter, walking along the road may yield Serins, Rock Sparrows and Bramblings that are attracted to the cafes and hotels that line the road. If there is no snow in spring and summer, a more pleasant walk is to cross the barrage and walk along the southerly edge of the Lac to the flat grazing lawns. A stream follows the easterly edge of the lawns and along its route can be a good place search for flora including Broad-leaved Marsh-orchids and both butterflies and dragonflies in season. The vegetation here can also be home to Stripeless Tree Frogs.

2 The main ski-lift car parking area gives a good view of the valley floor and informs you about the snow conditions around the head of the valley. In both winter and early spring, it is best to consider the plan of action based upon the extent of the snow and scan the areas from here. In these seasons it is likely that the road is the only clear way to continue. Most birds are attracted to the snow edge, particularly where it is melting and this should be your target. If no snow is present, then look for activity and follow the birds. Often large flocks of Rock Sparrows are present, and these may be joined by Horned Larks and both choughs. Note that when skiing is possible the road is often barriered here and you will be charged for parking.

3 The road continues through a sharp left-hand turn and to a car parking and market area another kilometre along the valley floor area. If there is no activity at the first parking area this second area can be the place to focus attention. It is most likely that this will be the first area in which African Crimson-winged Finches are present and they are especially fond of the baskets of almonds if the nut vendors are present. The first of the ski-lifts have their base stations here, and most of the higher slopes can be scanned to establish where the activity is, both human and avian. Mules are often also found here, as they will take visitors up the track towards the Toubkal National Park for a fee. This area is one of the best to find the various finches that inhabit the valley. In recent years, the Crimson-winged Finches appear to have adopted the last,

'Atlas' Horned Lark is common in the areas of short turf.

ROUTE 1: OUKAÏMEDEN

disused ski-lift as their vantage point and they can be seen sitting on the lift cables.

The small stream in the valley bottom attracts flocks to drink and is also home to Dipper and Grey Wagtail. Two small areas of woodland, sheltered around the scattered buildings, are worth scanning carefully as they will attract migrants and other birds including flycatchers and Moussier's Redstart. Birds are also attracted to the 'metal forest' of spars for the ski-lift and these spars and columns make for easier viewing than the trees, but the birds seem to like them just as much.

4 The track continues upwards towards the Toubkal National Park, and although the track is wide it is normally blocked to vehicular traffic, even if clear of snow. Therefore, if driving, leave your car at the last parking area by the ski-lifts and walk up the track. The next 1-2km of track gives a good introduction to the Alpine zone specialities including African Crimson-winged Finch and Atlas Wheatear, although in high summer some species will retreat higher still on the mountains. The scree slopes are home to the Berberia Graylings and other butterflies in late spring and summer. It is also a place to look for some special reptiles including Vaucher's Wall Lizard, Atlas Dwarf Lizard and Moroccan Rock Lizard.

Once you have gone as far as you wish, turn around and return to the sharp bend near point 3.

5 At the junction on the bend, a drivable track heads northwest up from the valley floor. This track heads past apartments and shepherd's huts and up to the communications mast above the ski resort. This area is a known hotspot for Alpine Accentor in the winter and early spring. It is still worth exploring in later seasons as the rocky edges can attract butterflies, especially if the little stream that flows in this side valley is still carrying water.

The African Crimson-winged Finch, the iconic endemic of the High Atlas and this is probably the best place in the world to see them.

The only way out is to retrace your route to Oukaïmeden and back to the Marrakech area below.

Route 2: Imlil

**FULL DAY, 11 KM
MODERATE-STRENUOUS**

Pine forests and Sub-alpine zone of the Toubkal Massif.

Habitats: High Atlas pine forest, Sub-alpine grasslands and river
Selected species: Juniper, Thuja, *Digitalis transiens*, Levaillant's Woodpecker, 'African' Chaffinch, 'Atlas' Coal Tit, 'Atlas' Crossbill, Atlas Flycatcher, Levaillant's Woodpecker, Black Wheatear, Rock Bunting, White-rumped Swift, Moroccan Ocellated Lizard, Moroccan Rock Lizard, *Berberia* Graylings, Vaucher's Heath, Moroccan Meadow Brown, Barbary Featherleg, Atlas Goldenring, Large Pincertail

Views up the valley from Imlil give glimpses of Jebel Toubkal.

Imlil is a busy and commercialised village as it is the main trekking centre for the Toubkal massif. There are plenty of places to stay and eat and it is possible to pick up guides for a trek in the High Atlas Mountains. Imlil lies at around 1800m above sea level and set in a picturesque river valley above the main route to Tizi n'Test – one of the major mountain passes across the High Atlas Mountains.

The whole area is therefore relatively easy to access. There is an unspoilt habitat with a flora and fauna of the pine woods and Sub-alpine meadows of the middle sections of the Atlas Mountains. For birdwatchers, it is the place to track down the endemic Levaillant's Woodpecker (among other species), while for those interested in butterflies and reptiles, there is a whole array of interesting species, particularly from mid-May into summer.

PRACTICAL PART

ROUTE 2: IMLIL

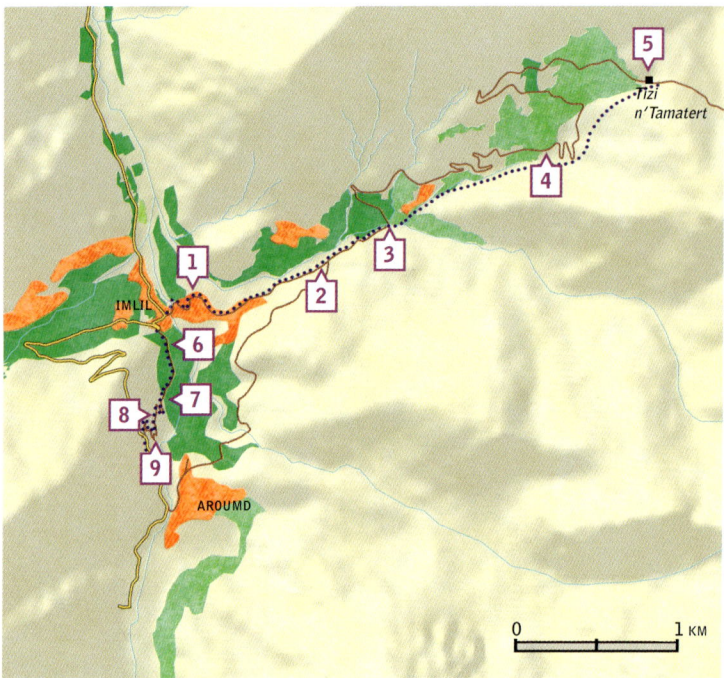

The river valley both above and below the village historically has been a good spot for dragonflies including records of Atlas Goldenring and Barbary Featherleg. The Sub-alpine meadows are good for butterflies including Vaucher's Heath and Moroccan Meadow Brown and higher still a wealth of graylings can be found.

This route consists of two short and easy walks, one towards the south of the village, and another heading east. Although the paths are well-trodden out, the marking of the routes can be a bit hit and miss. Although nominally way-marked in the same red and white marking adopted on French GR footpaths, many are missing or faded so can be tricky to find the way through.

Starting point Centre of Imlil (GPS: 31.136, -7.919) or parking area as directed.

Getting there Self-drive car, Grand Taxi or bus from Marrakech.

Walk 1: Imlil to Tizi n'Tamatert

This walk is a good introduction to a cross-section of elevations and their habitats in the High Atlas Mountains. The primary targets are the Sub-alpine zone and the scree slopes that both have a mix of local and endemic species. This is also one of the routes as part of the well-trodden Toubkal ascent, so if you have time and the desire it can be the start of a longer expedition into the mountains.

1 The best place to park is after the bridge at the start of the road to Tamatert. This is along the wooded banks of the river where in spring and summer you can hear the sound of Levaillant's Woodpeckers. After breeding the birds head higher to feed on ants' nests in the rocky areas above the village. The massif that towers over the village is the best location for White-rumped Swift and there are a pair or two of Bearded Vulture in the area.

2 The first section of the route sticks to the road and passes the small arable fields. These can be good for butterflies, especially blues, coppers and whites. African Chaffinch, Cirl Bunting and Spanish Sparrow can all be present.

3 The road turns sharply left, but a footpath into the village of Tamatert follows the valley line. Take this and continue to climb through the village until reaching the eastern end. House Buntings are plentiful along this stretch. Look out for Blue Rock Thrushes and Black Redstarts too.

The path continues to the south of the road until the first of the hairpin bends are passed. After another 200m the path leads up to the road. Now cross the road and follow the path along the stream bed

Whilst Red-billed Chough regularly wheel above the village (top), Atlas Pied Flycatcher (bottom) should be searched for in the riverine trees.

ROUTE 2: IMLIL

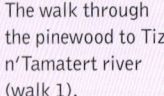

The walk through the pinewood to Tizi n'Tamatert river (walk 1).

steeply uphill. It continues to pass through Aleppo pines. To your right, you can just see the second set of switchbacks on the road to the pass. The footpath then crosses the road again as the pines thin out and the pass comes into view. The footpath covers the last section in a series of switchbacks itself and then arrives at the col at 2,358m.

4 The last section of the climb is an area of Sub-alpine meadow and it is worth looking for Vaucher's Heath and Moroccan Meadow Brown. The meadows can be attractive to both Moorish and Lataste's Vipers and Moroccan Ocellated Lizard. Look carefully for them around rocks and open patches.

5 The col looks down the double valley on the other side and is on a meeting place of tracks for the full Toubkal trek. In summer, the scree slopes are the habitat of choice for a number of Graylings including both Berberia species and Moroccan Grayling. High Atlas Day Gecko and Moroccan Rock Lizard can be obvious, sunning themselves on the boulders. You can walk further, but keep in mind that the way back is along the route by which you arrived.

Walk 2: Imlil to Cascades

This is more of a pleasant stroll that gives a short introduction to the area and a mix of localised habitats focused on the river valley. The route to the 'Cascades d'Imlil' is well signposted and a popular stroll for locals. If in any confusion simply head to the main north-south running river and head uphill. A waymark of the well-signposted Kasbah du Toubkal can also be used for direction finding. Stepping only a short distance to either side of main path provides an introduction to the local specialities.

6 Look for dragonflies on the river edge. More widespread Moroccan species such as dropwings and damselflies are commonest, but the rocky riverbed attracts the more specialist species such as Large Pincertail, Barbary Featherleg and Atlas Goldenring as well.

7 The woodland here is a known breeding location of Levaillant's Woodpecker which is especially fond of the riverside Poplars for nesting sites. These wooded slopes have also historically been a site for breeding Atlas Pied Flycatcher, although they can be surprisingly difficult to find and as they only arrive in May and leave by September, it is not known if the lack of recent sightings is because they are no longer here or because few birders visit at the right time of year.

The endemic Levaillant's Woodpecker enjoys the riverside poplars.

8 Climbing up beyond Kasbah Toubkal, the woodland ends and the hillsides are barren with a few Sub-alpine plants. This area is good for Black Wheatear and Rock Bunting. In autumn, Levaillant's Woodpeckers come to feed on the ants' nests. They move out of the trees into the more open area. The view up to the mountains above can be good for raptors and keep an eye out for White-rumped Swift in the summer. Both Red-billed and Alpine Choughs like the open hillside from here to the small village of Aroumd above.

9 Continue to the waterfalls. They are normally in full spate during snow melt but can be much reduced in summer and autumn. Return back to Imlil by the same path, but only after searching the riverside for dragonflies and butterflies.

Additional remarks
The route up from Asni to Timlil has orchards where Red-necked Nightjar breeds.

Route 3: Escale Forest

1-2 HOURS, 1-2 KM
EASY

An easy introduction to the High Atlas forest of Aleppo Pine and Thuja. Quiet, unsurfaced road, ideal for easy walking.

Habitats: High Atlas pine forest
Selected species: Barbary Thuja, Dwarf Palm, Yellow Bee Orchid, Moroccan Lavender, African' Chaffinch, Atlas Coal Tit, Atlas Crossbill, Moroccan Orange Tip

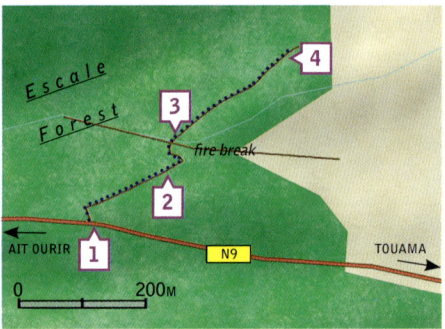

Escale Forest offers, like the previous route, an exploration of the High Atlas forests. Escale comprises mainly of Aleppo Pine intermixed with typical species of lower altitudes. There is nothing to suggest that this area is special, but grazing is light and there is free access which makes all the difference. On the opposite side of the N9 the much larger Iggeroka forest is fully fenced, ungrazed and probably better for wildlife but access is not possible.

Spring is best for the flowers and for the birds. Bird migration can be spectacular, in addition to the resident species. As the N9 valley leads to the col of Tizi n'Tichka pass over the mountains, there is often visible migration in both spring and autumn. In autumn particularly, migrants will hold up in the forest to feed or to wait for suitable conditions to cross the High Atlas Mountains.

Starting point Layby on the N9 by the road junction (GPS: 31.5434, -7.5350) between Ait Ourir (15km) and Touama (5km)

Getting there Self-drive car or Grand Taxi from Marrakech.

ROUTE 3: ESCALE FOREST

1 The layby on the roadside of the N9 gives views across the fenced woodland that extends upwards to the ridge to the south. Before entering the forest, it is worth scanning the area for any visible migration. Booted Eagle and Black Kite are the commonest raptors passing and the resident Bonelli's Eagles may also show themselves. Flocks of swifts, swallows and martins and Bee-eaters can also fly through.

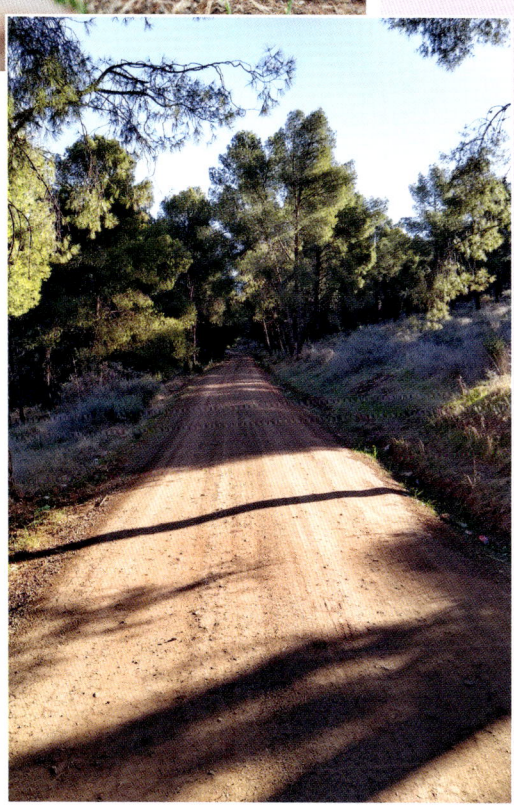

The route through the pine woods (bottom) where the *africana* form of Chaffinch is common (top).

2 The unsurfaced road heads north-east from the N9. Look for Cirl Bunting in the forest edge. Further into the trees, you should be able to find African Chaffinch, Coal Tit, and African Blue Tit amongst others. The pines throughout can attract Crossbills, which range widely and are best found from their calls. Below the trees where the canopy does not completely block out the sun, Moroccan Lavender, Branched Asphodel and Yellow Bee Orchids (one of the commoner orchid species in southern Morocco) can be plentiful in the Spring.

3 Further along the track, an overhead power line runs through the forest. The fire break can be attractive to birds hunting along the edge. Although not staying to breed,

ROUTE 3: ESCALE FOREST

The vista at point 4 (top). The flowers here are attended by Moroccan Orange Tip (bottom).

Common Redstarts, Spotted and Pied Flycatchers can be found on migration. Woodlarks are resident, as are Great Grey Shrikes that will perch on the wires. This break in the canopy means that circling birds can be seen, such as Sparrowhawk and Goshawk. The stretch from here onwards is best for Crossbill.

4 Further on, the track doubles back on itself and a vista overlooking the valley edge and the High Atlas can be seen. The viewpoint means that any visible migration is best viewed from here and more open country species such as Serin and Woodlark are more prevalent. Butterflies, including the three 'Moroccan' named species (Hairstreak, Copper and Orange Tip) can also be plentiful in early Summer.

Return to your parking area.

Route 4: The Sub-alpine zone above Zerkten

1-2 HOURS, 7.5 KM

An easy introduction to the High Atlas sub-alpine zone.

Habitats: Sub-alpine zone of open juniper woodlands and meadows
Selected species: Hoop-petticoat Daffodil, Barbary Nut, Levaillant's Woodpecker, Tristram's Warbler, Moussier's Redstart, Atlas Coal Tit, Ring Ouzel, Lataste's Viper, Moroccan Ocellated Lizard, Allard's Silver-line, Vaucher's Heath, Moroccan Meadow Brown, Desert Orange Tip

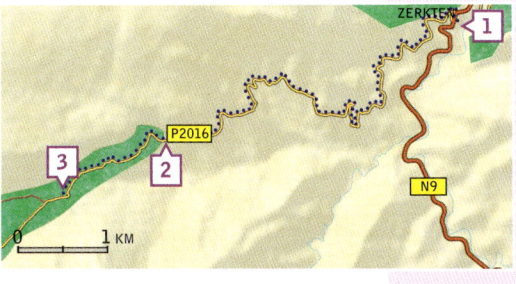

Although the N9 passes through the Sub-alpine zone, the immediate areas on either side of the road are heavily disturbed and degraded. Fortunately, it is a simple matter of turning off the main road to find relatively pristine habitat close by. The P2016 is one such road and, although it does eventually descend to the Zat valley (see additional site D), it shortly leads through open Juniper woods with often Sub-alpine meadows. There are no waymarked trails; the best approach is to drive slowly, pulling off the road by good looking meadows and start exploring. There are no access restrictions. The overall habitat is similar to the area above Imlil (see route 2 above) although the juniper woods here are more extensive.
Spring is the best time for visiting the area, but it is interesting in all seasons and in winter this habitat is the main wintering area for Ring Ouzel, a migrant from European uplands

Starting point The P2016 junction on the N9 in the village of Zerkten (GPS: 31.439, -7.405).

Getting there Self-drive car or Grand Taxi from Marrakech. From the village drive in the direction of the col.

ROUTE 4: THE SUB-ALPINE ZONE ABOVE ZERKTEN

1 The P2016 climbs out of the village of Zerkten passing the mosque and immediately follows the ridge up to the west. The first 4 km or so you will pass through a series of hamlets. Dependent upon the level of grazing these may be worth a stop but the best areas lie ahead.

In the roadside woods, Thuja is present as well as the three local species of Juniper. The larger valley trees attract Levaillant's Woodpecker which nest there and then move up to feed on ants on the rocky slopes later in the year.

The road continues up to the head of the valley after 6 km. Stop here and walk the meadows on both sides of the road.

2 The Juniper itself is favoured by (Atlas) Coal Tit and the more open edges by both Ring Ouzel and the local endemic form of Mistle Thrush. The meadows can be attractive to Lataste's Vipers and Moroccan Ocellated Lizard. If nectaring plants are present then look for Vaucher's Heath, Moroccan Meadow Brown, and Desert Orange Tip. Moroccan Orange Tip and Moroccan Copper, which are more common lower down, can also be found here. The meadows are good places to look for Aetherie's and Desert Fritillaries and Morocco Red-underwing Skipper, although Rosy Grizzled Skippers are often more plentiful. The

Atlas (or Seebohm's) Wheatear is an endemic breeder from these Sub-alpine meadows upwards.

ROUTE 4: THE SUB-ALPINE ZONE ABOVE ZERKTEN

most sought-after species is Allard's Silver-line which is an early season flyer. Flowers include Barbary Nut, Hoop-petticoat Daffodil, *Narcissus broussonetii* and later in the season, the endemic yellow foxglove, Digitalis transiens.

Continue over the col 2km until you can see the Zat Valley ahead and to the north. Park off the road and follow a track that runs east along the contour line for a few hundred metres.

3 This has similar species as stop 2 above, but the grazing and flowering timing is often different. Again, wander the slopes looking for the target species. This area around and above the col is best to search for breeding Tristram's Warbler and Moussier's Redstart.

Return to Zerkten or if your ultimate destination is Marrakech, you can follow the winding road north and downhill to Tighedouine and the Zat Valley (see site D on page 157).

African Knapweed Fritillary (top) and Hoop-petticoat Daffodil (bottom) are two species found along the road above Zerkten.

PRACTICAL PART

Route 5: Source de Tichka

1 HOUR, 1-2 KM
EASY

An exploration of the Alpine zone and its flora and fauna

Habitats: Alpine meadow and rocky slopes
Selected species: Atlas Wheatear, Water Pipit, Northern Raven, Alpine Chough, Red-billed Chough, Vaucher's Wall Lizard, High Atlas Day Gecko, Sooty Orange Tip, Vaucher's Heath, Atlas Blue, Hoop Petticoat Daffodil

Within the Alpine zone and not far from the col of Tizi n'Tichka, this previously was an unmissable location and one that is easily accessible, being bisected by the main N9 highway from Marrakech to Ouarzazate. However, with the twin impacts of the highway upgrades to the N9 and the overgrazing by sheep and goats, it is not as productive as it once was. Despite this, in terms of ease of access and the elevation it is worth stopping to catch up on high altitude species and any migrants that use the pass as a route on migration.

Starting point Layby on the N9 (GPS: 31.2910, -7.3800). There are large parking areas on both sides of the road.

Getting there Self-drive car or by Grand Taxi from Marrakech.

1 The area to the west of the road rises across Alpine meadows to the peaks behind. The rocky areas by the layby have boulders that attract Vaucher's Wall Lizards. Dependent upon season and the number of grazing sheep and goats, you may find flowering plants of the Sub-alpine and Alpine zone. If there is snow, birds are pushed into the area from the peaks above and can include both species of chough. Northern Raven and Atlas Wheatear is present regardless of the snow state. Later in spring, the butterflies will be obvious flitting across the meadow. Vaucher's Heath

CROSSBILL GUIDES • SOUTHERN MOROCCO

ROUTE 5: SOURCE DE TICHKA

and Atlas Blue are local endemics that can be found here. Three species of Orange Tip are possible with Moroccan and Desert joining the more localised Sooty Orange Tip in the meadows. There are no set paths but wandering, and scanning should be fruitful.

2 Returning to the eastern section, the area below the layby is the actual source of the Tichka river. The land around here is boggy and more vegetated. Beyond, the hillsides are rocky and attractive to day-active geckos, lizards and of course, they will attract the snakes, especially Southern Smooth Snakes that prey upon them. If the hillsides are parched, the damp hollows hold any remaining flowering plants and therefore will attract butterflies. The stream forms downhill from the parking area and although wagtails are often the only birds here, this area can attract Water Pipits and rarely a Dipper. In spring and autumn, these areas are attractive to migrants crossing the High Atlas Mountains, and if there is low cloud they can be grounded and find shelter here. Again, there is no set path but follow the sheep tracks to cover the habitat.

The endemic Vaucher's Wall Lizard (top) can be found in the boulder's around the barren Alpine zone (bottom).

PRACTICAL PART

Additional sites in the High Atlas

For the locations of the sites described below, see map on page 138.

A – Marrakech

Although not strictly in the High Atlas, Marrakech and its environs are likely to be the base for most people accessing the areas and therefore it makes sense to include them here. The old town shows its roots as a cultural and historic centre of the Berber rule and there are a number of palaces and madrasas with intricately carved interiors to visit. The Souk is extensive and a destination in its own right, but most visitors are attracted to the main square, the Jemma el-Fna, which is by day and by night the beating heart of the city. Full of stalls, hawkers and performers including snake charmers and henna tattooists, it is a mixing place for the whole city.

There is wildlife in the city, most obviously in the form of many White Storks. Other species to look out for include Little Swift, Laughing Dove and Common Bulbul. The ornamental flowers in the parks and in the new town attract Painted Ladies, particularly after their return migration in October/November.

The Menara Park is a formal garden in the Islamic style and is walkable from the town centre The main tank here attracts swifts and swallows, including Alpine and Little Swift and Red-rumped Swallow. The surrounding Olive groves are a migrant trap with flycatchers and chats present in season.

House Bunting is a typical species of urban areas, often entering the houses themselves.

For those who want to go a bit further, the N9 north crosses the Oued Tensift (GPS: 31.693000, -7.992000), just beyond the edge of the city and south of the town of Ouahat Sidi Brahim. It is a Petit Taxi or bus ride from the centre and here you can wander along the banks of the wadi, especially by heading west. Brown-throated Martins can be found amongst the other swallows and martins. A good mix of waders regularly turn up

CROSSBILL GUIDES • SOUTHERN MOROCCO

ADDITIONAL SITES IN THE HIGH ATLAS

on migration. Otherwise, typical low steppe species can be found (e.g. Barbary Partridge, Mahgreb Magpie and Moussier's Redstart in winter). As with many of the sites in this guide, it helps if there is water in the wadi, and due to road repairs, the habitat immediately by the bridges has been degraded.

B – Zat Valley

GPS 31.427, -7.529. The Zat Valley is a large, picturesque area south of Marrakech, situated on the north-facing slope of the High Atlas Mountains between the valleys of the Ourika and Tichka. Access is from the N9, taking the P2016 in the direction of Tighedouine. The road initially follows the bank of the Zat river itself, sticking to the lower elevations of the High Atlas, where the river flows through a wide gravel bed. Beyond Tighedouine the road climbs steeply into the Sub-alpine zone before crossing the col and back to the N9 at Zerkten, described in Route 4 above.

The habitats are typical of the lower slopes of the High Atlas Mountains and have a mix of species that are typically 'Mediterranean' in character. Common Chameleon, Spanish Terrapin and Large Psammodromus can be found along the river below Tighedouine, and also it is worth searching for amphibians here. Any flowering plants are attractive to butterflies including Two-tailed Pasha, Moroccan Copper and Spotted Fritillary. Beyond Tighedouine the character changes, and the forest opens out with more juniper bushes present and the fauna also changes to being typical of the Sub-alpine zone. Both Tristram's Warbler and Moussier's Redstart breed in the area.

The Common Bulbul is a familiar sight in and around parks and gardens.

C – Oued Nfis on the road to Azzaden

GPS: 31.199, -8.074. The P2022 road to Azzaden leaves the R203 and drops from Ouirgane below the main barrage built on the River Nfis. This area is typical of the lower levels of the High Atlas Mountains with the area dominated by pines. As

ADDITIONAL SITES IN THE HIGH ATLAS

Ancient Junipers and Thujas are a feature of the Nfis valley.

this area is often left ungrazed, it can be good for endemic flowering plants and these, in turn, attract butterflies. Plain Tiger, Two-tailed Pasha, African Grass Blue and Babel Blue are all relatively common together with a mix of fritillaries. Endemic reptiles are also plentiful with Moroccan Wall Lizard and Moroccan Ocellated Lizard. The birds are similar to those found at Escale Forest, see route 3 above. If the streams are flowing or even if there are just puddles in the streambed, it can be good for dragonflies, especially the Barbary Featherleg. To access the river, you can either park at the beginning of the track that starts at the above-mentioned grid point and follow it to the dam spillway, approximately 2 km distant.

Alternatively, you can continue to the R203 crossing of the Nfis river, 11km further on, but note that currently, the road turns to gravel after c5km. Continuing to Amizmiz will offer more good habitat on the edge of the Haouz plain, although it is unlikely you'll add any more species.

D – Sti Fatma waterfalls

GPS: 31.221, -7.671. The Sti Fatma waterfalls are a well-known tourist destination 24 km south from the turn to Oukaïmeden near the head of the Ourika valley. At 1600m, the seven waterfalls lie in the Sub-alpine zone. The marked track up to the waterfalls is a good introduction to the Sub-alpine habitat and the almost permanent water means that it is attractive to a wide range of particularly butterflies and dragonflies. They include most of the species found around Imlil (route 1). It is a popular beauty spot and if you arrive on a busy day, it may be sensible to move a little way further on, continuing along the P2017 further up the Ourika headwaters and explore. The road runs out after 10km or so.

ADDITIONAL SITES IN THE HIGH ATLAS

E – Tizi n'Test

GPS: 30.868, -8.379.
One of the main crossings of the High Atlas Mountains from Marrakech rises to the col of Tizi n'Test at 2,093m. The scenic route up to the pass enables access to the high Sub-alpine zone before continuing on to Taroudant. Although once a major trading route, this is a much narrower and more difficult road across the mountains compared to the Tizi n'Tichka, but in consequence, the habitats are better preserved along the route. You can simply drive up and stop where the vegetation looks promising. This approach not only is successful for botany but works for butterflies, with Vaucher's Heath, Atlas Blue and Desert Orange Tip all possible. The shrubby hillsides are the breeding habitat of Tristram's Warblers and Moussier's Redstart. There is a good section of Holm Oak woodland just by the col itself.

There are a number of release sites of Barbary Sheep and Cuvier's Gazelles in the area so you may find these animals along the road. The side roads should not be ignored either. The P2036, for example, which turns off 1.7 km north of the col heads down to a river valley that is excellent for the Atlas Goldenring, an endemic dragonfly.

The Holm Oaks at the Tizi n'Test create another habitat to explore.

PRACTICAL PART

ROUTES IN THE HIGH ARID STEPPE

Routes in the High Arid Steppe

The area to the south of the High Atlas is one that immediately shows the transition to the drier areas further south. The relatively flat plain is cut by wadis and cliffs, that away from any river valleys have sparse and dry vegetation. The setting between two mountain ranges is nonetheless spectacular and empty although, especially after rain, not so barren as you may have thought. Due to the elevation, above 1100m asl, the high arid steppes have cool nights and mornings and hot afternoons. The whole area can be plagued by high winds. These are northerlies in the winter and spring and desiccating southerlies in the summer. At both times, these winds are against the main direction of migration and therefore birds will often hold out here until the conditions improve.

The meagre plant life is dominated by drought-adapted species and these are normally small and scrubby. Only in the river valleys and in some wadi washouts will there be trees. Migrant birds and insects congregate in the more vegetated areas and these can be rewarding to visit.

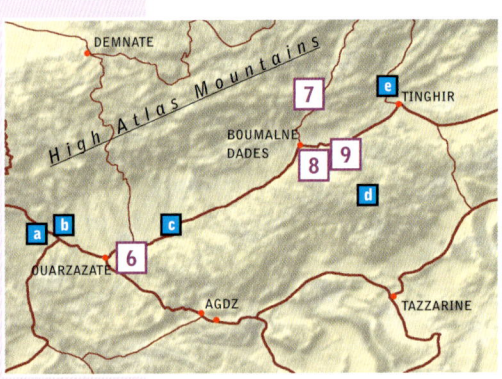

On the steppes themselves finding the areas which are attractive to special species requires an understanding of their particular needs and an element of luck. Population densities are low and vary in size and place from year to year. Therefore, some areas seem empty but with searching can hold a wide mix of interesting species, whilst others are simply as empty as they first appeared. There are two approaches to finding the birds. The first is to go to the locations that people have visited and found fruitful before and thus have stood the test of time. The second is to simply keep your eyes open and when you see something, to stop and explore. A mix of the two strategies is often the best way of tracking down the unique wildlife of the high arid steppe.

The routes included here are representative of the wider area and include sites that are easily accessible along the main roads between the Atlas and the desert. These are places that have proven to be successful over the years, however, as mentioned above the nomadic nature of many species means that they are not always as plentiful each year.

Route 6: Ouarzazate Reservoir

4 HOURS, 88 KMS
EASY

One of the few areas of open water in this part of Morocco. A magnet to migrating birds.

Habitats: Lake side, arid steppe
Selected species: Greater Flamingo, Ruddy Shelduck, Marbled Duck, Little Swift, Glossy Ibis, Black Stork, Western Marsh Harrier, Eurasian Stone-curlew, migrant waders, Spectacled Warbler, Spanish Terrapin, North African Water Frog, Vagrant Emperor, Lesser Emperor

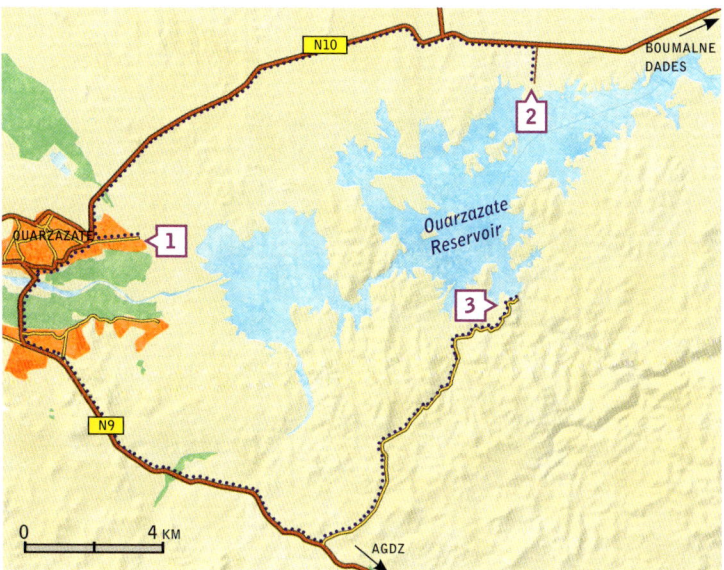

The *Barrage el Mansour Eddhabi* or Ouarzazate Reservoir lies to the east of Ouarzazate and the dams in the Drâa at the confluence of the Dadès and Asif Tidili rivers. The reservoir forms a patch of freshwater habitat in what is otherwise an arid area. In addition, being at the northern head of the Drâa, it is on a main inland migration route, so you can

ROUTE 6: QUARZAZATE RESERVOIR

imagine what a great site this can be for birdwatching. The numbers of birds and species present vary greatly with the seasons and the level of the water. Recently the water's edge has been several kilometres from the outskirts of the city, whilst in November 2014 it was at the edge of the built-up area.

Access to the western end of the reservoir is simple as it is right on the edge of Ouarzazate itself and a short trip by car or Petite Taxi. However, it may be dry. The other locations are further from the city but going there increases the likelihood of finding water. The dry reservoir bed is now covered in scrub, and in some areas, local farmers have started to cultivate small arable fields. This habitat is still interesting as it has an attractive mix of birds and dragonflies.

Some species can be looked for anywhere or by simply scanning from suitable vantage points. Ruddy Shelduck, Greater Flamingo, Black Stork, Black-winged Kite, Black Kite, Western Marsh Harrier are all often seen flying around the area without the need for searching in a particular place.

Starting point At the eastern end of Rue Ait Kdif (GPS: 30.9266, -6.8727)

Getting there Self-drive car or Petit Taxi from Ouarzazate. The starting point is also a simple walk from the city centre.

The Desert Wheatear is a familiar sight around the reservoir.

1 The informal parking area at the end of the tarmac road becomes a dusty track that continues eastward into the reservoir bed. Assuming there is no water, then simply follow the track. It will soon cross a heavily polluted stream with a series of linked pools. These can be attractive to waders, especially in the autumn with Little Stint, Curlew Sandpiper, Wood Sandpiper and Ruff all present.

There is a small makeshift crossing that enables the track to continue and pass an area of small agricultural fields. This area is good

ROUTE 6: QUARZAZATE RESERVOIR

for Spanish Sparrow, Yellow Wagtails and pipits. Moroccan Wagtail can be present but is scarce. Beyond here the area is a mix of tamarisk and cistus scrub and can be good for warblers, wheatears and chats, together with Stone Curlew. Migrant Quail are often flushed in spring. Overhead, the area is good in the morning for finding three species of swift, namely Pallid, Common and Little, that hunt over this area before climbing higher as the day progresses. The whole reservoir bed can be good for quartering dragonflies, with Vagrant and Lesser Emperors often very numerous. The track continues on to the shore of the western basin, but it can be a long and unproductive walk.

Return to the N10 and head east from the city (direction Skoura/Boumalne Dades). The second location gives views of the reservoir's central basin and can be found by turning south off the N10 after 15.3km through a Eucalyptus grove to an elevated parking area (GPS: 30.9681, -6.7579).

2 The shore and water can be distant but with a telescope you can usually see some birds (best arrive early or late because of the heat haze). The shoreline often has one or two Great White Egrets, a recent addition to the Moroccan avifauna but the most plentiful species on the water is Great Crested Grebe. However, it is the area just inland from the shoreline that can be most rewarding. Desert Lark breeds in the gravel plains around the reservoir and this can be one of the easiest places to find it. Also, Desert Wheatears are conspicuous and normally confiding. You don't need to leave the parking area to see them, although you can stroll all the way to water's edge if you choose. The Eucalyptus grove between the N10 and the parking area is a raptor roosting site, and it is worth checking the trees on the way in or out, Long-legged Buzzards and Bonelli's Eagles use this throughout the year plus Booted Eagle and Black Kite during migration.

The Desert Lark is adapted to the rock foreshores.

PRACTICAL PART

ROUTE 6: OUARZAZATE RESERVOIR

For the third location, go back and cross Ouarzazate, leaving the town via the N9 southeast bound towards Ait Saoun. Approximately 13 kms from the bridge over the Drâa in Ouarzazate, go left onto the P1513 towards the main dam (the barrage is signposted), which is another 13 kms further (GPS: 30.9112, -6.7609).

3 The area around the dam is guaranteed to have water and is the best spot when overall water levels are low. You are also much closer to the water, so even though the bird species here are not necessarily different from those on points one and two, views of waterbirds are usually better than on the other sites.

In addition, other waterbodies in the Ouarzazate area can attract waterbirds when the reservoir level is low. These are often small and disturbed but can be surprisingly fruitful. For example, the small Barrage Tamight (GPS: 30.8871, -6.9423), less than 10km south of Ouarzazate on the P1507 south of the village of the same name, has a mouth-watering list of waders and ducks including Marbled Duck and Red-knobbed Coot. Other small irrigation pools in the valley have the same potential.

View at point 2 of the route, where the water edge can be quite distant.

Route 7: Dadès Gorge

1-2 HOURS, 2 KM
EASY (IF WALKING DOWNHILL)

A renowned scenic area with a gorge formed by the Dadès river.
The southern edge of High Atlas Mountains with interesting geology.

Habitats: river gorge
Selected species: Barbary Ground Squirrel, Barbary Sheep, Barbary Partridge, Golden Eagle, Bonelli's Eagle, Crag Martin, Black Wheatear, Blue Rock Thrush, Rock Bunting, Tristram's Warbler, Austaut's Grayling

Together with the Todra Gorge (see additional sites C), the Dadès Gorge is typical of the dramatic southern edge of the High Atlas Mountains where they hit the High Arid Steppe. The ecosystem, therefore, has components of both zones. There is a well signposted road, the R794, from Boumalne Dades that lies some 30km to the south. There are plenty of restaurants and accommodation in the area. This area is conveniently linked with a visit to the unmissable Boumalne Dades plains in route 8.
As the only route is walking along the R704 itself, take care of the traffic. Normally this is light and respects walkers.

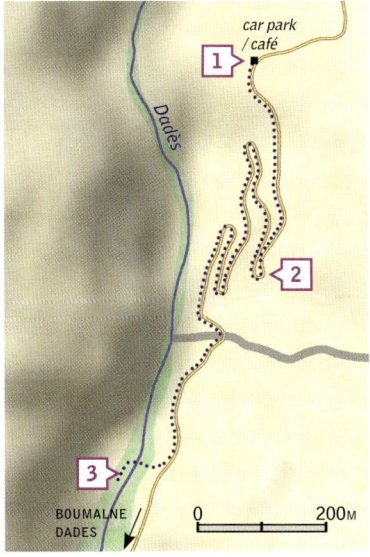

Starting point Parking area/Layby on the R704 by café-restaurant Timzzillite Chez Mohamed at the top of the switchbacks (GPS: 31.5297, -5.9253).

ROUTE 7: DADÈS GORGE

The switchbacks of the road give easy access to the gorge side habitat (top), where the endemic Tristram's Warbler can be found (bottom).

Getting there Self-drive car or Grand Taxi from Boumalne Dades.

1 The parking area and viewpoint gives stunning views at the high point of the road up the gorge. The area around the restaurant usually has a pair of resident Blue Rock Thrushes in the vicinity and the higher slopes are normally best for Rock Bunting. Careful scanning of the upper levels of the gorge can offer views of Barbary Sheep. Hhowever, care must be taken not to confuse them with the numerous goats that also graze the precipitous cliffs. Overhead, eagles can appear at any time. A pair of Bonelli's Eagles is resident in the area, but other species can be found as well.

2 Walk down the road around the switchbacks that give close views of the cliff faces. This is a good location to get close views of Barbary Ground Squirrels that forage on the rocky areas close to the road. Tristram's Warblers hold territory in season and the cliffs have many holes that are used by Rock Doves, all of which look 'pure' enough to be

ROUTE 7: DADÈS GORGE

considered wild birds rather than Feral Pigeons. In late summer and autumn, this route is normally alive with Austaut's Grayling, a High Atlas endemic butterfly. Also, look for Dodder, this area has an infestation of this parasitic plant.

3 Approaching the bottom of the gorge, explore the river which normally keeps flowing year-round. The river banks are popular among Barbary Partridges both for drinking and picking up grit that they need in their crops to digest the hard seeds they live on. Crag Martins can be seen anywhere in the gorge, but approach more closely near the water. The riverside vegetation, which is mainly Oleander, may attract other insects and birds. This is one of the few locations where the dragonfly Western Spectre has been found.

If visiting by car you need to return to the parking area, otherwise head downstream to a café to pick up a Grand Taxi and return back to Boumalne Dades to the south.

Additional site
The *Pattes de Singe*, about half way between this route and Boumalne Dades, are a series of cliffs that have been eroded by exfoliation and appear to resemble monkey hands. They are worth a stop. There is an overlook at Tamellalt, 12 km south of the stop described here.

The bizarre *Pattes de Singe* (monkey hands) rock formations are a local tourist attraction.

PRACTICAL PART

ROUTE 8: PLAINS OF BOUMALNE DADES

Route 8: Plains of Boumalne Dades

2-4 HOURS, 40 KM

The classic location to access the High Arid Steppes.
Great for birdwatching, within easy access of Boumalne Dades.

Habitats: High Arid Steppe, stony plain with scattered dwarf shrubs
Selected species: Fat Sand Rat, Temminck's Lark, Thick-billed Lark, Hoopoe Lark, Thekla's Lark, Cream-coloured Courser, Black-bellied Sandgrouse, Red-rumped Wheatear, Desert Wheatear, Boehme's Agama, Moroccan Spiny-tailed Agama

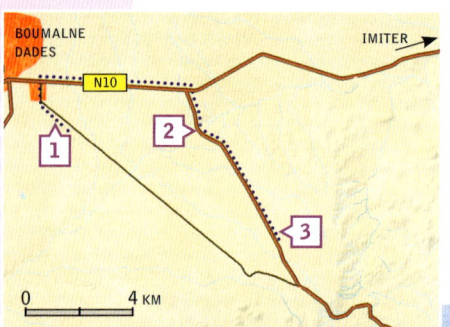

This is the area of the legendary 'Tagdilt Track', a route that had previously been the only 'road' heading south towards the easterly spur of the Anti-Atlas Mountains. Since the construction of the tarmac road to Ikniouen, this is not an access road, and the northern end of the track has progressively been built over but remains accessible. As it is now largely unused the

The gravel plains stretch for as far as the eye can see.

CROSSBILL GUIDES • SOUTHERN MOROCCO

ROUTE 8: PLAINS OF BOUMALNE DADES

old track is in poor condition and especially in the sandy areas, driving along it risks bogging down. Early spring is the best for the widest range of species, however, it is worthy of a visit in any season. As always, this area close to town is a tipping ground for both building waste and ordinary rubbish, and the whole area is strewn with plastic, although arguably less than it has been historically. It still gives the odd juxtaposition of great species next to human detritus. Only by moving further east and south can you escape the rubbish. It must be said, though, that many species appear not to mind the rubbish!

Along the new road, the access is simpler and in reality, the best way of finding species is simply to wander the steppe or scan for movement. Although often appearing lifeless, with patience there is often plenty to see. Of course, it is possible to walk out from the edge of town and follow the line of the old track, however, distances are quite large and there is no protection from the sun. Most visitors drive and then after stopping walk short loops to find the available species. Most species range widely over the whole plain and, therefore, there are not specific areas for particular species.

Red-rumped Wheatear (top) and Temminck's Lark (bottom) are typical High Arid Steppe birds found in the plains of Boumalne Dades.

Burrows of Fat Sand Rats and Moroccan Spiny-tailed Lizard dot the steppe. Care should be exercised not to collapse their burrows not only for the sake of these animals but for the Red-rumped Wheatears which nest in them.
Long-legged Buzzard, Trumpeter Finch, Red-rumped Wheatear, Desert Wheatear, Black-bellied Sandgrouse, Greater Short-toed and Thekla's Larks can be found almost anywhere.

Starting point Park on side of the track off the N10 after leaving Boumalne Dades to the east (GPS: 31.359, -5.962).

Getting there Self-drive car or Petit Taxi from Boumalne Dades. It is possible to walk to the first stop, however, note that it would be a walk of c.20km to cover all of the stops here.

ROUTE 8: PLAINS OF BOUMALNE DADES

1 The first area is around where the old track hits the N10. This used to be marked by the Inov Petrol Station, but further building work has pushed this further east. Follow any track heading south into the steppe, heading to the vicinity of the walled area. This gives you a good introduction to what is around. The wall itself offers an elevated vigil location for hunting shrikes and wheatears.

The typical view of Black bellied Sandgrouse - when you flush a family party.

2 Returning to the N10, the turning onto the road to Ikniouen is 5 km from Boumalne Dades (4km from the turn off to Stop 1) and a further 1 km along the new road there is a depression on the left-hand side. This natural bowl attracts whatever moisture there is and also is normally covered in ground-hugging herbs. This 'different' area appears to be particularly attractive to the birds. Temminck's Larks are normally the most common species, but wheatears, both Desert and Red-rumped, are also present. If there's any water, then this can attract waders. Although Little Ringed Plover and Green Sandpiper are the most regular, other waders have been seen.

3 A further 4.8km along the road, there is a track to the right which heads WSW. This passes over a short rise before dropping down to a dry river bed. Park up and repeat the approach used elsewhere. This is normally a good area for both Cream-colored Courser and Thick-billed Lark. The area toward the Anti-Atlas to the south is the most likely area to find Crowned Sandgrouse. Their morning drinking flights are the simplest way of seeing them, but care is needed to distinguish them from Black-bellied and Pin-tailed Sandgrouse both of which may also be present. In the sandy stream bed, there is a large colony of Fat Sand Rats. These charming rodents can be seen changing bedding and interacting around their many burrows.

Route 9: Gorges near Imiter

1 HOUR
EASY

Gorges with birds not found elsewhere in the flat steppe.

Habitats: High Arid Steppe gorge and wadi
Selected species: Maghreb Wheatear, Black Wheatear, Pharaoh Eagle Owl, Lanner Falcon, Long-legged Buzzard, Bosk's Fringe-fingered Lizard, Böhme's Agama

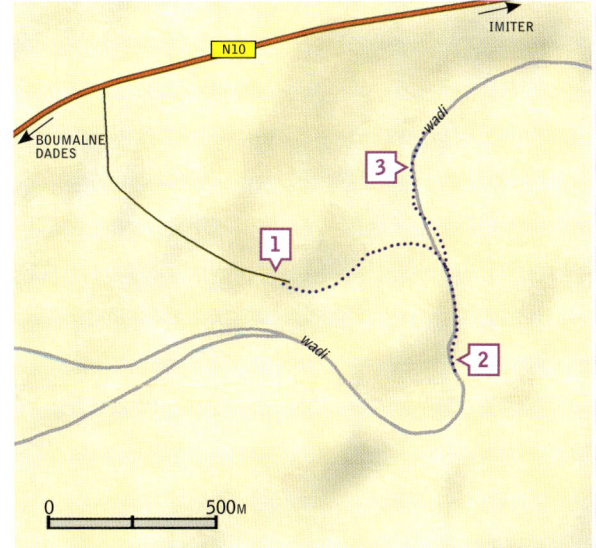

The gorges near Imiter are probably not very different from many other incised wadis or gorges in the High Arid Steppe zone. What makes them stand out is not the habitat, but their proximity to the N10, offering easy access to a habitat where many sought-after bird species live, hence its inclusion in this itinerary. Early spring is the best for the widest range of species as there is likely to be vegetation in the wadi and the local nests will be active.

Starting point
The turning to the location is 16.5km east of Boumalne Dades, a further 8.8km from the Ikniouen turning or 4.5km west of Imiter. Park at GPS 31.370, -5.826 and then walk over the crest of the 'col' to the north-east to access the 'gorge' itself.

Getting there Most visitors visit this area either by self-drive car or by Grand Taxi from Boumalne Dades.

ROUTE 9: GORGES NEAR IMITER

1 Before leaving the parking area, scan the old gravel workings and wadi below. This area normally has parties of Trumpeter Finches and breeding White-crowned Wheatears.

Follow the track to the north-east over the ridge until you can see into the valley with the gorge cliffs in front of you.

2 Continue into the wadi bed and head south. Search the gorge for cliff loving species. Long-legged Buzzards are nearly always present. Lanners or Pharaoh Eagle Owl may be present as well, but as they do not tolerate each other's company, it is either one or the other. Cliff-loving wheatears can be present including Black and White-crowned, but the prize here could be Maghreb Wheatear. This is a species that is becoming scarce in recent years and although the route east of Boumalne Dades has always been a good place to look, pairs tend to move around the available habitat.

3 After searching return to the entrance of the wadi and follow it north, back towards the N10. The valley bottom can have local resident species such as Cream-colored Courser or Desert Lark. The vegetated runnels attract migrants, such as redstarts, warblers and chats. The route back can be either to return to the original parking spot or head up the wadi side to a parking spot on the edge of the N10 which is the alternative location to stop.

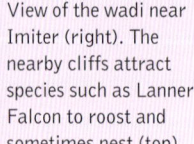

View of the wadi near Imiter (right). The nearby cliffs attract species such as Lanner Falcon to roost and sometimes nest (top).

Additional sites in the High Arid Steppes

For the locations of the sites described below, see map on page 160.

A – Amerzgane

GPS: 31.037, -7.217. The main N9 passes through the village of Amerzgane after crossing the High Atlas Mountains via the Tiz n' Tichka, 35km northwest of Ouarzazate. In the centre of the village is an obvious junction with the P1505 road that heads south. Stop on the roadside just south of the wadi crossing. The habitat is typical of the High Arid Steppe in close proximity to a wadi and rocky bluffs. And the small fields and unaltered gravel plains should be searched in addition to the cliffs and the wadi edges. This is one of the most reliable places to find Maghreb Wheatear, which is otherwise increasingly hard to find. In addition, other wheatears, Trumpeter Finch and a whole mix of migrants can be found in the area especially if poor weather higher up is delaying the passage of birds.

The unprepossessing cliffs at Amerzgane are one of the few hotspots for the Maghreb Wheatear.

B – Ait Ben Haddou

GPS: 31.047, -7.132. Overall 30km north-west of Ouarzazate, the world heritage site of the former Ksar of Ait Ben Haddou, is well signposted along the P1506, which turns off from the N9 at Tazentout. The Ksar used to protect the trade routes from the Sahara that crossed to High Atlas Mountains via the Tiz n'Tichka pass.

It is a picturesque setting and has been widely used in many Hollywood blockbusters, including Time Bandits and Gladiator. It sits in an area of high arid steppe with both bluffs and the Ounila river, meaning that it is a good location for exploration. Parking is well marked and there are plenty of paths along the river, whilst most visitors limit themselves to the Ksar itself.

Although the village of Ait Ben Haddou attracts the crowds, it the surrounding wadi and cliffs that are interesting to the naturalist.

ADDITIONAL SITES IN THE HIGH ARID STEPPES

The species typical of the area include Desert and Thekla's Larks, Black and White crowned Wheatears, Rock Buntings and Black-bellied Sandgrouse are known to sometimes come to drink to the river. During migration, almost any species can turn up and raptor passage overhead can sometimes be strong as birds are funnelled by the need to cross the mountains via the pass.

C – Skoura Palmerie

GPS: 31.048, -6.573. An extensive palmerie in the High Arid Steppes to the west of Skoura along the N10, 35km east of Ouarzazate. The main part of the palmerie is separated from the main N10 by a tributary to the Dadès river, however it is normally dry and access is straightforward except after rain. The area is a migrant trap and also holds a number of birds through the winter. Booted Eagle often winter and Blue Rock Thrush and Moussier's Redstart can also be common. During migration, a mix of warblers, chats and flycatchers stop off to feed and these can include Woodchat Shrike and Golden Oriole. All of these are attracted by the small agricultural fields below the palms and their irrigation system. It is a pleasant place to wander in the shade for a few hours.

These same fields are attractive to a mix of amphibians, including Moroccan Painted Frogs and Moroccan Toad and both butterflies and dragonflies, mainly a mix of whites and Epaulet Skimmers, in the spring and summer. The palmerie is dotted with Kasbahs, many of which are now converted to small hotels and, together with the views up to the High Atlas Mountains to the north, makes this an attractive place to wander.

D – Jebel Saghro

GPS: 31.150, -5.650. On the eastern edge of the Anti-Atlas, the Jebel Saghro range rises to 2,712m and forms a dramatic horseshoe of old volcanic peaks that have eroded into massifs, pipes, steep cliffs and flat-topped mountains. The core of the range has become much easier to reach since the building of the tarmac road to Ikniuoen (see route 8) and this means straightforward access from Boumalne Dades, 47km away.

The highest peak, Amalou n'Mansour is a two hour (or so) walk above the village, starting at 1940m asl. The path is straightforward but at times a bit unclear on the ground. The path leaves the village by a clear trail

ADDITIONAL SITES IN THE HIGH ARID STEPPES

heading south from the Mosque (GPS: 31.17088, -5.67433) and up a zigzag path to the heads up the cliff face, a climb of 400m or so. Once at the top of this cliff (GPS: 31.14553, -5.67550) the final summit is to the east, but there is no need to head that far, except for the exhilaration of reaching the highest point. This first section of the trail gives a good cross-section of the local habitats and the specialities of this area of the Anti-Atlas. This is a good spot for Streaked Scrub Warbler and Desert Lark and the Anti-Atlas has a range of rare, often endemic drought-adapted plants, some of which can be found on this route.

E – Todra Gorge

GPS: 31.587, -5.592. Arguably even more dramatic scenically, The Todra Gorge is narrower and has steeper cliffs than the Dadès Gorge but is less convenient to get to and more difficult to work as the road stays in the valley bottom. The overall area has very similar species, and dependent upon your specific itinerary the two sites could be considered interchangeable.

Todra gorge is reached along the R702, 15km north of Tinghir and the 2km section is most interesting for the geology and landscape. The surrounding mountain edges hold Black Wheatear and Tristram's Warbler, whilst the river valley can be attractive to Barbary Partridge. The general area holds Bonelli's Eagles, whilst other large raptors show up with some regularity. To stand any chance of seeing almost anything beyond the ubiquitous Eurasian Crag Martin and Grey Wagtail, you need to scramble up the herding tracks south of the narrowest part of the gorge and achieve a wider vista.

The dramatic Todra gorge is narrow and difficult to explore.

PRACTICAL PART

Routes in the Sahara

The route south from the High Arid Steppe takes you down to the edge of the Sahara, dropping below the 1000m contour line into an increasingly arid landscape. Accurately, it is part of the neo-Saharan biome, but simply called Sahara in this book.

In the Sahara, there are even fewer towns than in the arid steppes, and only a couple of lightly trafficked tarmac roads cross the region. This makes access to this remote region relatively simple, at least when one explores sites close to the main roads. Further afield, there is a vast, remote area that needs a full expedition to explore, which is beyond the scope of this book.

This is an area to be treated with respect – a very harsh environment where minor troubles can lead to serious issues if you don't have water. It is also a challenging environment to watch wildlife as well, but for many visitors, this is the highlight of the trip to Morocco.

Most mental images of the desert are ones of endless sand dunes, but this sort of landscape is relatively uncommon in Morocco. The majority of the area consists of stony plains and wadi washouts amongst rocky bluffs. The (accessible) areas of sand dunes are restricted to the region of Merzouga in the east and M'hamid in the south, which require the longest drives to get to.

Even more than the arid steppes, this is a place where bird densities are low and many species only appear when conditions are right. Some areas need specialist help, both for access and to track down the nomadic species one needs up-to-the-minute local knowledge. This is the case with the dune areas, and these areas should not be attempted with a single vehicle, unless backup can be arranged, and need a four-wheel drive anyway.

The Drâa valley cuts through this desolate landscape and this naturally becomes the focus of any visit. The water supports an oasis and palmerie-type habitat in an otherwise arid environment. However, as on the arid steppes before, the really special species are adapted to the desert itself and need to be looked for away from the watercourse.

ROUTE 10: DESERT WELL NEAR JORF

Route 10: Desert Well near Jorf

**1 HOUR, 1-2 KM
EASY**

A desert well with a concentration of Saharan wildlife.

Habitats: Saharan desert edge
Selected species: *Asphodelus tenuifolius, Euphorbia calyptera, Cleome africana*, Sodom's Apple Milkweed, Maghreb Lark, Hoopoe Lark, Bar-tailed Lark, Spectacled Warbler, Scrub Warbler, Trumpeter Finch, Greenish Black-tip

Only a few metres off the most popular route to Erg Chebbi, a well structure and the nearby rocky outcrop are obvious from the road. This is usually the first area of truly Saharan habitat reached when arriving from the arid steppe. As with all desert, the habitat here is marked by low diversity and small populations. However, the presence of the well and therefore water seems to attract whatever is around.
Overall, the attractiveness of the plain is dependent upon the extent of the rains, and the amount of vegetation that has been brought by them. Early spring is the best for the widest range of species, however, it is worthy of a visit in any season.

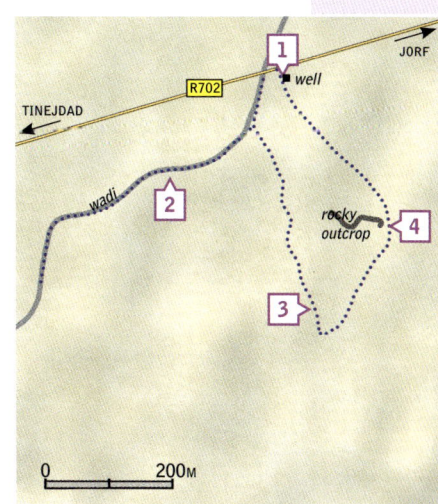

Starting point The R702 road between Tinejdad and Erfoud, roughly 14 kms west of the village of Jorf (GPS: 31.522, -4.541).

Getting there Self-drive car or Grand Taxi from either Boumalne Dades or Erfoud.

1 The well is hand-drawn and the overflow is often attractive to the smaller desert birds and migrants that come to drink. Particularly Trumpeter Finches are frequent here. White-crowned Wheatears nest in the well itself and can be seen diving down the shaft.

PRACTICAL PART

ROUTE 10: DESERT WELL NEAR JORF

Head down into the wadi and follow it for a kilometre or so. The edges are marked by tall Sodom's Adam Milkweeds.

2 If there are water pools in the wadi this spot can be very rewarding for birdwatching including Yellow and Morocco Wagtails and waders. You may find Maghreb Lark, for which these wadis are the ideal habitat (other 'crested' larks are very scarce here). They often sing close to the road. This location also holds Scrub Warbler, although the best area for this species is a bit further west along the same valley line. If time allows, explore as far as possible.

Return and just before the road, climb out of the valley and head broadly south. Your target should be any area of the plain that is vegetated.

3 You cross a sandy wash out plain with scant vegetation that can become surprisingly flowery after autumn rains, with *Euphorbia calyptrata*, *Asphodelus tenuifolius* and *Cleome africana* sometimes forming large drifts. If this is the case, the plants and their seeds attract many species, especially Trumpeter Finches and Spectacled Warblers. Greenish Black-tips are often common, especially amongst any crucifers.

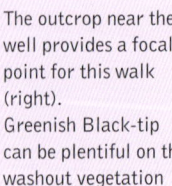

The outcrop near the well provides a focal point for this walk (right).
Greenish Black-tip can be plentiful on the washout vegetation (top).

ROUTE 10: DESERT WELL NEAR JORF

Larks can be plentiful in the more open areas with Hoopoe and Bar-tailed Larks, two Saharan specialities, often being the most numerous.

Head towards the conspicuous rocky outcrop on your left.

4 The outcrop attracts sentinel hunters that use the elevation over the plains to scan for prey. Kestrel and Little Owls can be found, and there are usually some wheatears around, with Desert being the most likely. Mason bees are a feature of the rock faces, their nesting tubes can be seen on the underside of the rock overhangs.

Return to the road and well, which are clearly visible from the rocky outcrop.

A short distance south of the well along the R702 is an ad-hoc museum which offers a presentation on the water systems (Khetteras) and gives a different view on man's attempts to survive in this harsh environment.

Spectacled warblers breed in the wadi side vegetation.

PRACTICAL PART

Route 11: Erg Chebbi and its environs

1-2 DAYS

The dramatic Erg Chebbi dunes and a mix of other Saharan habitats.
Spectacular birdlife and wildlife.
Local guide needed to find most of the species.

Habitats: sahara sand dunes, gravel plains, tussock grass dunes, cliffs, palm groves, open water
Selected species: Desert Bitter Melon, Fennec Fox, Rüppell's Fox, Jirds, Jerboas, Houbara Bustard, African Desert Warbler, Desert Sparrow, Egyptian Nightjar, Spotted Sandgrouse, Crowned Sandgrouse, Cream-colored Courser, Bar-tailed Lark, Brown-necked Raven, African Green Toad, Western Sandfish, Dumeril's Fringe-fingered Lizard, Long-footed Fringe-fingered Lizard, Sand Geckos, Desert Monitor, Horned Viper, Desert Swallowtail, Vagrant Hawker, Oasis Bluetail, Black Pennant

Erg Chebbi is an extensive and moving sand dune complex 28 km long, up to 7 km wide and up to 150m high. The name is also generally used for the surrounding area. Although the dunes are the major attraction for most visitors, these are not the main target for naturalists. It is the area around the dunes that is interesting and holds many desert specials. Any time of year is good to visit however early spring has the widest range of spe-

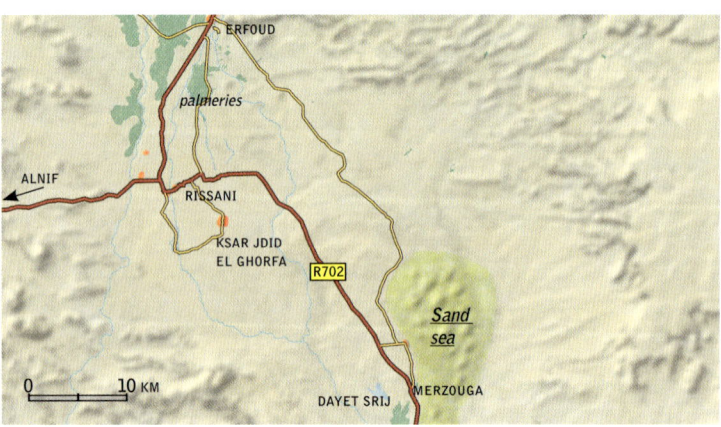

ROUTE 11: ERG CHEBBI AND ITS ENVIRONS

cies, and it can be dangerously hot in summer. The desert is far from uniform. The nature and the amount of vegetation makes a huge difference to its attractiveness to species and this changes from month to month and year to year. The habitat is very fragile and it is increasingly being used for a wide range of 'adventure sports' so keeping away from the areas that they generally use is also recommended. Lastly, this area is very close to the Algerian border. This has historically provided some protection to the area and reduced its attractiveness to grazing and general access. The border zone is politically and militarily sensitive and care must be exercised if going off track.

Species are very difficult to find without local and up to date knowledge and therefore, we suggest that specialist access is arranged with a 4x4 vehicle and a guide. Rather than describing Erg Chebbi as a self-drive route, we provide information on what occurs in the different habitats. Your local guide will pick you up from your hotel and take you to the best areas based upon current knowledge. This will involve travelling off-road to cover a cross-section of the micro-habitats in this area. The evening is by far the best time for mammals and reptiles, especially the period just after dusk. Staying at one of the camps at the foot of Erg Chebbi and going out on foot after dark is another good strategy to connect with the species.

The sands of the Erg are relatively devoid of life (top), but Hoopoe Larks can be found where the sand meets the gravel plains (bottom; shown in display flight).

PRACTICAL PART

ROUTE 11: ERG CHEBBI AND ITS ENVIRONS

In in some parts around Erg Chebbi Halfa grasses have stabalised the sands.

Sand dunes
The majority appear relatively lifeless but provide a home for the sand specialists such as Western Sandfish, Sand Geckos and sidewinding snakes such as Horned Vipers.

Gravel plains
These consist of dark gravel on a light, sandy base and are the classic areas for Houbara Bustard, Crowned and Spotted Sandgrouse, and Cream-colored Courser (although coursers like the edges of the sandy tussock grass as well). Although this type of habitat surrounds Erg Chebbi, for the bustard the most likely area is further towards the Algerian border. Where there are trees, there can be large flocks of Trumpeter Finches. In the wadi washout zones, small bushes provide cover and these are the places to search for Egyptian Nightjar. In reality, it is better to invest a few Dirhams and tip a local who has staked out a roost site. In winter, these plains can hold flocks of Thick-billed Larks plus, in some years, Dunn's Lark.

Almost impossible to find, the Egyptian Nightjar relies on its camouflage at its day time roost.

Tussock Grasses

Tussock grasses grow on small ridges of sand and form the classic habitat for breeding African Desert Warbler and feeding area for Fulvous Babbler. The grasses form a popular habitat for lizards, jirds and jerboas. The most suitable areas are between Erg Chebbi and Erfoud, east of the R702.

Palmeries

These add a mix of natural vegetation and low-intensity arable crops. They are also critical nesting areas for Desert Sparrow and Fulvous Babbler, although these only appear to like the smaller and remoter palmeries to the east of Erg Chebbi. Many of the more modern palmeries use drip irrigation but where traditional water channels are still used, they are good for African Green Toad, North African Water Frog, plus dragonflies such as Violet and Orange-winged Dropwings, Desert Darter and various skimmers. The flowering plants attract butterflies including Desert Swallowtail and Plain Tiger. The most productive for finding amphibians and dragonflies is the Palmerie d'Igrane at Hassilabled, just west of Erg Chebbi (see site C on page 194).

New Palm groves

Increasing numbers of palm trees have been planted immediately to the east of Erg Chebbi and are mostly associated with the tourist camps. These have been good for Desert Sparrow and Fulvous Babbler and the surrounding trees are excellent migrant traps and hold Tristram's Warblers in the winter. There is some evidence that the maturing trees have enabled House Sparrows to gain a foothold and therefore the Desert Sparrows have been forced into more marginal habitat, such as the acacias on the surrounding plain.

Houbara still hangs on to the east of the Erg, although views are invariably distant.

Drinking troughs

The increase of Camels in the area for tourist rides has increased the use of drinking troughs, which attract sandgrouse that come here to drink. Both Crowned and Spotted Sandgrouse normally drink around two hours after sunrise.

Desert Sparrow is fond of the new palm groves, and nesting boxes have been provided to support their recovery.

Cliffs and escarpments

The cliffs attract Brown-necked Ravens and Lanner Falcons, while the area of tamarisks at the foot of the cliffs should be explored for Tristram's Warbler throughout the winter. The whole area is very good for fossils and simply by walking along the foot of any cliffs it is possible to find many specimens. The best known cliffs lie to the west of Rissani, a short distance along the N12 (see site D on page 194), but there are many others around the edge of the gravel plains.

Open Water

Although it may seem improbable, in periods after the rains, the desert floods and there is a semi-permanent lake at Dayet Srij (GPS: 31.108, -4.053). This can continue to hold water through the summer months and into the next rainy season. It is not unusual to find that this is over 1km long and 500m wide, and at those times it seems improbable that it will dry out. However, it only takes one dry winter for the lake to revert to dry desert.

If there is water, it can be spectacular for birdwatching. Flocks of 500+ Greater Flamingos, large numbers of Ruddy Shelduck, Marbled Duck, Black-winged Stilts and large numbers of migrant waders can all be found. The lake also has a long list of rarities associated with it including Blue-winged Teal, Franklin's Gull and Grey Phalarope.

The area is attractive to insects. Dragonflies can be abundant, particularly the Vagrant, Lesser and Blue Emperors. Black Pennant has been found in recent years. In turn, these attract insect-eating birds, such as Blue-cheeked Bee-eaters and Whiskered Terns.

In wet winters, other pools and lakes form, especially around the foot of Erg Chebbi. These in turn will attract water birds and the results can be spectacular.

The water courses are normally dry, except immediately after rains. Only Oued Erfoud seems to hold water longer than many. This river forms another migrant trap and is a reliable location for finding Moroccan Wagtail. North African Water Frogs can also be plentiful in the remaining pools.

Route 12: The southern Route – Tazarine

2-3 HOURS, 5 KM

Splendid landscape with lat-topped acacias and palm oases.
Great birdwatching, with several 'African' species and many migrants.

Habitats: Gravel plain, isolated limestone bluffs, palm oasis
Selected species: African Rock Martin, Blue-cheeked Bee-eater, Fulvous Babbler, Barbary Partridge, Migrant warblers and chats, Plain Tiger

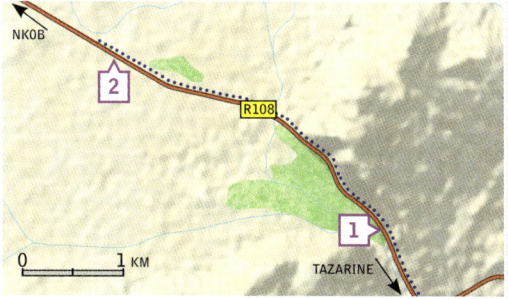

Although there are choices for the route that connects Erg Chebbi with Ouarzazate, the southern N12 route along the edge of the Saharan biome has much to recommend it. The scenery is surprisingly different from that further north and it is much less populated. The plains appear very 'African' and this is reinforced by the current attempts to reintroduce Ostrich, Addax, Scimitar-horned Oryx and other ungulates, though there are no facilities to view them.
As with the other routes and sites in this part of Morocco, the list of possible species is impressive, but all of them occur in very low densities. The main tactic is to stop when something is seen or to go to suitable places and search. It is with this second approach in mind that these two locations just west of Tizarine are included. This area around Tizarine is not dissimilar to many others along the route, however it has been found to be productive and is a sensible 'mid-point' for a stop.

Starting point Tazarine (GPS: 30.789, -5.573). Leave the town westwards (Ouarzazate). Stop after 1 km in a pull-off by the road.

1 The Acacia and Palm oasis on the (dry) Oued Tazarine (GPS: 30.789, -5.573) provides some dense shade in the otherwise sun-baked plains. Overlooked by high cliffs of the wadi walls this is a migrant trap in spring

ROUTE 12: THE SOUTHERN ROUTE – TAZARINE

and especially in autumn. The acacias here bloom in September and this attracts invertebrates to the sources of pollen and nectar. In turn, birds heading south find this the last opportunity to feed before crossing the Sahara. The oasis can seem full of birds at this time, with flycatchers as well as a wide mix of Sylvia warblers and both Eastern and Western Olivaceous Warblers being present. Away from this peak time it is quieter, but still worth a stop. Drift migrants from further south include African Rock Martin, which needs careful separation from Crag Martins, and Blue-cheeked Bee-eaters that may stay and breed locally. Barbary Partridge are resident and Moussier's Redstart and Tristram's Warbler winter here having bred in the mountains to the north.

2 A further 3.5km west (GPS: 30.804, -5.603) along the N12 is a line of acacia in a gravel plain. This area extends across the road to the wadi bed and the whole area is worth searching for open country species. Among the butterflies, Plain Tigers can be commonplace in addition to the normal desert species of Greenish Black-tip. Wheatears can be plentiful during migration, with Northern, Western Black-eared and Desert Wheatears joining the resident White-crowned. Note that some of the acacias here are Camel thorn (*Vachellia erioloba*). These are not native but have been planted as browsing food for livestock, which eat the leaves (despite the wicked thorns) and the seed pods.

The palmerie at Tazarine provides welcome respite to migrants in this parched landscape.

Route 13: The Drâa Valley

3-4 HOURS, 44 KM

Main river basin in the southernmost part of Morocco, attracting a lot of wildlife.

Habitats: Saharan River Valley, palmeries
Selected species: Barbary Partridge, Blue Rock Thrush, Cetti's Warbler, Nightingale, Rufous-tailed Scrub Robin, Blue-cheeked Bee-eater, Vagrant Emperor, Sahara Bluetail, Oasis Bluetail, Red-veined Dropwing

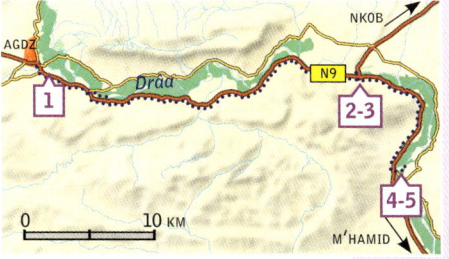

The Drâa is the longest river in Morocco and is formed from the confluence of the Dades and Imini rivers near Ouarzazate and then flows south to the Algerian border before heading almost due west to the coast. The main N9 crosses the Anti-Atlas Mountains south of Ouarzazate and returns to the banks of the Oued Drâa at Agdz. It then follows the course of the river all the way to M'hamid, 190km away. The section of the Drâa referenced in this route is the 35km section south of Agdz. It is an ancient trading route and the landscape that developed was to support the caravans that crossed the Sahara. Despite it being closer to Ouarzazate, it has been less developed for tourism as has the area south of Erfoud and around Erg Chebbi. Yet the road improvements in 2015-16 have made access simpler.

The landscape is still dominated by the Ksars and Kasbahs and their surrounding palmeries. The water level varies tremendously from year to year and season to season. There have been centuries of human intervention. Weirs, reservoirs and irrigation systems mean that the river is rarely in full flow. In the driest part of the year, it is often reduced to a series of pools and damp stretches where the wildlife concentrates. For naturalists, it can be quite difficult to know where to concentrate your efforts. Sites that were rewarding one year can become dry and devoid of life the next. The three locations on this route have been shown to

ROUTE 13: THE DRÂA VALLEY

be worth a stop and are typical of this area, but on travelling along the N9 it is best to keep looking for wherever there is still water and seek access.

The whole of the river valley is a magnet to migrating birds and bee-eaters, both Eurasian and Blue-cheeked, and Rufous-tailed Scrub Robin stay to breed. Other dry area species can be drawn to the water to drink, such as Trumpeter Finches and Barbary Partridges. The mud-brick Kasbahs are a favoured hang out of Blue Rock-thrushes. The whole of the river is good for Moroccan Wagtail.

Starting point Agdz GPS: 30.688, -6.193

Getting there Self-drive or Grand Taxi from Ouarzazate.

Blue-cheeked Bee-eater is a breeding summer migrant.

Follow the N9 eastwards. Five km south of Agdz, there is a turning to the village of Tamnougalt (GPS: 30.674525, -6.407475). Cross the river and park immediately after the bridge

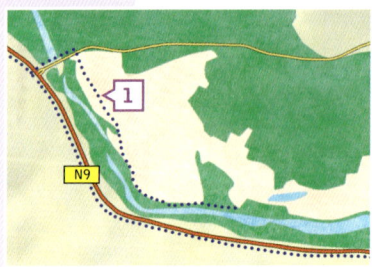

1 In this area, the Drâa runs through a series of pools with sandy banks and areas of low-intensity gravel extraction. Follow the eastern bank of the river downstream, and search the river banks for dragonflies. This site is particularly good for all three species of dropwings; i.e., Violet, Orange-winged and Red-veined, together with Sahara Bluetail.

The dense riverside vegetation holds good densities of Cetti's Warblers and Nightingales.

CROSSBILL GUIDES • SOUTHERN MOROCCO

ROUTE 13: THE DRÂA VALLEY

Continue along the N9. 33 km south from Agdz, turn left on the R108 and park on the edge of the R108 just to the north of the river bridge (GPS: 30.688, -6.193).

2 From the bridge you look out over what is normally one of the widest and deepest stretches of the Drâa. Most birds can be found simply by walking along the roadside and crossing the bridge. The deep water here attracts Cormorants, herons including Purple, Night and Squacco, and migrant waders. The riverine palmerie is a migrant trap and most warblers (including both Western and Eastern Olivaceous), chats and flycatchers can be found by walking around the field edges. As elsewhere in the Drâa, you should keep an eye on the skies as many of the larger migrants pass overhead including many species of raptors.

3 400m north of the bridge is a track that heads approximately 1 kilometre east and back to the river bed. If there is water in the pools behind the weir, this can be good for dragonflies, including Vagrant Emperor and Sahara Bluetail. Other Damselflies should be searched for along any areas of riverside vegetation, as this is as about as far north as Oasis Bluetail can be found. The

The palmeries in the Drâa valley.

PRACTICAL PART

birds here are more typical of the surrounding desert and both Fulvous Babblers and Desert Larks have been found.

Continue further along the N9 for another 12 km. Turn off the N9 just north of an Afriquia fuel station (GPS: 30.620361, -6.165528).

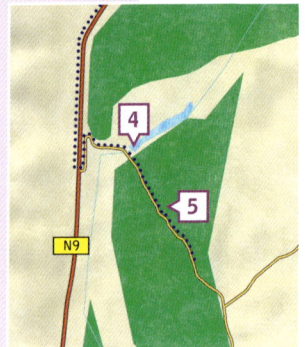

4 This third location along the Drâa is a length of the river that usually holds water behind a small dam. The track loops around to the north before heading eastwards and crossing the Drâa after 500m. Walk northwards along the edge of the water upstream of the dam. This is another dragonfly location, particularly for Sahara and Oasis Bluetails, although other species could also be found.

5 The track continues to an area of palmerie and as you are heading further south, you've entered the distribution range of Desert Hedgehogs and Kuhl's Pipistrelle. Birds include Desert and Maghreb Larks and Fulvous Babbler. These are joined by breeding migrants such as Blue-cheeked Bee-eaters and Rufous-tailed Scrub Robins.

Fulvous Babbler is a characteristic species of the palmeries edges.

Route 14: M'Hamid

8+ HOURS

Sand dunes and oases on the Drâa valley.
Wild and little visited area at the end of trafficable roads.
Rich wildlife, but hard to explore area.

Habitats: Sand dunes and Desert Oasis
Selected species: Egyptian Nightjar, Fulvous Babbler, Eastern Olivaceous Warbler, African Desert Warbler, Desert Sparrow, Desert Hedgehog, Fennec Fox, Jirds, Jerboas, Western Sandfish, Dumeril's Fringe-fingered Lizard, Long-footed Fringe-fingered Lizard, Sand Geckos, Desert Monitor, Horned Viper, Sand Viper

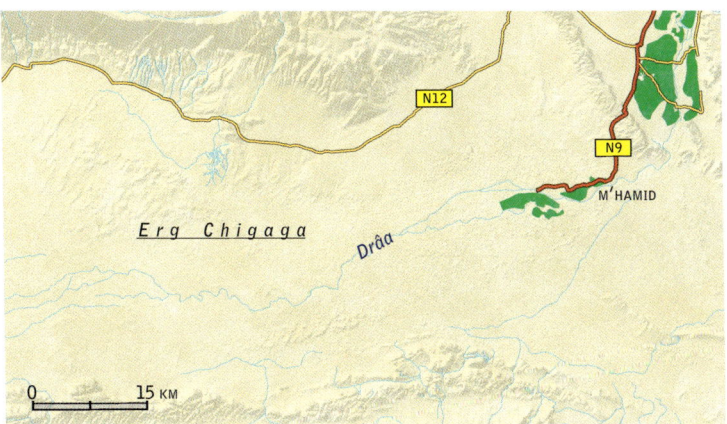

M'hamid is a desert oasis town only 40km from the Algerian border. Local tensions meant this area was out of bounds for a long time, but recently it became a hub for a burgeoning adventure tourism economy. Here, travellers transfer to 4x4 for the off-road drive to the dunes of Erg Chigaga.
In theory, M'Hamid has the same species as those found at Erg Chebbi (route 11) although this area doesn't have the open water equivalent of Dayet Srij, nor is Houbara Bustard found here. Furthermore, there isn't the same number of eco-visitors, and so there are fewer people looking

and fewer local guides. That being said, even with the fewer visitors there is a mouth-watering list of species that have already been found and with disturbance increasing around Erg Chebbi, it is likely that M'Hamid's popularity will increase.

The comments on various habitats and species described in route 11 apply to M'hamid as well, only here there is more sand and less gravel. You will need to ensure that your guide knows what you are looking for and the mix of habitats to visit. For the nocturnal species, the best approach is to stay at one of the 'glamping-style' accommodations and wander locally from there at dusk. Driving off-road at night is very dangerous and cannot be recommended.

African Desert Warbler is limited to the sandy desert area and prefers the Halfa grass zones.

Palmeries

The area around M'hamid can be explored from the end of N12 without resorting to a guided day out. Fulvous Babbler, Desert Sparrow and the damselfly Oasis Bluetail are the key resident species. It is possible to see Spotted and Crowned Sandgrouse at irrigation pools. Eastern Olivaceous Warbler is fond of Tamarisks and is a breeding summer migrant.

Sand dunes

Immediately south of Oued Drâa lies an area of sand dunes. This area is best for the Western Sandfish, Sand Geckos and both Horned and Desert Vipers. Although it is a few kilometres away, note that this area can be sensitive depending on the state of tension with Algeria, so seek advice before you start exploring. Some 30 km to the west lies a vast sand sea, or Erg.

Tussock grass and wadi washout

This is the main habitat west of M'hamid itself and this is best for reptiles, especially the fringe-fingered lizards, Fennec Foxes and Desert Hedgehog. African Desert Warbler nests in the tussock grass areas and Egyptian Nightjar prefers the Oued edges with scattered bushes.

Other sites in the Sahara

For the locations of the sites described below, see map on page 178.

A – Goulmima wadi

 GPS: 31.755, -4.837. There is a shallow, broad wadi east of Goulmima that has long been a good location to find the rare Streaked Scrub Warbler. They seem to be around throughout the year. Other desert species are possible including Maghreb Lark, Cream-coloured Courser and a mix of wheatears and larks.
Road N10 crosses the wadi at 13.3 kms from the bridge over the river at Goulmima. From here you can explore.

B – Ziz Gorge

 GPS: 32.158, -4.362. North of Errachidia, the N13 crosses the High Atlas Mountains and provides the easterly route back to either Marrakech or to the Middle Atlas and the cities of the north. This is the Eastern High Atlas, which has a character of its own. There are species here that only just extend into Morocco from Algeria. One such species is the North African Gundi, a short-tailed rodent that can be found on the rocky slopes of the Ziz Gorge. The best approach is to park off the main N13 road wherever it is safe to do so and scan the rock faces above that overlook the valley. The Ziz river itself holds the typical amphibians and you may find Painted Frog, a species that is localised in this part of the High Atlas and further east in Algeria.

The stark landscape of the Sahara makes this region the highlight of any trip to Morocco.

OTHER SITES IN THE SAHARA

Whilst the Brown-necked Raven (bottom) can be found almost anywhere, local help is invaluable is finding a roosting Pharaoh Eagle Owl.

C – Palmerie d'Igrane at Hassilabled

(GPS: 31.143, -4.023) A palmerie in the shadow of Erg Chebbi has the advantage of being accessible from the tarmac road and is a good location for a couple of hours of exploration. This well-established palmerie follows the traditional model with chickpeas and lentils grown under the shade of palms and pomegranates. The vegetation and water attract a number of species. Birds include wintering Tristram's Warblers and Moussier's Redstarts, and you may see Desert Swallowtail as well. In the water channels, African Green Toads and North African Pond Frogs are plentiful and dragonflies include three species of dropwing.

D – Rissani Escarpment

(GPS: 31.275, -4.336). Ten km west of Rissani and on the main N12, there is a large escarpment that runs parallel to the road for approximately 5km. At the easterly end, the main road runs to the back of the cliff and you need to leave the road to see the cliff face. It is a good place for birdwatching when travelling to or from Erg Chebbi.

CROSSBILL GUIDES • SOUTHERN MOROCCO

OTHER SITES IN THE SAHARA

The first access point is at a wadi crossing and goes straight into an area of acacias and tamarisks. This area is good for wintering Tristram's Warbler and can be a good migrant trap. The second access point is 3.6km further west, where a track takes you round to the front of the cliff. This cliff face is often a nest site for Lanner Falcon or Pharaoh Eagle Owl. It also has a den for Rüppell's Foxes in some years. The whole area is good for Brown-necked Raven and Desert Lark. The wash out plain to the south of the N12 can hold a good mix of larks, including Thick-billed.

E – Oued Tarkal near Zawyat Sidi Blal

GPS: 30.468972, -6.977194. This is a remote wadi 79km from Agdz that is often dry. Its claim to fame is that two species of dragonfly that were new to Morocco were found here, namely the Desert Darter and Desert Skimmer. Other dragonfly species are present, and of these the most notable is the Sahara Bluetail. The whole area is accessible from the R111 road that runs parallel to the riverbed before rising into the Anti-Atlas.

The best area is along the riverbed to the south of the R111 bridge, although the whole area can be explored as far north of the mosque at Ait Hammou. Look particularly around any rocky pools, where reservoirs have been constructed and where the irrigation ditches hold water.

Oued Tarkal as a whole is reputed to be one of the better places to look for Moroccan Spiny-tailed Lizard.

View from the Rissani escarpment.

Routes in the Souss Valley

The Oued Souss is a triangle of land that lies to the west of the Arid Steppe and is sandwiched between the High Atlas and Anti-Atlas Mountains. It extends all the way to the coast. It was always the centre of agriculture in Southern Morocco, but in recent years the extent of the areas under cultivation has increased. There has also been an enormous increase of land that is under intensive cultivation under greenhouses. This is particularly the case nearer the coast between Taroudant and Agadir and therefore most of the better locations are inland from Taroudant or close to both the High Atlas and Anti-Atlas Mountains. The areas we describe retain the special flavour of the Oued Souss and its character of being different and more verdant than other parts of Southern Morocco. It is here that the remaining Argan forest is found (see page 92). In this park-like woodland not only the main tree (the Argan) is an endemic, but the whole ecosystem is full of surprises, including relict populations of African Ground Squirrel and a number of endemic reptiles. It is also here that the mass migrations of Painted Lady butterflies originate (see page 128) in a near annual event that sends this butterfly across Europe as far as the Arctic Circle.

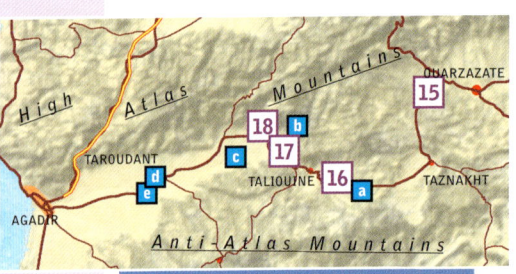

Unlike some of the other regions in this book, this is not a remote area and consequently, the routes are never far from villages and other human influences. The habitats are driven by the rivers that flow through the areas and are dependent upon the presence of water to attract the species of note here.

The distinctive bridge nr Aoulouz marks excellent dragonfly habitat (Additional site B on page 208).

Route 15: Iriri fields and Tiouiyine

1-2 HOURS
EASY

High Steppe and arable plots adjacent to the Asif Tidili river.

Habitats: Fields and riverine habitat
Selected species: Little Crake, Spotted Crake, Bonelli's Eagle, Corn Bunting, Cirl Bunting, Rock Bunting, Cetti's Warbler, Moroccan Toad, Bosc's Fringe-fingered Lizard, Orange-winged Dropwing

Travelling from Ouarzazate to Taroudant on the N10 the road initially follows the course of the Asif Tidili, a tributary of the Drâa. This is the first point in that journey where the influence of Oued Souss can be seen in the make-up of the species present. The fields at Iriri are watered from a dam above the site. They are also known by the name of the nearest village, Tiouiyine.

Despite the elevation, the small agricultural fields here attract a series of species that become more prevalent with the drop in altitude and the more fertile areas further west. However, they are joined with wildlife more normally found in the High Arid Steppes. In addition, the permanence of the water attracts a number of species to the river and riverside vegetation, including both Spotted and Little Crakes and Jack Snipe. There are plenty of narrow paths that can be followed although care is needed not to walk on the crops.

Orange-winged Dropwings are frequent along the river.

PRACTICAL PART

ROUTE 15: IRIRI FIELDS AND TIOUIYINE

Starting point The bridge over the Asif Tidili on the N10 between Ouarzazate and Taroudant (GPS: 30.942, -7.209). This is 15km west of Tazentout and 2km east of Tiouiyine. There is a pull-off on the roadside before the bridge.

Getting there Self-drive or Grand Taxi from Ouarzazate.

The Asif Tidili (top) usual holds water and is attractive to amphibians such as this Spanish Terrapin (bottom).

1 The layby on the N10 is by the track that goes up to the dam, and is well-placed for scanning along the power lines. Surprisingly often a Bonelli's Eagle perches here.

Cross the road and enter the fields across from the irrigation ditch.

2 Amphibians like this area, so a search for Moroccan Toad can be fruitful. Walk the edges of the small fields to search for birds. Depending on the time of the year and the progression of crops there can be plenty of activity. Corn Buntings jangle in spring and these can

ROUTE 15: IRIRI FIELDS AND TIOUIYINE

be joined by Cirl Buntings, Linnets, Yellow Wagtails and a mix of migrants. In winter, pipits and chats are present, including good numbers of Moussier's Redstarts. The crops, especially if cabbages are being grown, attract a number of butterflies including festoons, Scarce Swallowtail, Sooty and Desert Orange Tips and a mix of whites, including Scarce Green-striped White.

3 The tamarisks that line the river and the water course itself are a draw in this otherwise dry area. North African Water Frogs and Spanish Terrapins are common, and a mix of dragonflies including Sahara Bluetail, Orange-winged Dropwing and Broad Scarlet appears in the course of spring. Ruddy Shelduck, Cormorant, Little Grebe and other water birds can be found here, and during winter and on migration both Common and Jack Snipe have been found. The thick vegetation is the place to seek out crakes during spring migration. The sandy banks and areas can be searched for fringe-fingered lizards and the most likely to be found is Bosc's.

4 The bridge is the best place to scan the area for anything different. Crag Martins breed in the abutments and will whizz close overhead. The riverside vegetation can be scanned for warblers and other species including crakes during migration. Raptors can appear overhead including Osprey, eagles and falcons, including Lesser Kestrels.

Walk back via the road.

The agricultural fields are a magnet for migrant birds such as this Woodchat Shrike.

PRACTICAL PART

Route 16: Crocus fields of Ighri and Tinfat

1-2 HOURS, 1-2 KM
EASY

Orchards and arable fields in the Souss Valley.

Habitats: Fields and orchards
Selected species: 'Atlas' Great Spotted Woodpecker, Great Tit, Greenfinch, Goldfinch, Scarce Swallowtail, Spanish Festoon, Spotted Fritillary, Scarce Green-striped White

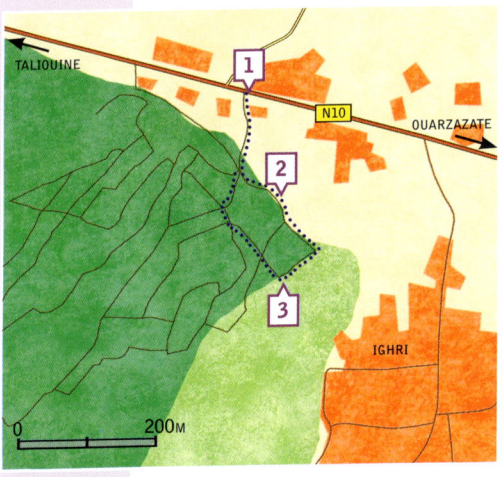

The area along the N10, east of Taliouine is renowned as the Saffron capital of Morocco. Saffron is the anther of the Autumn Crocus, *Crocus sativus*. Although this plant isn't native to Morocco, it grows here well at the altitude of 1200m and above. It flowers from mid-October to mid-November, and outside this time there is little to see of the plants themselves.

The area here is one where traditional low-intensity agriculture has resulted in a good mixed habitat that is particularly attractive for butterflies and several species of birds that, although familiar in Europe, are of distinctive local subspecies that can be tricky to find. The orchards provide dappled shade for the crops and fallow areas have a number of 'weeds' including Pheasant-eye (previously known as Red Morocco) that provide both nectar and food-plants for the local butterflies. There are plenty of paths to explore, but as with all agricultural areas, make sure you do not walk through the crops and stick to the narrow paths.

Starting point Roadside café in Tinfat on the N10 between Ouarzazate to Taroudant (GPS: 30.474, -7.740). Ighri is 2km further east and Taliouine 26km further west.

ROUTE 16: CROCUS FIELDS OF IGHRI AND TINFAT

Getting there Self-drive or Grand Taxi from Ouarzazate or Taroudant.

1 The layby on the N10 is by a café, where you can sample the Saffron tea. Behind the café is a flat area where Saffron is grown in season. The rest of the time the fields are fallow and hold a mix of butterflies. Difficult to ignore are the large well-marked species, which include Scarce Swallowtail, Spanish Festoon, and several fritillaries.

2 Cross the dry riverbed and enter the orchards and fields beyond. The larger poplars here are particularly attractive to Great Spotted Woodpecker (ssp. mauritanus). Other birds like the lightly wooded environment and Great Tits (ssp. excelsus) and Jay (ssp. minor) are the noisiest. Between the trees, Speckled Wood is the commonest butterfly, however if cabbages are being grown (or allowed as weeds) look for different species of 'whites' too. Careful searching could offer Scarce Green-striped White amongst the commoner species.

The orchards at Ighri (top) attract arboreal migrants like this Western Bonelli's Warbler (bottom).

3 The whole area is a patchwork of crops and fallow fields and the best solution is simply to go where things of interest pull. The fields are extensive and dependent upon time and inclination you can either return or look further. Wherever you wander off to, simply heading north brings you back to the N10, and from there find your way back to the café and your vehicle.

PRACTICAL PART

ROUTE 17: THE ARGAN FOREST

Route 17: The Argan forest

2-3 HOURS, 5 KM
MODERATE

The classic Argan forest.

Habitats: Argan forest
Selected species: Argan, African Ground Squirrel, Many-scaled Skink, Egyptian Cobra, Moorish Viper, Puff Adder, African House Snake, birds of prey

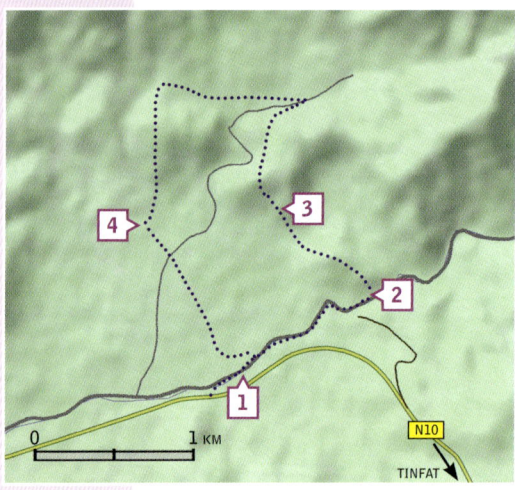

The Souss is the place to see the Argan, the endemic tree that forms a park-like ecosystem of its own. It is, for those who know it, it bit like the Spanish dehesa and Portuguese montado, but with Argan instead of oak. Despite losing half of its former range, the Argan still covers large parts of the Souss from sea level up to c1100m asl, however much of it is heavily exploited and overgrazed. The area explored here is almost pristine and has the advantage of being close to the main N10 road.

As with the Argan itself, this habitat has its ancestry in the Rift Valley of East Africa and many of the species are more typical of that area. The flora alone is represented by over 1000 species, of which 140 or so have evolved to endemic forms. Most of these are difficult to identify and are annuals flowering only after rain. Other sub-Saharan species have persisted such as the African Ground Squirrel, African House Snake and both Tawny Eagles and Dark Chanting Goshawk. Unfortunately, these latter too have all but disappeared, the first being very scarce and the latter appears to have become extinct in the Maghreb, but still may be hanging on somewhere.

The forest is exploited for grazing and wood, while the Argan tree itself

CROSSBILL GUIDES • SOUTHERN MOROCCO

ROUTE 17: THE ARGAN FOREST

has recently been recognised as a 'super product' for the oil from its seeds (see page 92).
On this walk, the Argan Tree takes centre. There is no clear route. Rather, you should wander through the forest which sits in a natural bowl so that you can walk up to the forest below the ridge (a climb of approximately 200 m). The forest is densest near the road but opens out higher on the slopes. The area is mainly open access and wandering through the trees gives an appreciation of the woodland.

Starting point Pull-in by the side of the N10, 21.2 kms west from the centre of Taliouiline and 13km east of Aoulouz (GPS: 30.621, -8.101).

Getting there Self-drive; Grand Taxi from Ouarzazate or Taroudant.

1 The pull off on the N10 provides an ample parking area. Here you can have a good look at the Argan trees at close range. The nuts take a year to mature, therefore look at a number of trees to see the various stages of development. Keep an eye on the ridge lines and the skies above the forest, where raptors of various species can be expected to drift by. You may also be greeted by a friendly local goat herder.

The Argan trees form an open 'park-like' forest.

PRACTICAL PART

ROUTE 17: THE ARGAN FOREST

2 The easiest route into the forest is eastwards along the old N10 about 500m before heading up across the wadi line and up the hill. The wadi is nearly always dry so look for a sensible track to cross the banks as they can be steep. Each area on this route has a subtly different soil type and humidity. Look for where plants are in flower. The shrubby endemic greenweed *Genista ifniensis*, the spurge *Euphorbia echinus*, the broom *Teline segonnier* and the lavender *Lavandula pedunculata atlantica* can all be found. Annuals are also possible but are dependent upon recent rain.

3 Continue through the forest which has a varying density and a mix of sandy and rocky areas before arriving at a more open, park-like woodland. There is a second wadi line after about 500m and this can be followed upwards as far as you wish to go. This habitat is rich in reptiles, although finding them is a challenge. Egyptian Cobra is at its most numerous in this habitat and Puff Adder, Moorish Viper and African House Snakes are present. Skinks, including Many-scaled and Orange, can also be found, even Chameleon is possible.

The immature Argan nuts are red and become green as they mature.

100m or so below the ridge line there is a clear route to the west. Follow the contour line for 600m or so until you can see a clear way down before picking your way down the slope.

4 After heading south for 500m or so, you will cross the second wadi line that you reached at point 3. This needs to be crossed and then the parking area is a further 600m beyond as you head south/south-east. Dependent upon the wadi edges you may need to cross the final wadi near the car park 100m or so downstream.

Other good areas of Argan forest can be found, especially to the north-east of Agadir, especially along the route of the Autoroute A3 and the Route National N9 to Marrakech. Note it is impossible to stop along the Autoroute.

Route 18: Aoulouz barrage and river

1+ HOURS, 1-2 KM
EASY

Well-vegetated, riverine habitat at the beginning of the lowland Souss valley.

Habitats: Well-vegetated river, fields
Selected species: Purple Heron, Squacco Heron, African Reed Warbler, Little Crake, Spanish Terrapin, Copper Demoiselle, Broad Scarlet, Blue Emperor

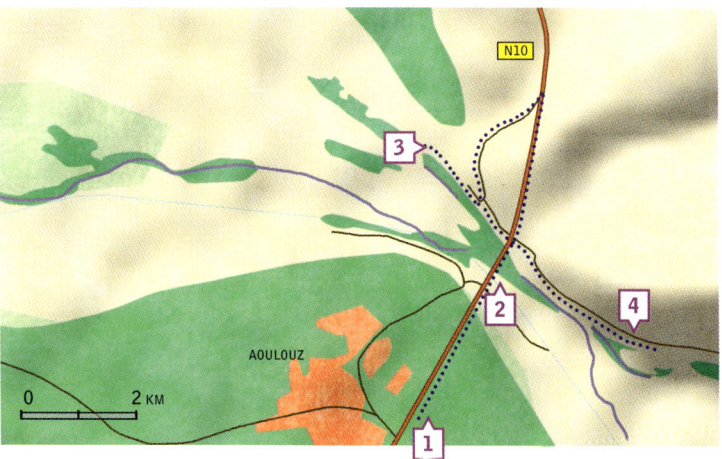

The Aoulouz river lies in the far eastern extent of the true Souss valley. The river is dammed a short distance from where the N10 crosses it and the waterworks provide for a steady release of water throughout the year. This permanent presence of water turns this section of the Aoulouz into a hot-spot of biodiversity. Birds, dragonflies and reptiles are particularly well-represented.
The river is well-vegetated and the N10 bridge provides a vantage point where you can see along the waterway itself. It is possible to walk down to the river to explore its banks.

Starting point Pull-in by the bridge on side of the N10, 3 kms northwest of the centre of Aoulouz (GPS: 30.695, -8.155).

ROUTE 18: AOULOUZ BARRAGE AND RIVER

the Souss at Aoulouz (top) is thick with vegetation beloved of herons and dragonflies such as this Violet Dropwing (bottom).

Getting there Self-drive or Grand Taxi from Ouarzazate or Taroudant.

1 The layby on the N10 to the east of the bridge overlooks agricultural fields where Spotless Starling, Wood Pigeon, Blackbird and Bulbul can be found. Spanish and House Sparrows are plentiful on the edge of town.

Walk in a northerly direction to the bridge.

2 The bridge gives panoramic views over the river. Take your time here as the riverbanks are well-vegetated and it normally requires careful scanning to pick out the species here. Herons, including Squacco and Purple, can be found in the reeds, and the edges can hold Little Crake during migration. It is worth looking out for reed warblers at this site. Although during migration the vast majority will be familiar Eurasian species of Reed and Sedge Warblers, early season visits have shown that African Reed Warblers are present and will start singing before the migrant species pass through. In early summer, the African Reed Warblers will be the only ones present and it is currently believed that they stay all year round. One species that is more obvious, is the Red-rumped Swallow that patrols the area, often at head height for those standing on the bridge. There can be huge numbers of Spanish Terrapins lazing on the banks.

Take a note of the state of the river and vegetation both upstream and downstream of the bridge.

On the other side of the bridge follow the track that leads down to the river. From here you can walk both upstream and downstream. Dependent upon the level of the river and the actual course it takes, one side is normally better than the other. Choose which is the better based upon activity viewable from the bridge.

3 Heading downstream gives better views of the more vegetated areas and the river normally flows slower. Walk the river edge as far as you can see water. The same birds you saw from the bridge are present but it is normally difficult to see them as they remain hidden. This is a good place to look for dragonflies. Early in the season Broad Scarlet and Blue Emperors are the most plentiful dragonflies and these can be joined by a mix of Copper Demoiselle and damselflies, including Mediterranean and Blue-eye (Goblet-marked). Later in the season, all three dropwings and Epaulet Skimmers emerge.

Squacco Herons pass through on migration (top). The Moroccan Wagtail is a distinctive form of White Wagtail and can be found along the Aoulouz river.

4 Returning to the access track enables you to head upstream and under the bridge to the other side. Normally there is less vegetation here, but the area holds similar species as the previous point. However, this is the better side for Sahara Bluetail. The deeper pools here are often used by villagers for swimming so disturbance can be high.

ADDITIONAL SITES IN SOUSS VALLEY

Additional sites in Souss Valley

For the locations of the sites described below, see map on page 196.

A – Tizi n'Taratine

(GPS: 30.456, -7.674) Tizi n'Taratine is an unremarkable col at 1835m along the N10 road from Ouarzazate to Taroudant. It superficially looks like any other along the road, but it marks the last high point on the road and to the west the slow descent begins into the Souss valley proper that eventually leads to the sea. This area of Precambrian volcanic rocks is only 7 km east of Route 16 (see above) but, uniquely, is the only site for Dupont's Larks in the book. Here, the wormwood scrub is replaced by tussock grass and the combination of elevation, soil and flora is obviously to their liking. As is typical with this species, knowing that they are here and finding them are two very different things, and your best chance is around dawn in spring when the birds are singing. The area immediately by the track to the telecom mast has recently been ploughed, but the same tussock grass habitat extends a couple of kilometres in both directions along the N10 and more so to the south, so you may need to explore a wider area.

The steppe at Tizi n'Taratine.

B – Barrage Mouktar Soussi

GPS 30.701, -8.153. Accessed from the N10 adjacent to route 18 above, the Aoulouz river above the barrages holds water throughout the year from the headwaters of the Souss river. This is an ideal location to look for species that cross over between the Souss valley proper and the lower reaches of the south-facing slope of the High Atlas Mountains.

To get there, follow the minor road that leaves the N10 eastwards, 500m north of the N10 road bridge. The road is signposted to Iguidi and ultimately Lac Ifni at 74km. The road nominally follows the course of the

ADDITIONAL SITES IN SOUSS VALLEY

The Aoulouz river below the Barrage Mouktar Soussi.

Souss (Asif Tifnoute), initially passing the waters behind the Barrage (dam) Aoulouz and then reaches the Barrage Moukthar Soussi after 19 km. The river and the reservoirs are generally invisible from the road and in any case, it is not the reservoirs themselves that are of interest but the stretch of the river that runs circa 10km between the two reservoirs. Access is only straightforward at two points.

At 16.5 km from the N10, a side road descends through olive groves to a bridge (GPS: 30.725060, -8.012000). There is a track that runs downstream that gives access to the riverbed which is a mix of channels and pools.

At 19km from the N10, it is possible to park below the Moukthar Soussi dam itself (GPS: 30.736691, -7.987108) and explore the river for approximately a kilometre downstream. This section has a series of cascades and pools, so a good mix of aquatic conditions, however, there are construction works ongoing on the dam so whether this area will be impacted remains to be seen.

These areas hold most of the dragonfly species that are possible on route 18, but in addition, are good locations for Red-veined Dropwing and Yellow-veined Skimmer. The area has potential for reptiles and amphibians as the waterflow is consistent here, being released slowly from the reservoirs. Moroccan Painted Frog and Brongerma's Toads are possible amongst the more plentiful North African Water Frogs and Spanish Terrapins.

PRACTICAL PART

ADDITIONAL SITES IN SOUSS VALLEY

C – Iguidar

Made famous in the birding community under the name of Igoudar, this was the place to look for Dark Chanting Goshawk. Although this bird has disappeared, the area still holds many birds representative of the Souss valley and remains a hotspot for raptors.

There are two approaches to searching the area. The first is to enter the area via the P1733 that leaves the main N10 1km east of Oulad Berhil, and 40km west of Taroudant, the turning being by a petrol station. The village of Iguidar is 5 km along this road, however, it is the small hill to the north of the road before you enter the village that should be your target. Scanning for raptors should offer views of Long-legged Buzzard, Black-winged Kite, Booted Eagle, Lesser Kestrel and maybe something scarcer. This northern bank of the Souss has become increasingly farmed in recent years. The southern bank along the P1706 is less converted to agriculture and has stands of Argan. This is now probably the better place to explore.

Alternatively, head for the Souss river (GPS: 30.592, -8.398) which, although over 1km wide at this point, rarely holds any water. This is 11.4 km from the N10, continuing along the P1733 though Iguidar. The last 2.5km stretch is on gravel track.

In habitat it is closer to a sandy desert and therefore holds species more typical of the Sahara hundreds of kilometres further away. Egyptian Nightjar and Fulvous Babbler are two of the most exciting birds. A search along the riverbanks should also produce Desert Wheatear and Hoopoe Lark. It is normally possible to drive the whole way across, and due to the disturbance on the north bank, exploration closer to the southern bank is more likely to be successful. You can link to the P1706 on the southern bank and from there head on to Taroudant or Aoulouz.

D – The parks and walls of Taroudant

Taroudant is the main city and administrative hub in the centre of Souss valley and forms a good base for explorations. The historic, walled city is itself attractive and worthy of a visit. Just outside the city walls, there are several pleasant parks, including the Jardin Brahim Roudani, where Spotless Starling, Common Bulbul and Little Swift are common. Maghreb Owl (formerly regarded as a subspecies of Tawny Owl) also breeds in the parks. A visit after dusk should at least produce the calling birds, and with a bit of effort, you should be able to see them.

ADDITIONAL SITES IN SOUSS VALLEY

The parks just outside the ancient city walls at Taroudant can host a number of key species, such as Maghreb Owl.

E – Ain el Madiour

GPS: 30.433, -8.896. The lower Souss valley has been heavily degraded as a wildlife site by the conversion to intensive agriculture, often involving greenhouses that produce food for the export market. However, some areas still exist that give an impression of how the valley was before. This is one of such areas, five kilometres to the west of Taroudant city and just north of the village of Ain el Madiour. The wadi bottom is approximately 500m wide and it is easy to access as a bridge on the main N10 road crosses the Souss river here. Park by the bridge next to the telecoms mast and walk the main course upstream. You may find Red-necked Nightjar, Black-winged Kite and even Fulvous Babbler. The north bank is degraded by the expansion of Taroudant, but the south bank is more unspoilt once you have cleared the N10 petrol stations. During migration, and particularly if there is a good amount of water, a whole host of herons and crakes can be found.

Black-winged Kite at Ain el Madiour.

PRACTICAL PART

Routes in the southern Anti-Atlas

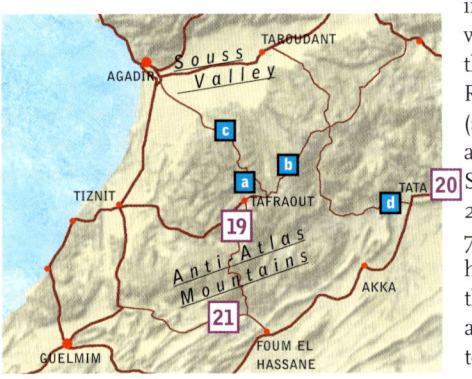

The extremely arid southern Anti-Atlas route is the most remote location in this guide, and it is rarely travelled. It is bounded by the Anti Atlas Mountains to the north and the Drâa valley to the south. Access has been improved enormously with the completion of the N12 road, that starts in Rissani near Erg Chebbi (see site D on page 194) and ends on the coast at Sidi Ifni (see site E on page 243), a total distance of 746km. The sites included here are in two groups, those that are in easy access to Tafraoute, a small town with amenities and a good centre to explore the Anti-Atlas, or those that are on the N12 or very close to it.

Superficially, the Anti-Atlas is similar to areas that surround it. The southern and eastern areas reflect the Saharan zones, while the northern area abutting the Souss has Argan forest, whilst the northeastern part resembles the High Arid Steppes just to the north of the mountains. In the far west, the influence of the Atlantic comes into play. So, for the visitor, each zone has a recognisable theme, but due to altitude, and to some extent geology, the flora and fauna is slightly different and in many cases unique. Pioneering visits have shown that the Anti-Atlas is a mammal hotspot, with truly wild Cuvier's Gazelle still surviving and a long list of special species including North African Sengi, Algerian Hedgehog and African Wild Cat. Reptiles are also diverse and plentiful and show a mix of species from the rock lovers through to those than prefer sandy soils from the Sahara as you progress southwards to the Drâa valley. Some species such as the impressive Saw-scaled Viper are only found here. By contrast, there are few birds that cannot be found elsewhere. However this is the only area where Lichtenstein's Sandgrouse can be considered regular, and you're more likely to find African Rock Martin here. This area is also a hotspot for endemic flora, but as access is limited and flowering can be only once every three years, it is difficult for a casual visitor to time their visit right.

Route 19: Tafraoute

4+ HOURS, 21 KM
EASY-MODERATE

Rocky hillsides and arid valleys of the Anti-Atlas.

Habitats: Rocky plains and outcrops
Selected species: North African Sengi, Cuvier's Gazelle, Sundevall's Jird, Trumpeter Finch, Moroccan Spiny-tailed Lizard, Oudri's Fan-footed Gecko, Small-spotted Desert Racer, Vagrant Emperor, Desert Fritillary, Aetherie Fritillary, Allard's Blue

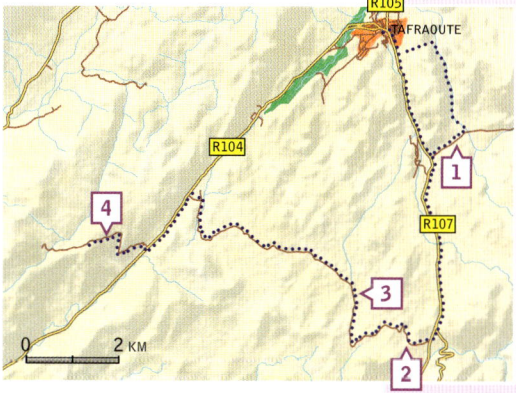

Tafraoute is a thriving town that has become the main centre for exploring this part of the Anti-Atlas Mountains. It gives excellent access to a range of habitats that are typical of a granite massif in the Anti-Atlas. There is a sense of being a pioneer here and every visit can bring surprises. Vegetation is mainly influenced by the Souss valley just to the north, with Argan being the main native tree.
The headline species are the Sengi and the Cuvier's Gazelle. The latter is best searched for at dusk or by spotlighting after dark. The best locations are in the flat valley bottom that surrounds 'les roches peintes' (painted rocks), a local landmark of large boulders that were painted mainly blue by a Belgian artist Jean Verame in 1985.
The route here covers three distinct areas that can be visited separately or combined as here, however note that time of day is important for both the gazelles and the Sengi. For the former, dusk is the best period and for the latter dawn.

Starting point Tafraoute town, the roundabout at the meeting of the R104, R105 and R107 (GPS: 29.720, -8.972).

ROUTE 19: TAFRAOUTE

Getting there Self-drive; accommodation available in the town.

Head south on the R107. Just after passing the village of Agrd Odad, turn left and park on the edge of the oued just to the east of Agrd Odad (GPS: 29.7003, -8.9563). On foot, follow the line of the watercourse northwards.

1 After c1.5km there is a series of pools where the oued narrows between the granite hills on either side. These run for nearly a kilometre and this water attracts birds and insects alike. The pools can be full of North African Pond Frogs. Most of the plant life is concentrated on the lower slopes and close to any water. Recent rain will have encouraged the Anti-Atlas annuals to bloom. The acacias and Argans attract birds and the characteristic resident species here are Trumpeter Finch, Desert Lark and White-crowned Wheatear. During migration, the trees can be alive with warblers, flycatchers and chats. Butterflies are common if plants are flowering. Look for Scarce Green-striped White, Desert Swallowtail, African Knapweed Fritillary, Desert Fritillary, False Baton Blue and Allard's Blue. Dragonflies are most likely to include Vagrant and Lesser Emperors and Violet Dropwings. Among the reptiles, search for Common Fringe-fingered Lizards, and in the rockier areas; Small-spotted Desert Racer and Algerian Dwarf Gecko, the latter occur where trees shade the rocks.

Böhme's Agama is a familiar species in rocky areas.

You can either return the way you came or continue on for a further kilometre or so before heading west to the edge of Tafraoute itself. It is then

ROUTE 19: TAFRAOUTE

The oued to the east of Agrd Odad often holds water.

possible to walk back along the R107 to the parking area. A second oued runs along the roadway itself, but this one is less likely to hold water. When it does, it is worth taking this route and making a circuit. The road is relatively quiet so, although care is needed, it is a pleasant walk.
Back at the car, continue along the N107 and after a few kilometres, turn right to the 'Roches Peintes' (clearly signposted).

2 The valley floor south of Tafraoute is a sandy plain, dotted with granite outcrops. Most visitors have found that the best spot to find the gazelle is along the gravel road that connects the R107 to the R104, that surrounds the 'Roches Peintes' (GPS: 29.669, -8.979). Cape Hares and African Wildcat have also been seen here, and Algerian Hedgehog and Common Genet are probably present as well. In the sandy wadi edges look for Sundevall's Jird, a species known from a few sites in this area. The plain also has a good population of Moroccan Spiny-tailed Lizards.

3 From the Roches Peintes you can continue along the same gravel road to the R104, which leads through more good habitat for the Cuvier's Gazelle.
The track reaches the R104 where you turn left (southwest). After 1.5 kms, a track leaves the R104 by two telecom masts (GPS: 29.678523, -9.026377)

ROUTE 19: TAFRAOUTE

and runs up from the valley floor to a further telecoms mast on the hilltop above. The initial steep section of 2.2km is mainly concreted and arrives at a place where it is possible to park. You can either walk or drive further on the track for another 900m or so, roughly following the 1200m contour just below the ridge line, where again parking is possible (GPS: 29.678472, -9.041000).

4 The habitat here is a boulder-strewn hillside under stunted Argan Trees. Close to the second parking area there are abandoned fields, each bounded by a dry stone wall. Anywhere between these two parking points and on both sides of the track you should look for the Sengi, one of the strangest mammals of Morocco (see page 98). Most recent reports have been from near the second point. Early morning is best but even then, they are not easy to see, in part because they move extremely quickly. Walking the track between the two parking areas will also give wonderful views of this part of the Tafraoute area and enable a search for the other inhabitants of the area, such as Oudri's Fan-footed Gecko, Böhme's Agama and Algerian Whip Snake. If there are still flowers on the hillside, it can be good for a mix of butterflies, including Allard's Blue and Aetherie and Desert Fritillaries.

The granite outcrops form a distinctive landscape just south of Tafraoute.

Route 20: Tissint

4+ HOURS
4-6 KM WALK, EASY

Arid wadi on the edge of the Sahara. Sandy river banks and rocky slopes.

Habitats: Wadi
Selected species: Western Sand Skink, Böhme's Gecko, Oudri's Fan-fingered Gecko, Moorish Sand Gecko, Böhme's Agama, Lichtenstein's Sandgrouse, African Rock Martin, Eastern Olivaceous Warbler, Sahara Bluetail, Faded Pincertail

Tissint is a small and remote town nestled below a ridge that towers 500m above it. Oued El Maleh, a tributary of the Drâa, has cut a short gorge through the ridge and the N12 passes at the same point. The ridge is formed of igneous rocks and this forces the groundwater to the surface. The mixture of water, sandy wadi, palmeries and rocky cliffs means that this area attracts a good range of birds, reptiles and insects in the arid landscape.

Two additional sites are included east of the town. These should be checked out, but as they are both on the N12 and are up to 18km distant, a car is needed to reach them.

Starting point East of the N12 roundabout at the north end of Tissint. Take the minor road to the east that drops into the oued (GPS: 29.9064, -7.3145). Cross the valley bottom and park in a clear layby off the road. Walk back along the wadi edge and then east to the palmerie.

Getting there Self-drive

ROUTE 20: TISSINT

1 This area can be very good for migrants that congregate in the oued and in the tamarisks that line the watercourse. In late spring, there are many Eastern Olivaceous Warblers. It is also good for reptiles with Böhme's Gecko and Böhme's Agamas both present.

2 Head to the palmerie and continue through to the sandy valley beyond. This south-easterly edge is best for Fulvous Babbler and in the irrigation channels, you can find all three species of dropwing (Violet, Red-veined and Orange-winged). It should be possible to find Oasis Bluetail as well as the plentiful Sahara Bluetail. The sandy areas have Western Sandfish, Sand Geckos and Fat Sand Rats. Both Dumeril's and Long-footed Fringe-fingered Lizards can be looked for as they are both diurnal but will still hide from the heat of the day.

Once at the most southerly point of the palmerie, head back across the streamline and head south-west.

3 When walking over the other palmerie, you cross the oeud bed. Unlike the area around Point 1, there is rarely water here. This is because this section of the watercourse runs over permeable rocks so the water is underground.

Explore this second palmerie. In spite of being close to the first, it has different species. Rufous-tailed Scrub Robin seem to favour the northern one, whilst conversely Blue-cheeked Bee-eater is found in the southern. Turn north and walk between the stream bed and the village to return to your parking spot checking the flat-topped acacias if they are in flower as this attracts insects and the birds that feed on them.

Tissint sits below a granite ridge cut by the Oued al Maleh.

ROUTE 20: TISSINT

4 Walk the oued upstream. It is possible to walk along on both banks between the tamarisks and the bottom of the cliffs where there is a mix of pools, runnels and even lakes. The only guaranteed crossing point is the road at Akka Nait Siddi which crosses both branches of the oued. The overall loop is 4.5km and the cliffs here are favoured by African Rock Martins. Note that they are easily confused with Eurasian Crag Martins or even the Brown-throated Martins that also occur here. The latter usually stay closer to the watercourse. The is the best area for Eastern Olivaceous Warbler and the pools attract amphibians and a surprising array of migrants including waders and even Black Tern.

Where water is present at Tissint, Sahara Bluetails (top) will breed and Lichtenstein's Sandgrouse come to drink (bottom).

5 Eleven km east of Tissint is one of the few known drinking sites of Lichtenstein's Sandgrouse (GPS: 29.850437, -7.264300).
The sandgrouse drink in the river but often fly in and stop by the N12 before dropping down to drink. Look on the little flat area below the gully in the cliffs. Note that unlike the other sandgrouse species, Lichtenstein's drinks in the evenings, often not appearing until after dusk and when it is almost too dark to see.

Additional site
Eighteen km from the town, the N12 crosses the Oued el Mahel (GPS: 29.822213, -7.196884). This is a dragonfly hotspot. Most numerous are the dropwings, particularly Orange-winged Dropwing. The rare Faded Pincertail and Sahara Bluetail are also present. It is a simple matter to park off the road and wander the oued on both sides of the road, focusing on where the vegetation and water remain. The water can be extensive, but it is often masked by the dense planting of Tamarisks. Eastern Olivaceous Warblers can be found in the denser areas.

Route 21: Taghjijt

2-4 HOURS, 4-6 KM
EASY

Birds and reptiles on the border of the Anti-Atlas and the Sahara.

Habitats: rocky hillsides, wadi wash out plains, sandy plains
Selected species: Streaked Scrub-warbler, Desert Lark, Bar-tailed Lark, Spectacled Warbler, Fulvous Babbler, Böhme's Agama, Moroccan Spiny-tailed Lizard

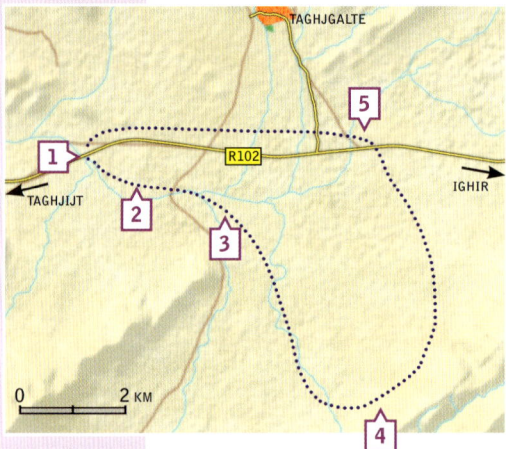

Taghjijt is close to the main east-west route where the influence of the Sahara is more strongly felt rather than the Anti-Atlas Mountains. The mix of rocky hills, sandy plains and cliffs are the remains of a basalt dyke that crosses the plain. They are home to a mix of species, mostly birds and reptiles. Among the former is the darker south-western subspecies theresae of Streaked Scrub-warbler – a rarity that is likely to be promoted to species level.
There are no set paths across the plains so be prepared to wander where your sightings take you.
Taghjijt village itself is nestled in a wadi below steep cliffs in a pleasant oasis palmerie and has stunning scenery as well as local amenities. Keep an eye open for raptors as both Bonelli's and Golden Eagle have been found here and almost anything can turn up during migration.

Starting point Taghjijt
Drive east from the village on the R102. After 28 kms just off the R102 road to the east at the wadi crossing to the west, you see a low hill to the south of the road (GPS point 29.1079, -9.1534).

Getting there Self-drive

1 Explore the immediate area of the wadi crossing for both Fulvous Babbler and Spectacled Warbler. In winter these may be joined by Tristram's Warbler.

2 Walking to the south-southeast, climb the low hill and search the slopes for the Scrub-warblers. They are best looked for on the steeper slopes, but they can wander down to the wadi edge.

3 Walking back down into the wadi and heading eastwards takes you into a washout from the hills to the north. This is the area most likely to have annual plants, depending upon season and rain of course. Look for *Asphodelus refractus*, Yellow Cistanche and Desert Melon.

4 After about a kilometre head south into the sandy plain. It is an area rather than a location and is bound by a steep cliff face to the south. Scan for the burrows of Moroccan Spiny-tailed Lizards. Hoopoe Lark, Bar-tailed Lark and other lark species may be present. The cliff which races to the south can attract African Rock Martins and provide nest sites for Brown-necked Ravens and Lanners. Pharaoh Eagle Owl is likely to be present as well.

Streaked Scrub Warbler – a charismatic species of dry slopes.

Walk in a wide arc to ensure that all the habitat is covered before heading back north to the R102 and then back to your car. You will cross other wash out areas and rocky hillsides so depending on success to this point, these can be searched for the remaining targets.

5 A larger hillock to the north of the R102 can also be climbed if there is no sign of the Scrub Warblers to the south. These rocky slopes hold Böhme's Agama and Small-spotted Lizards.

PRACTICAL PART

Additional sites in the southern Anti-Atlas

For the locations of the sites described below, see map on page 212.

A – Jebel Lkest

GPS Point 29.785603, -9.010113. One of the high points of the Anti-Atlas, Jebel Lkest, is just one of a series of peaks that forms the granite 'wall' to the north of the town of Trafaoute (see route 20). A trail starts 15km north of the village of Tagdicht, which lies at the end of a road that turns off the R105 near Tadart. The first 2.5km are tarmac, and the whole stretch is narrow. Also, parking is at a premium in Tagdicht so check at the café/auberge in Tadart before heading on.

Jebel Lkest is a hotspot for endemic and relict flora and new species are being found regularly here. The endemic *Phagnalon latifolium* can be found almost at the summit, whilst Spanish Fritillaria has been found lower on the same mountain and is the only location south of Rif for this species. A good range of other Anti-Atlas plants can be found along the trail to the summit. This is also a good site for butterflies. One of the sought-after species found here is Allard's Silver-line. Regular sightings of Barbary Sheep have also been made from this area.

There is a walking route described on Wikiloc (**www.wikiloc.com**), but it is still best to hire a guide at the village to walk up with you. The local name of the peak is 'Afan Ntimzgadiwine', so this is what you should ask

Jebel Lkest is one of the peaks that forms a granite 'wall' just to the north of Tafraoute.

for. The climb is almost 1000m from 1407m to the summit at 2339m; a serious day trip in a remote area and takes 8hrs to complete. The best period to visit is in winter and early spring, especially after rains.

B – Tighrman

 GPS: 29.876905, -8.719681. The village of Tighrman is at the southern end of a north-south col across the Anti-Atlas Mountains. It is 51km north of Tafraoute along the R106 to Irherm and on to Taroudant. The natural topography of the region encourages migrating birds to channel through the wadi. In addition, the permeable sand and limestones mean that the hillsides are naturally only vegetated with stunted wormwoods, so the almond trees and other cultivated fields act as a magnet to wildlife. The main oued runs along the road and it is a simple matter of pulling off the R106 east of the village, walk to the oued bottom and follow it northwards parallel to the road.

Whilst Lanner, Trumpeter Finch and Desert Lark are resident in the region, the funnelling effect pulls in a wide range of species to this area especially during spring migration. Flycatchers, chats and warblers (including Western Orphean, Western Sub-alpine, and Melodious) can all be found in trees beside the oued. Most of the migrant wheatear species also pass through this area, including Atlas Wheatear. The sandier oued bottom is the right habitat for crepuscular Sundavall's Jird but it is likely that the larger Fat Sand Rat will be more obvious. The hills above here are also the home to Barbary Sheep, but, as always, they are elusive.

C – Askar

 GPS: 30.058024, -9.086813. Askar is a known location for North African Sengi, the only member of the elephant-shrew family found north of the Sahara. As such it has long attracted mammal enthusiasts to the area. The area is along the R105 as it heads eastwards from Ait Baha, which is 70km from both Agadir and Taroudant. The road climbs as it heads east beyond the village of Askar across broken rocky habitat with both cactoid spurges and stunted trees. Sightings have been concentrated in the vicinity of the road 2km above the village around the 800m contour. Park off the road at the above-mentioned grid point and walk up the slope to the hillside above. The Sengi is most active around dawn. The area is also home to Algerian Hedgehog and Common Genet, both of which are nocturnal.

Facilities including fuel and accommodation can be found at the nearby Ait Baha.

ADDITIONAL SITES IN THE SOUTHERN ANTI-ATLAS

D – Tata Pools

GPS: 29.708500, -7.996833. This site is approximately mid-way between Tissint and Tafraoute. Oued Tata runs alongside the N12 and has a mix of habitats that attracts a range of wildlife. The prime location is where the R109 crosses Oued Tata, 2.1 km from the junction with the N12, which is about 4km south of the town of Tata itself. Park by the crossing and wander into the wadi bed both north and south, taking in the mix of irrigation reservoirs, ditches and the natural stream bed and pools.

Over fourteen species of dragonflies and damselflies have been reported here, including Sahara Bluetail, Blue-eye (or Goblet-marked Damselfly), Green Hooktail, Desert Skimmer and Black Pennant. The last species has recently colonised Southern Morocco and it is likely that it is more widespread than realised, although this is one of the few known regular sites. Fulvous Babblers are also present in the wadi and surrounding fields and Spotted Sandgrouse have been seen coming in to drink. Reptiles include Moroccan Spiny-tailed Lizard and Saw-scaled Viper. In fact, Tata is one of the few localities where the latter has been found.

If you have time, wander through the palmeries here. Breeding Rufous-tailed Scrub Robin and various butterflies can be found and the irrigation channels also attract some of the dragonflies, especially the dropwings.

The Tata pools formed as the oued crosses impervious rocks (bottom). This is a dragonfly hotspot but also holds butterflies, such as this Mediterrean Blue.

Routes near the coast

The coast is a populous place and one where there is an increasing tourism infrastructure. It is a popular winter sun destination and resort complexes are being developed to cope with the expansion around Agadir itself. The entire area has a cosmopolitan feel and a more international pace of life. Traffic is often heavy and the coast road can be painfully slow.

To the naturalist, however, this is definitely a prime location. The general biodiversity is higher than deeper inland, as there is more water and temperatures are nearly 10°C lower (see page 26). This means that it is a pleasant place to visit in all seasons although the area can get very busy in summer.

If you follow the coastline from north to south (c300kms), the ecosystem changes from Mediterranean around Essaouira, to fully Saharan south of Sidi Ifni. The changes are not just a simple matter of getting hotter and drier, but other influences come into play, including the Canaries' influence on the flora. The recommendation is to sample these areas and focus on the species that interest you most. The routes here are arranged in the same way allowing you to see this progression from the north to south but not ignoring the hinterland either. In this way they cover most of the ecological niches along the coast. As elsewhere, you can stop at places that look promising, but unlike the other areas in the book, this is a modified habitat with tourism and intense agriculture rapidly eroding the remaining natural areas. This human impact is continuing apace. Although still possible, this makes it less likely that a visitor will discover the sort of hidden gems that are so much part of exploring Southern Morocco. In the hinterland, behind the coastal strip, there are still good sites to be found, and with the western end of both High Atlas and Anti-Atlas Mountains being just inland, there is a wealth of places to look. The zones where the mountains are influenced by the ocean have a different character again and therefore it is worth making the effort to visit.

PRACTICAL PART

Route 22: Tamri

**2-4 HOURS,
3-5 KM WALK, EASY**

The spot for seeing Northern Bald Ibis, in addition to migratory birds. Great example of a blind estuary.

Habitats: Estuary, coastal cliffs, coastal scrub
Selected species: Northern Bald Ibis, Audouin's Gull, Plain Swift, Margarita's Fringe-fingered Lizard, Desert Bluet

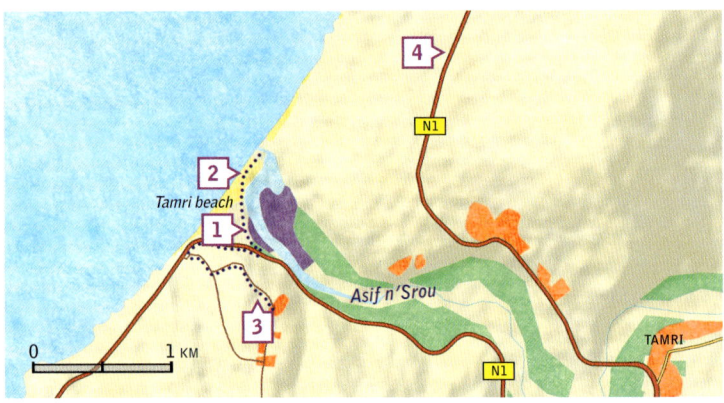

Tamri is the name of the village at the centre of a series of habitats that are the home to one of the last breeding colonies of Northern Bald Ibis. Although not part of the Souss-Massa National Park where this species also breeds, the same people that look after the birds there also oversee the colony of Tamri. Although the Tamri colony is smaller, the birds are more easily seen.

For the visitor, there are two key areas near the village, namely the estuary of the Asif n'Srou river and the coastal maquis that stretches onto the cliffs. There are plenty of other points of interest around the estuary and its relatively small size makes it easy to access and walk around. The Bald Ibis can range widely and is often seen flying along the cliffs and across the estuary. They feed on the dry heaths around Tamri and finding them is usually a matter of scanning along the hillsides from the beach. Do

ROUTE 22: TAMRI

not try to search the sea cliffs to find the nests – their breeding grounds are deliberately closed to visitors to avoid disturbance.

Starting point The beach car park on the N1, the direct route from Agadir to Essaouira (GPS: 30.709, -9.858) This is 4.5km before the village of Tamri if coming from Agadir, just after the coastal road headed inland.

Getting there Self-drive; taxi or bus from Agadir or Essaouira.

Park in the large car park on the N1, which is mainly used by surfers and others accessing the beach. There may be a fee to pay for someone to 'guard' your car and the by-product is that they normally have some idea of where the Bald Ibises are.

1 Head for the river, cross the scrub and scan the upper reaches of the estuary and the reeds opposite. Coots, ducks, herons and waders are normally present in this part of the river, and during migration Glossy Ibis or Night Heron may be found. The reeds attract Marsh Harriers and there is a general feeling that anything can turn up.

This area is worth searching carefully for lizards and other reptiles, especially at the back of the small dunes and around the tamarisks. Margarita's Fringe-fingered Lizard, in particular, is endemic to this area of the coast. This is also a known location of Desert Bluet that occur in the vegetated river edges both here and closer to the village.

The blind estuary of Asif N'Srou (top) is at the centre of the foraging area for the northern group of Northern Bald Ibis (bottom).

PRACTICAL PART

ROUTE 22: TAMRI

2 Walk along the river edge to the beach. The freshwater lagoon behind the beach is popular with gulls which come here to bathe, washing the accumulated salt off their plumage. The flock here often consists of thousands of birds, the majority of which are Yellow-legged and Lesser Black-backed Gulls, but Audouin's Gulls are normally present in good numbers too (up to several hundred).

The Bald Ibises often forage around the white buildings visible to the north on the slope rising towards the northern fields. These can be in small family parties or at times forming a single flock of up to one hundred birds.

3 If there is any difficulty in finding the Bald Ibis, try the new untarmacked road just south of the estuary car park. This heads along the top of the cliffs overlooking the estuary and accesses further coastal maquis and fields, where the birds frequently are. This road also gives you a good view of the whole site. Asif n'Srou is a typical example of a blind estuary where a sandbar has cut the river from the sea. Blind estuaries are a feature of arid regions, where flowing water is rare. When the river flows (after deluges higher up in the mountains), it carries enough water to carve out a river channel, which is subsequently closed off in dry periods by sand deposited by the ocean currents.

Margarita's Fringe-fingered Lizard is common in the coastal scrub.

4 If you still haven't found the Bald Ibis, they could be feeding in the 'northern fields'. This is an area of abandoned and low-intensity agriculture surrounded by original maquis along the road from Tamri in the direction of Essaouira. You will need to drive 7-10km from the beach car park along the N1 northwards through the village of Tamri and towards the high ground beyond. The Bald Ibis forage close to the road and are normally visible from the roadside. Thekla's Larks and Tawny Pipits can be found here as well. There is a track down to a promontory on the coast (GPS point 30.719390, -9.840944), and this can be taken if the Ibis are still elusive, but do not go further north.

Route 23: Paradise Valley

**4+ HOURS, 8 KM
MODERATE**

Scenic river valley, renowned for its waterfalls, rock pools and lush vegetation. Rich dragonfly fauna and some attractive birds.

Habitats: Steep river valley, scrubland, riparian vegetation
Selected species: Bonelli's Eagle, Moussier's Redstart, Rock Bunting, Ringed Cascader, Red-veined Dropwing, Blue-eye Damselfly, Moroccan Orange Tip

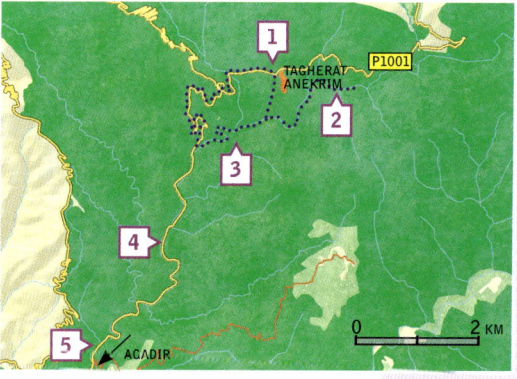

North of Agadir lies the valley of the Tamraght river. It is both very scenic and a good introduction to the western High Atlas. The valley was actually given the name 'Paradise' by visiting tourists in the sixties and is a well-known beauty spot within easy reach of Agadir, so it can get very busy at peak times. There are many cafes along the P1001 road and in the valley itself. The main selling point of these cafes is that the tables and chairs are actually in the river and associated pools. It does not take much effort to go beyond the easily accessible areas by the car parks and this is where you can find both peace and wildlife.

The area is really only green and a 'paradise' after winter rains when the river runs through a series of cascades and the vegetation has a spurt of growth. The valley has palms and oleanders at the bottom and the hillsides have Argan, Thuja and Wild Pistachio. The flora is rich in thymes and other herbs and these, in turn, will attract butterflies.

The Tamraght river is known for its dragonflies, with the Ringed Cascader the top prize. This beautiful species is difficult to find elsewhere in Morocco. As often, the occurrence of dragonflies is dependent upon the water levels. In the right conditions, you'll find that the river has three distinct habitats, – small isolated pools, areas of slowly flowing water and

ROUTE 23: PARADISE VALLEY

sections where it flows rapidly. Ideally, you should explore all these three habitats as each will have different species.

Starting point Car park on the P1001 just west of the village of Tagherat Anekrim (GPS 30.596633, -9.522516).

Getting there Self-drive; taxi or bus from Agadir or Essaouira.

The Tamraght river has cut a rocky path through the valley (top) and Booted Eagles patrol the skies above (bottom).

1 The walking trail begins above the valley itself on the P1001. There are two routes here. Don't follow the '*Circuit Route de Miel*' (which follows the road), but instead take the trail that heads down into the valley below, heading south. On the first stretch you have good views of the area. Scan for raptors that can drift over the ridges above. Most likely ones are Bonelli's and Booted Eagles and Barbary Falcon, now considered a race of Peregrine. Here, and on the rest of the route, check the slopes for Moussier's Redstart and Rock Bunting.

The path arrives at the valley floor upstream from a series of bathing pools. Take the path upstream, away from the pools.

2 This part of the valley is quiet and takes you towards the higher reaches. Search for Barbary Featherleg and Ringed Cascader.

ROUTE 23: PARADISE VALLEY

3 Return and follow the valley to the bathing pools. This part is quite heavily commercialised. The path arrives back at the P1001 road at a car park. The river edge below the car park is again good for dragonflies and all three of the local dropwing species can be found together with Blue-eye. The good habitat continues for approximately 1km.

Turning right on the P1001 it is a 3.3 km walk up to the other car park, but you can also take a taxi.

Two additional locations can be visited. Both are along the P1001 road in the direction of Agadir, and really are only viable if you have your own car or are prepared for a hike.

4 5.5 km south of the original starting point is another section of the Tamraght river that is worth searching for Ringed Cascader (GPS: 30.572250, -9.538510). As with most sections, this is a roadside location and access is simple once you have found a safe place to park.

5 A further stop can be made after another 1.8km downhill from point 4. The river is even more heavily vegetated and includes sections that are slower moving. These lower reaches are less disturbed and around the lowest limit the Ringed Cascader and Red-winged Dropwings can be found. Historic records include Yellow Clubtail and Orange-spotted Emerald and both species may still occur especially in wet years when the river continues to flow through the summer.

Typical species are Barbary Ground Squirrel and Moussier's Redstart.

PRACTICAL PART

ROUTE 24: THE SOUSS ESTUARY

Route 24: The Souss Estuary

1 HOUR, 1-2 KM
EASY

Coastal marshes and scrub within easy reach of Agadir.
Great bird-watching, both along the river and in the scrubland.

Habitats: Estuary and coastal scrub
Selected species: Greater Flamingo, Spoonbill, Osprey, waders, Lesser Crested Tern, Red-necked Nightjar, Golden Fringe-fingered Lizard, Helmethead Gecko

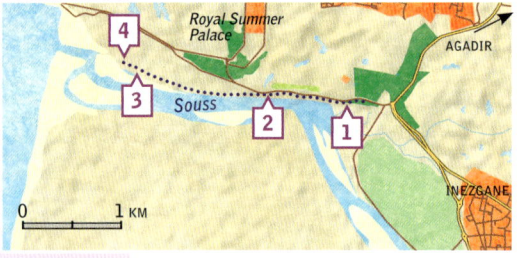

The Souss estuary, unlike the others in southern Morocco is not a 'blind' estuary (i.e closed off from the sea by a sand bar) but has a permenant outflow to the ocean. The estuary is therefore under the influence of the tides, with large sand and mudflats exposed at low tide. It is a coastal hotspot for birds, particularly on migration. Most of the wetland species seen in Morocco can be found here and there is an impressive list of vagrants. In addition, some coastal maquis remains where birds can be found, altough most of it has been cleared for golf courses that surround the Royal Summer Palace that sits on the north bank of the river.

The Souss estuary lies on the southern edge of Agadir and the outskirts of the next town to the south, namely Inezgane. For the visitor, it is not obvious where Agadir ends and Inezgane begins as it appears to be a suburb of the city lined with a series of golf courses.

The Golden Fringe-fingered Lizard is limited to the coastal strip.

CROSSBILL GUIDES • SOUTHERN MOROCCO

ROUTE 24: THE SOUSS ESTUARY

The Souss estuary is easy to reach from the tourist hotels in and around Agadir and forms the northern edge of the southern section of the Souss-Massa National Park.

Note that the estuary is relatively wide and birdwatching is dependent upon the tide. High tide is best avoided. You'd better visit as mud is exposed during a falling or rising tide. Furthermore, visits in the evening and Friday (the holy day for Muslims) are best avoided as it tends to be crowded then. The site can be sensitive as it is overlooked by one of the Royal Palaces and if any of the family are in residence, there can be issues with binoculars, long-lens cameras etc. Furthermore, construction work is continuing on the sea wall and access can change as the work progresses.

Starting point The car park area before the Royal Palace (GPS: 30.362, -9.587).

Getting there Drive 3.5 km east from N10, where you leave the main road in the direction of Ocean Golf/Golf Med les Dunes. You can get there with your rental car, taxi or bus.

1 From the car park it is possible to walk c500m eastwards, following the estuary upstream. This first section is a marsh that can hold herons, egrets and a good mix of waders which are visible in the channels exposed at low tide. This area also holds a gull roost, which can hold good numbers of Mediterranean Gulls that tend to be scarce

the Souss estuary at high tide.

ROUTE 24: THE SOUSS ESTUARY

Greater Flamingos are common in the Souss estuary.

elsewhere on this coast. Look out for Slender-billed, and more rarely Little Gulls which sometimes mix in with the commoner species. Also scan the pylons around this part of the estuary as two or three Ospreys are normally present, except during the summer months. Don't forget to look at the golf courses to the north. The well-watered fairways and greens can attract a number of birds and butterflies although they can disappear behind the walls into the complex. Large flocks of Maghreb Magpies can loiter around here.

2 Return to the car park. If the tide is either very high or very low, it is normally more productive to head west towards the coast itself. The bend of the river here holds most of the waders and the numbers are impressive. The birds can be quite distant and a telescope is an advantage. One species that doesn't need a telescope is the Greater Flamingo; the large flock of up to 500 birds couldn't be more obvious.

3 It is not necessary to walk the whole way to the ocean, but certainly walk to the last bay before the coastal sand dunes. This area is popular with terns and waders. It is the best location to look for Lesser Crested Terns that are regular during the year but most plentiful in the autumn.

4 The maquis between the river and the Royal Palace attracts migrants, especially warblers and shrikes. The sandy soils are home to Golden Fringe-fingered Lizard and Helmet-head Gecko. It is also a renowned site for Red-necked Nightjar, although they can be elusive and getting close to the Palace boundary (where they are best seen) cannot be recommended for reasons as noted above.

Route 25: Oued Massa

6 HOURS-FULL DAY
MODERATE

Estuary, surrounded by desert, scrub and agricultural habitats.
One of top birding sites in the country.

Habitats: Estuary, coastal scrub, sandy steppe, fields, riverine woodland
Selected species: Desert Thumb, Egyptian Mongoose, Marbled Duck, Northern Bald Ibis, Mediterranean Short-toed Lark, Brown-throated Martin, Black-crowned Tchagra, Golden Fringe-fingered Lizard, Forskal's Sand Snake, False Mallow Skipper, Vagrant Emperor

Oued Massa National Park is a collection of sites around the Oued Massa estuary and agricultural fields. Historically, it held some real desert species, but these have become scarcer as the extent of the agriculture has increased. Nevertheless, the National Park remains a really interesting location as there is a good mix of habitats within a relatively small area. This route contains several such locations where you can sample the variety of the whole area. The main focus of this route is the estuary, but it is worth exploring a wider area, including the extensive coastal maquis, where interesting flora and fauna can be found throughout. Note that the locations

ROUTE 25: OUED MASSA

Oued Massa runs through agricultural fields (top) where Zitting Cisticola is a constant companion (bottom).

of this route are mostly widely spaced and really requires a car to travel between them and potentially visit other interesting areas to achieve full coverage of habitats around the river valley.

Starting point Sidi Rabat village (GPS 30.086, -9.664).

Getting there Self-drive; grand taxi or bus from Agadir.

1 Sidi R'bat is a small village on the Atlantic coast (but one with a hotel and café). You reach it via the town of Ardbalou. The road between the latter and Sidi R'bat crosses coastal maquis, most of which is unfenced and overgrazed by goats to the point that in places no vegetation remains. This is nevertheless attractive to Lesser (or Mediterranean) Short-toed Larks and a few pairs breed here. Just before the village, there are some fenced areas that give a good impression of what this would look like if the plants were allowed to regenerate.

ROUTE 25: OUED MASSA

Drive through Sidi R'bat and park just past the hotel where the road overlooks the sea (GPS: 30.086, -9.664).

2 Wander the area between here and the sea cliffs. The last maquis before the cliffs hosts Stone Curlew. After the breeding season, the birds gather here and the flock often totals more than 50 birds.
The Northern Bald Ibis breeding cliff is north of this point, but access is restricted beyond the caves of 'les grottes ifrane' and you mustn't go further for risk of disturbing this endangered species. Flocks of birds can be seen in this area, generally flying between foraging areas or to the nest colony. Gannets and shearwaters may be found offshore in the autumn.

3 It is possible to walk south from here, down the cliffs to the river mouth and then to the western end of the National Park where there are a couple of bird hides over-looking the pools behind the sand bar that cuts the Oued Massa from the sea. These pools can have Flamingos, herons, waders and ducks (including Marbled Duck). This is a minimum of 5 km walk (return) and you need to decide whether it is worth the effort.

Return to Sidi R'bat and follow the road back Ardbalou and turn right at the roundabout on the edge of town.

4 The formal National Park entrance is on the northern edge of Ardbalou (GPS Point 30.043, 9.644), although there is little to say you have arrived, just a simple archway and a faded sign. The road continues on for c3km to the car park at the museum (GPS point 30.057217, -9.654734). Although it is possible to drive to the museum, it is the riverside vegetation here that is productive and it is best to walk at least some of the way. The road follows the right-hand bank of the river and heads northwest towards the sea.

5 Walking along with the river, the view to your left is the riverine cliffs that run to the coast. The area of natural vegetation at this part of the coast is one of transition between Mediterranean and a more 'Canary-type' maquis, where cactoid spurge *Euphorbia officinarum* and the succulent *Kleinia anteuphorbium* join the cistus. The main target here is the Black-crowned Tchagra. This bird is not uncommon along the coast and you will hear them soon enough. However, its skulking

PRACTICAL PART

ROUTE 25: OUED MASSA

The Oued Massa eco-museum.

behaviour often makes it difficult to see. In these riverside tamarisks, you have the best possible chance to find it, especially if you can find two territorial males battling for the stretch of river.

After 1km or so there is a patch of small agricultural fields, nestling beneath the riverside cliffs. There are many Moussier's Redstarts and Thekla's Larks here that often perch and sing on the cliffs and slopes above the road.

It is, of course, possible to walk the whole length of the river to the sea and reach the hides noted in site 3. It is an 8 km round trip. The more productive approach is to return to your car and drive to the centre/museum car park at the end of the track (GPS point 30.057217, -9.654734) and walk the short loop at this end of the estuary.

Return to Ardbalou and turn right in the village to the bridge over the Massa river.

6 From the bridge, check the birds and dragonflies. The river attracts substantial numbers of swifts, swallows and martins. With them are Brown-throated Martins, an African species. This is one of the easiest places to see them north of the Sahara. As they are often in mixed flocks, you have the opportunity to directly compare with the other swallows and martins. Crakes, Great Snipe and all kinds of European waders are all possible during migration. The dragonfly fauna has a Mediterranean feel, with Blue, Lesser and Vagrant Emperors and Red-veined Darter the most likely species.

Return to Ardbalou and continue in a southwesterly direction to the town of Massa, which is like a southern extension of Ardbalou. Four kilometres upstream from the previous stop, you can turn right and drop back down to the river in the direction of Imallalen. There is a parking area in a glade of Eucalyptus just before the river crossing (GPS: 30.004, -9.656).

7 Walk the eastern bank, following the line of a now disused elevated irrigation channel. The 'river' usually comprises a series of pools rather than a flowing stream and along the edge is a mix of riverine scrub and small plantations. To the east are arable fields. Black-crowned Tchagra occurs here (but is hard to spot) and Brown-throated Martins are often found above the pools. The river is good for Spanish Terrapins and amphibians, including Stripeless Tree Frog, Brongersma's Toad and African Green Toad. In spring, the strange parasitic plant 'Desert Thumb' (also called Maltese Fungus) can be plentiful on the sandy banks.

The field edges should not be ignored as Yellow Wagtails of various races, Black-winged Kites, Woodchat and Great Grey Shrikes can all be found. Basically, it can be buzzing with life, with butterflies, birds and dragonflies.

You can follow the riverside for 1.3 kms to a third bridge. Then return back to the car and drive back to Massa, turn left to the centre of Ardbalou, where you turn right towards the N1. After 1.5 kms you reach a low hill (GPS: 30.024, -9.617).

Black-crowned Tchagra is found in the riverine vegetation but more often heard than seen (top). The Oued Massa is also the haunt for the rare False Mallow Skipper (bottom).

8 This is an old rubbish tip that is slowly being converted into farmland. This area is drier than the Massa valley a few kilometres away and this is reflected in the species typically found here. Follow one of the tracks along the low hill and into the hinterland overlooking the valley. Tawny Pipit, Stone Curlew and possibly Cream-colored Courser and Black-bellied Sandgrouse can be found here. Little Owls like the dry stone walls and during migration anything can turn up. Red Fox is also often seen hunting the abandoned fields.

Additional sites near the Coast

For the locations of the sites described below, see map on page 225.

A – Essaouira

Essaouira is a burgeoning and popular resort town within easy reach of both Marrakech and Agadir. Based around the picturesque harbour with its seafront ramparts backed by the medina, this has become a tourist hotspot and much of the area around the town has steadily been developed to provide the supporting infrastructure for the growing numbers of tourists, especially the plethora of golf courses. However, this still remains a great location for exploring the local habitats which are typical of the cooler Mediterranean climate.

Oued Ksab near Essaouira has a Mediterranean feel and wildlife.

The maquis is dominated by cistus and broom species, and is a good area to search for *Ophrys* orchids, including Dull Bee, Mirror and Spanish Omega* (*O. dyris*) Orchids in February and March. Amongst the calcareous sands, the endemic pale blue sand crocus *Romulea engleri* can also be found and is one of the earliest flowers, often starting in December. Any remaining patches of vegetation should be searched as this area also holds a mix of reptiles including Common Fringe-fingered Lizard, Simon's Small Lizard and Oliver's Small Lizard. The small pools also hold Sharp-ribbed Newt.

The Oued Ksab estuary just to the south of the town is another 'blind' estuary (the stream almost but not quite reaching the sea) and this is a good area to look for birds. Walking along the beach will give you views of the lagoon and a mix of waterbirds, including Greater Flamingo, Ruddy Shelduck and waders is often present. Brown-throated Martin occurs, but is not as regular as further south. The offshore island of

ADDITIONAL SITES NEAR THE COAST

Mogador has a breeding colony of Eleonora's Falcons, and from April until October, hunting birds can be seen around the town and the nearby coast.

The valley just upstream of the Ksab bridge is a migrant trap, and when it holds water, it is especially good for amphibians and dragonflies. Park at GPS point 31.4643, -9.7595 and walk along the disused roadway or drop down to the riverbank to explore. Go at least as far as the conspicuous pipe bridge (c1km) and check all the pools, including the cross drains. Species include Moussier's Redstart, Western Olivaceous Warbler, and Black-crowned Tchagra. Be aware that the local Spotless Starling seem to have mastered mimicking the tchagra's song. Dragonflies include the emperors, Southern Skimmer and Mediterranean Bluet in season. Flowering plants attract butterflies including African Knapweed Fritillary.

The dunes and pines around Oued Ksab have historically been a good area for Red-necked Nightjar, although the expansion of golf courses over the last few years has reduced the places where they can be found.

The Lighthouse at Cap Rhir is an important landmark.

B - Cap Rhir

GPS 30.628, -9.881. 45 km north from Agadir along the main N1 coast road, the lighthouse marks the promontory and furthest westerly point on this part of the coast Cap Rhir. Its position, with an elevation of 30m or so, makes the location below the lighthouse a good spot for sea-watching. The lighthouse itself is c.500m inland, and by following tracks you can cross the sandy scrubland and get closer to the sea. A wide range of terns, skuas and shearwaters pass by, with Arctic Skua, Cory's Shearwater and Sandwich Tern present throughout most of the year. In autumn these are joined by Manx and Sooty Shearwaters, Great and Pomarine Skuas and both Lesser Crested and West African Crested Terns. With a strong onshore wind, more oceanic species can join them. Offshore cetaceans can also be seen. Dolphins and pilot whales are most likely, but great whales are possible too, especially Bryde's and Humpback.

PRACTICAL PART

ADDITIONAL SITES NEAR THE COAST

The landward side of the headland should not be ignored. Bald Ibis often fly past and flora around here includes the endemic garlic *Allium paniculatum* ssp *antiatlanticum* within the coastal maquis.

C – Sous-Massa National Park- Reserve de Gazelles

GPS: 30.287744, -9.560439. The central area of the Sous-Massa National Park (Parc Animalier) houses herds of large ungulates which are bred here for release into the wild. Addax, Scimitar-horned Oryx, Damas and Dorcas Gazelles, some of Morocco's iconic species that historically ranged the Saharan edge, are held in large pens and are readily observed in more or less natural settings.

The habitat attracts other 'wild' species including Barbary Ground Squirrel and a range of typical birds similar to those found in Oued Massa. It has also been attractive to wintering Dotterel with flocks of 40 or so birds being found there.

The *Reserve de Gazelle du Parc Souss Massa* is signposted off the main N1, 22km south of Agadir. The buffer zone before the park entrance is a good example of coastal Argan forest, and it is here that the African Ground Squirrel was re-discovered (see pages 84 and 97).

D – Jebel Imzi

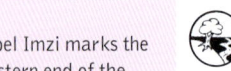

Jebel Imzi marks the western end of the Anti-Atlas.

GPS: 29.749, -9.288. Jebel Imzi and the associated peaks loom over the coastal plain to the east of Tiznit. At 1535m, Jebel Imzi is the highest peak at the Western end of the Anti-Atlas chain. This area is a showcase of the influence of the Atlantic on the native flora. It is the best place to seek the native Dragon Tree and Azores Laurel and also holds a mix of species typical of the Western Anti-Atlas including *Apteranthes joannis* (formerly called *Caralluma*), a succulent cactus-like member of the milkweed family with spectacular flowers in late summer) It is often found around the base of the spurge *Euphorbia officinarum echinus*.

Jebel Imzi is an out of the way place, although recent road improvements have aided access. You need to travel the R104 from Tiznit through Anzi to the end of the village of Agadir Ouguejgal (see grid point above). Most of the Dragon Trees are congregated in the gorges carved through the dramatic mountain landscape, so follow the tracks eastwards and upwards from the village.

E – Sidi Ifni

GPS: 29.449, -9.930. South of Tiznit, there is a 'plateau' of pre-Cambrian igneous rock just inland from the coastal town Sidi Ifni. This is the last area that shows the influence of the Souss valley and the Anti-Atlas before the topography drops down to the Saharan depression at Guelmim and further south. This is an area of distinctive flora and marks the zenith of the influence of the Canaries on the flora of the area (see pages 93-94)

Although the N12 crosses the plateau, most visitors will enter the area via the R104 from Tiznit, Sidi Ifni being 75 km from the N1 turnoff in the town. This road heads along the coast and therefore it is necessary to turn off this road along the P1903 or P1907 to get onto the plateau itself and from there is it simply a matter of stopping at suitable looking areas. The two roads meet at grid point given above.

The whole area is akin to a massive caldera, with the high ridges around the perimeter and a flat lower plateau within. The lower area is generally of little interest as most has long been adopted for agriculture and little of the natural vegetation remains. The steeper slopes around the 'rim' are where efforts should be concentrated.

The bushy King Juba's Spurge (*Euphorbia regis-jubae*) is a good indicator of where the natural vegetation remains and its ball-like bushes are simple to spot. With these you should find *Lavendula dentata* and the succulent *Kleinia* and other spurges. If visiting in autumn the blue flowering bulb *Autonoë latifolia* can be obvious.

The vegetation also changes from north to south and from east to west. In the north-east the vegetation sits under a tree layer, mostly Argan, whilst along the coast the natural vegetation is a version of low coastal scrub, where the spurges dominate.

This southern coastal area should not be ignored, as the area to the southwest of Sidi Ifni on the right bank of Oued Arksis south of the town along the N12 is the best location for the soapwort *Commelina rupicola*, a sub-Saharan species (although it has recently been found closer to Tiznit, in a valley 4km to the north of Sidi-Moussa d' Aglou).

King Juba's Spurge indicates where natural vegetation remains on the Sidi Ifni plateau.

TOURIST INFORMATION & OBSERVATION TIPS

Travelling to and in Southern Morocco

Via air As a visitor it is most likely that you will arrive in Southern Morocco by air via Marrakech, Agadir or perhaps Essaouira. There is a wide selection of flights often by low-cost carriers that have reduced the cost and increased the flexibility of visiting this part of Morocco. Recently a service has been offered to Ouarzazate from limited locations in Europe, enabling access to the desert without needing to drive over the High Atlas Mountains.

Other international airports in central and northern Morocco are in Casablanca, Rabat, Fez and Tangier. These are all a long drive away from the area described in this book and are only suited as an in or outbound destination when you have sufficient time and plan to visit other parts of Morocco as well.

Overland The distance and challenge of reaching this area overland should not be underestimated, although an increasing number of people do choose this route. They are generally of two types. There are those who are going on to cross the Sahara itself (and this is a comparatively simple first step) and there are those who are spending the winter in warmer climes usually in their own mobile home. The most popular route for drivers is via Algeciras-Tangier ferry (see www.frs.es), although there are other crossings, including from Genoa and Barcelona (see www.gnv.it). Even after reaching the African side of the Mediterranean, it is over 600km before you reach Marrakech which is in the northern part of the area considered here. This may not sound as a lot, but with average road journey speeds around 60km/h (except on the very few motorways), it is a long trip. In the mountains where it is difficult to drive, you won't be able to do more than 40km/h. In short, travelling overland really only works if your visit here is part of a prolonged trip.

The borders to Algeria have been closed since 1994 and no land crossing is possible. The border to Mauritania is only open near Nouadhibou on the main route to the capital Nouakchott. Even this border crossing can be suddenly shut, and you often need to hire a 'fixer' for the Mauritanian section. The best way of crossing is to buy a bus ticket between cross-border towns.

Trains Marrakech is the southern terminal of the Moroccan rail network run by the state rail provider ONCF (see **www.oncf.ma**). Trains can be used to get to southern Morocco from all the northern cities (including linking with the ferries from Europe), but no other places within our area are connected. There has been a plan to extend the network to Agadir via Marrakech, but no date has been set for delivery. Potentially confusingly, Moroccan railways offer tickets for the journey from Marrakech to Agadir, but this part of any journey will be done in a bus.

Coaches and Buses There is a good network of intercity coaches and buses connecting the main towns and cities in Morocco and every town has a bus station. It is possible to travel to many points here from the northern cities and this can be a way of travelling into southern Morocco once you are in the country.

The main three companies are Supratours, CTM, and SATA. Supratours is part of ONCF (the Moroccan railways and share the same website as above). CTM operates its sales fully online (see **www.ctm.ma**), so booking is relatively simple. SATA has the best network into the more remote areas in the south, but has a poorer reputation and no direct website, although apparently all routes can be booked via a third-party website (see **www.lagare.ma**).

Travelling in Southern Morocco

By far the simplest and most flexible way to travel is by hire car. Hiring a car is straightforward and there is a wide selection of providers from which to choose. It is likely that you will be offered a package deal with your flight, or even with your train ticket. Note however that most of the routes in this book are in remote areas and the majority are to the south of the High Atlas Mountains. Very few of the hire companies have offices in this area, and it is worth researching the network of support and recovery offices prior to finally selecting your rental company.

Once you have your car it is important to realise that distances are great, and the roads are few. They attract every kind of traveller from cars to bicycles, donkey drawn carts and livestock. Roads go from town to town and there are few bypasses, so although the open roads are often free from traffic, navigating villages and towns can be slow and nerve-racking. Expect to average no more than 40km per hour when travelling, even though the open stretches may allow speeds up to 100km/h.

It is also better to avoid driving at night. Many car drivers consider the use of headlights to be an optional extra whilst other road users will often be found going against the flow of traffic on the wrong side of the road and may not have any lights at all. In contrast, the very early morning is much easier as the roads are quieter.

The main routes are generally in good condition. The only issue is that roadworks are often done with little attempt to manage the flow of existing traffic. This often leads to delays. Side roads can be in poor condition, and many are not tarmacked. Note that most car companies' insurances do not cover driving off the tarmacked roads and therefore careful consideration is needed to drive on the tracks and minor roads here. The car routes in this book are therefore on tarmac roads, unless specifically stated otherwise.

Grand and Petit Taxis

Despite their name, Grand Taxis, (or G-Taxis for short) are not really taxis in a European model. As is typical across the whole of Africa they are shared transportation that supplements bus network in more remote areas. Grand Taxis used to be almost exclusively of old E-class Mercedes saloons, but nearly all have been replaced except in the far south. Dacia Lodgy seems to be the most popular make and model being adopted now and they are a familiar sight everywhere. They do not run to a fixed timetable but will leave when sufficient people want to go to the destination, linking towns and places along the route. These are often by far the most economical way of getting from place to place but is not for the faint hearted as they will not leave until they are stuffed full of people and goods, even livestock

As Grand Taxis will not go at regular intervals and may even stop running if there is no perceived demand, they are not best suited to reach the remote sites described in this guide.

However, they will be prepared to set down along their normal route and will also pick up if there is space. You can simply ask to be dropped off close to the needed location but note that fares are fixed for the whole route and this flat fare does not allow for discounts if you are going part way. Most Grand Taxi routes are from town to town via villages, which means that you need to ask if they go to where you want to before getting in. Once there, there is no guarantee when another Grand Taxi will be along to pick you up.

Some Grand Taxis will agree to do an exclusive trip for you alone, but you must negotiate the fee in advance. Also, if you want to be picked up from your drop off point later, ask the driver if there are limits on timings and if you can confirm when any others will be running that way. You may need to wait, or try to 'pre-book' you return trip.

Petit taxis are small hatchbacks and are exclusive to the hirer and usually reserved for travel within the town or host district, i.e. short journeys. Therefore, they are like 'real' taxis. They are often but not always metered and it is simplest to agree a charge for a journey. Expect them to be relatively expensive (but still cheap in European terms). They are limited by licence to 3 passengers.

Both Petit Taxis and older style Grand Taxis sport a distinctive colour or two-tone colour scheme. The colours used denote their host location and differ from district to district. Most of the colour schemes are chosen so they stand out and would not be selected by a normal car buyer – at least not in Morocco, making it is simple enough to tell the difference from normal cars. Petit Taxis will often use the same stands in the towns, so it is best to ask for the taxi stand if you want to hire one.

Traffic

Away from the coast and the cities, most roads are quiet by European standards. A large proportion of the road traffic is commercial vehicles; lorries, vans and the like. They are often aggressively driven and overloaded with cargo – be careful in other words. Leave plenty of space for other road users, even if they don't do so for you. The road between Marrakech and Agadir was rated as the most dangerous in the whole of Africa prior to the motorway being opened.

As there are few roads, navigation is straightforward. The road conditions on the main routes are generally fine, but backroads and those in the mountains (even the main crossings) can be tortuous and in poor condition. Routes away from the main N and R roads are often untarmacked and can be very poor. Driving standards deteriorate in poor weather and both rain and snow have a massive impact. Roads are generally poorly drained and most drivers simply have little experience of driving in the wet and cold. Demisters and windscreen wipers are often in poor working condition. The towns are visibly policed by the two groups, the *Sûreté Nationale* and the *Gendarmerie Royale*. They each have a different role, but it is generally the Gendarmerie Royale you will encounter. Many roads will have roadblocks at key interchanges and the Gendarmerie will stop cars and lorries to ensure that the rules are being obeyed. They tend not to stop tourists. Speed traps are commonplace, especially on the edge of towns and speed limits are rigorously enforced with on-the-spot fines. If you get stopped always ask for evidence and a receipt for any fines. There are stories of these being invented and bogus demands for money.

When stopping, pull completely off the road and park beyond the lines marking the road edges. In addition, be aware of the other road users. Animals, especially reptiles, can be attracted to the road surfaces in the evenings and care should be taken not to run them over. Agama and some other species will 'play dead' when threatened, a recipe for disaster on a desert road.

A final word on camels which, especially in the south, are a unique hazard. They can be extremely well camouflaged. Particularly at dusk they are almost invisible on the roadsides. All camels are owned by someone but they are left to wander so will walk onto roads. If you hit one, you will be expected to pay compensation. Worse is that such road accidents are often fatal to camel and car passengers alike. Due to the camel's long legs, it crashes through the windscreen and roof rather than the impact being absorbed by the car's bumper and crumple zones. In short, be warned...!

Planning your trip

When to go

There is no single answer regarding when to go. It depends on what you want to see and where you are prepared to go. Any season has its charms, although summer is, with the exception of the high peaks and the narrow coastal strip, too hot.

Only by being aware of the seasonal variations can you succeed in finding what you came to see. For most visitors focussed upon birds, the classic timing is early spring, which is from late February to early April. In this period, the Saharan areas are not too hot and most of the target species are present and relatively easy to find. The mountain birds can be found at sites and altitudes that are accessible, making them relatively easy to find. Keep in mind though that the weather here can still be poor, snow being known even in April.

The beginning of April is still too early for some migrant birds. Usually White-rumped Swift, Blue-cheeked Bee-eater and Eastern Olivaceous Warbler will not have returned to their Moroccan breeding sites by then. There is a good range of wildflowers and some butterflies present, but it is generally too early for the mountain species (except some of the Sub-alpine bulbs) and conversely too late for the Saharan flora which will have gone to seed by then.

For the mountain flora, the majority of the interesting species are in the Sub-alpine and Alpine zones, and here May and June are the prime months. It is the same timing that is good for butterflies and reptiles. Birding can also be good, but with the peaks free of snow, many of the special species range widely and little of this high Alpine zone is realistically accessible. By this time the steppes and the Sahara can already be uncomfortably hot, the flora desiccated and most animals hiding from the heat of the midday sun.

These high temperatures can continue well into September, although the flowering of the acacias along the edge of the Sahara means this can be a great time to see migrant birds and, additionally, a good diversity of dragonflies and butterflies.

The coast benefits from cooler temperatures and therefore the heat is manageable through most of the year. Note that by coast we refer only to the narrow band influenced by the Canary Current. In summer and autumn, fog banks are frequent here but the habitats avoid the desiccation of the inland zones. Flowering plants continue into the early summer and many animals are active for most of the day. Eleonora's Falcons only return to their breeding island in late April and from July onwards migrant waders start to arrive from their breeding locations in the arctic and the tern numbers build up, bringing both species of orange-billed terns to the estuaries. The winter period is very pleasant away from the mountains. Generally daytime temperatures are moderate and wildlife activity continues through the whole of the day. It can be very cold at night, and of course this is the period of the greatest risk of rain.

Rainfall rarely impacts a trip away from the mountains, and usually consists of short showers. Note that wadis can be dangerous after rains (see page 255).
Not only is there a question of the time of year, but also of the way to make the best of the visits to these areas. Certainly, it is simple to say that during the hot months, there is little activity in the middle of day due to the extreme heat. This is not only true of warm-blooded fauna, but, as insects and reptiles cannot regulate their body temperature, they also hide at these times. In the hottest time of year, it is simply not worth searching in the middle of the day as little can be seen and your health is likely to suffer.
The only exception to this rule is in the high mountains, where the mid-day temperatures are manageable and butterflies, dragonflies and reptiles are not often most active at midday.
The dawn is the coldest part of the day, and there is normally little activity until the first warming rays of the sun reach the area. There is not much of a dawn chorus in the steppes and Saharan-edge. About an hour after sun-up is peak time and territorial species will be in full song. Sandgrouse come to drink two hours after dawn and this is the best time to see them. The exception is Lichtenstein's Sandgrouse, which is an evening drinker, normally when it just too dark to see them!
Away from the mountains, most diurnal reptiles are active in this post-dawn period, but the better time to find these is at dusk. This period has the advantage of also crossing over into the emergence of the nocturnal species, including most of the mammals.

Weather and temperatures

Most of the time the weather is stable and sunny. The lowlands away from the coast are extremely hot during the summer months. Summer temperatures above 40°C are the norm inland. Note however that these are air temperatures in the shade so, in reality, the mercury rises quite a bit more (see page 27). In summer these high temperatures are also often matched with a desiccating wind and if this perpetuates then dust and sandstorms can make this doubly uncomfortable. Humidity is very low meaning that temperatures at night are substantially lower, but even with a 20°C swing means that the nights remain warm. It is only in winter that with the daytime highs being lower, the night-time can literally become freezing cold.
As already mentioned, the coastal strip is cooled by the Canary Current and therefore the high temperatures are substantially cooler than even a few kilometres inland. However, these areas are also susceptible to fog banks that reduce the normal 30°C+ by a further 10°C or so.
With this being the norm, it can come as a surprise when it does actually rain. Clouds can build with surprising rapidity, and what is most noticeable is the sudden increase in wind speed and drop in temperature. Rain does not always follow, and in

fact wind is often a signal that rain has fallen elsewhere. For example, early spring is often windy on the High Arid Steppes as a reaction to rain and snow in the High Atlas Mountains. When rain does fall it is usually short and intense, but this shouldn't be taken as saying prolonged rain never happens.

Accommodation

There is a wealth of accommodation across the whole of Morocco, and a large proportion of it is focused on the tourist market. Accommodation ranges widely in standard, facilities and costs and many places advertise online through their own web sites or through booking websites. Stays are still regulated through local police, so expect passport details to be collected at each location.

Camping, as distinct from wild camping, is not supported except along the coast. Even here, this is really only provided to hook up mobile homes rather than for a night under canvas. Nomad-style camping is offered in the desert for the more adventurous as part of a package of 'authentic desert experiences' offered to tourists. It is the desert version of glamping, so not to be confused with pitching your own tent, grabbing your roll of toilet paper on your way to the toilet block, as you would on European camp sites.

Wild camping is possible but note the requirement to notify the local police and ensure that it is safe to camp where you propose. Domestic animals are driven large distances and you could be on their route. Never set camp in a wadi, as a flash flood, although unlikely, could be devastating.

Opening times, shopping and eating out

Although it is a Muslim country, Morocco still follows the French business model of Monday to Friday. The exception is that the typical mid-day closing is extended on a Friday to allow for the prayers. Businesses open at 9am, closing from 13.00, and then opening again from 15.00 to 17.00 or 18.00. Shops generally are slow to open, but will be in business by 10 am, but then, after the afternoon break, will stay open until 21.30.

Shopping is an experience in Morocco. Away from the main cities, you'll get your groceries in small stores and souks (fixed market). The souks are usually based around the small streets in the medina (town centre) and are arranged so that the same goods are found in the one area. Butchers can be separated between white poultry and red meats but will nearly always hang up the whole carcass on show and some part of the original animal to illustrate what the meat is – a far cry from vacuum-packed portions sold across Europe. Vegetables are from local sources and therefore seasonal.

There will always be a spice shop or two, where great sacks of herbs and spices are displayed. These include both culinary and medicinal plant products.

Most towns will also have a market day when farmers from around the district bring in their produce to be sold, and often other travelling sales are available including clothes and electrical goods.

The souks are part commerce and part a social meeting place. They tend to open early and close late, with a break in the middle of the day. Markets are really morning affairs that close when the goods are sold, or customers have left so it is not so much of a fixed time.

Cafes are also popular meeting spots and there are always places open for food. Restaurants offer snacks and food through the day, and the main hours are familiarly similar to France with lunches around 1pm and dinner at 7.30 -8.00 pm. It is important to note that Morocco is in the same time zone as the UK summertime, but does not change its clocks in the winter months.

A more recent development is the number of 'Café Mobiles' that have sprung up. These are converted vans with an expresso machine in the back. Serving a limited range of coffees and other drinks they are more prevalent on major routes or on the outskirts of larger towns and designed for a 'grab and go' beverage.

It is important to note that all of this changes radically during the holy month of Ramadan, which is not at a fixed period in the year but moves forward by 11 days each year when compared with our western calendar. Observance includes fasting from dawn til dusk. Morocco does not strictly observe this in the way found in many Muslim countries, however some shops, restaurants and cafes will be closed during the day, or for the period. This will obviously affect your visit, so we strongly advise to check in advance whether this important period coincides with your visit. Ramadan is broken by the festival of Eid al Fitr, and this also will change opening times. During Ramadan, the clocks may be changed to bring forward the breaking of the fast to earlier in the day.

Typical meals

Most of the food is heavily based upon the Ottoman and Moorish cuisines found around the Mediterranean basin. Each area of Morocco has a slightly different style and approach based mainly on what can be grown locally. There is also still a French influence in the approach to food. The main dish is the tagine, a term that covers both the dish itself and the distinctive conical pot it is cooked in. The pots are ubiquitous, as the dishes are slow-cooked over small charcoal burners outside restaurants and cafes from the early hours each day. The meat is cooked with whatever vegetables (or fruits) are in season and the choice is between beef, lamb, goat or chicken. Nearly all restaurants offer a vegetarian option. Classic combinations include chicken and olives, or lamb and quince. Preserved lemons are a favoured flavouring especially in chicken dishes. Tagine dishes are normally served with bread and a chopped onion and tomato salad. Couscous is also popular. The steamed couscous is served with

vegetables and / or meat. There are also meat kebabs simply grilled over charcoal.
Most food is not very heavily spiced or hot with chilli. However, both cumin and a harissa paste or sauce will be offered on the side, so you can add them to your specific taste. A local spice mix, called Ras el Hanout, is used in some dishes and this is a blend of spices the composition of which changes from place to place but is cumin-dominated.
Berber omelette is also offered. It is a dish of slowly poached eggs with onions and tomatoes, spiced with Ras el Hanout. Berber omelette can also be cooked in a tagine and has its roots in the dish Shakshuka that turns up in various forms across the Middle East.
Desserts again show the colonial roots, and French style patisserie is widely available, but in addition there are a number of rose-water flavoured dishes especially in the Dadès area.
In common with France and against the perception of a Muslim country, alcohol is widely served. There are both vineyards and breweries in the north of Morocco and therefore local beverages are available and at substantially lower prices than those imported. However, especially south of the High Atlas don't be surprised if you find that the hotel, restaurant or cafe is dry and you have to rely on 'Berber Whisky'; i.e. Mint Tea.

Convenient travel and safety issues

Annoyances and hazards
We should start with saying that Morocco is a safe country for travellers. In fact, within the Muslim world, it is one of the safest countries to explore individually. For centuries Morocco has had a tolerant and welcoming society and certainly since independence, it has been a very stable country. Since Mohammed VI came to the throne in 1999, there has been a continuing drive for the country to meet both the demands of the modern world and the aspirations of its citizens. The tensions that have challenged the rest of North Africa and the Middle East have been notable by their near absence here. Being Berber, as distinct from Arab, helps with this sense of being different and, although there are still issues in particular regions and with some communities seeking greater autonomy, there is nothing that that hinders travelling in the country. That being said, there are several issues that require extra attention, either because they are a potential danger, a holiday spoiler or so different from European countries that they may worry you even if there is no reason to. These issues fall into risks from wildlife, climate and different social norms.

Wildlife

There are plenty of venomous snakes on the Moroccan list, including the iconic Cobra. They are unlikely to be seen, and more often they will rapidly move away from you rather than attack.

Most stings are actually from scorpions and some of the species are very toxic. They are nocturnal creatures that hide in borrows and crevices during the day. Occasionally, they crawl away in shoes, bags or clothing left on the floor. Shaking out shoes and not leaving bags on the floor (especially when camping or staying in simple rural accommodation) should avoid any problems.

Dogs are not as common as in Europe as they have a dubious status in Islam. However feral dogs are still found especially in the cooler areas and around towns. They are rarely aggressive and most packs will move off of their own accord as you approach. Nevertheless, it is important to remember that rabies is still present in Morocco, so keep clear of dogs and cats wherever possible.

Climate

The biggest issue is the heat, and the consequential need for water. Dehydration is a serious health issue and can be potentially fatal. Bottled water is widely available and is safe but comes with the environmental cost of the plastic bottles. Water in taps is from one of two sources. The municipal water systems are to French standard and are normally safe to drink, but if there is a local drought in the south this needs to be checked. Alternatively, they come from local boreholes, and these can become contaminated especially if livestock are farmed in the water catchment. You will need to ask or simply assume the worst and sterilise your personal supply.

Rehydration is important, either with bespoke sachets, or the WHO-recommended sugar and table salt. In addition, be aware that your salt loss may be much higher than at home, especially with the amount of sweat you will generate in the field. This needs to be replaced to keep yourself healthy. Many Northern Europeans have adopted a low salt diet, but here you will probably need to actively add salt or seek out salty food after a long day in the field.

In preparing for heat, some visitors are caught out by the cold in the high mountains, where snow can occur in any month but is most likely from October to March. Carrying suitable clothing is essential.

Social issues

There is an underlying western structure and approach to life, due to the French colonial heritage, that makes it easy to forget that Morocco has a very different culture. Especially in the far south customs and outlook are far more traditional. Tourism has grown to an important part of the country's economy and most Moroccans recognise and value this. Twinned with their cultural tradition of supporting travellers, it makes them wonderful hosts.

However, it is important to remember that because customs are different, it is easy to cross an invisible line and cause offence. For example, shorts and short skirts are not worn by Moroccans and are considered disrespectful and should be avoided in towns and villages away from the main tourist centres. Head coverings are the norm, but the climate is such that wearing a hat is needed anyway. This goes for both men and women.

Remember that the income of the average Moroccan is still less than 10% of most countries in Western Europe. As the typical naturalist is laden with cameras, optics and other equipment, he/she appears very wealthy in local eyes. This inevitably attracts attention from the unscrupulous, but probably no more than anywhere else. Women's rights have been transformed since the millennium, and it is not uncommon to find women heading businesses, especially in the tourism sector. However, it is still a patriarchal society and it remains unusual for local Moroccan women to travel unaccompanied by men and almost never to travel alone. Therefore, if you are a woman travelling alone, expect to attract unwanted attention every once in a while (besides the normal, courteous behaviour). Usually this doesn't go further than improper and annoying remarks and behaviour, but there have been occasions where it has escalated. The Gendarmarie Royale has a particular division to assist tourists, so they should be approached if you are unfortunate enough to suffer any difficulties.

Travel in times of rain and snow

Precipitation, both rain and snow, are a blessing and a curse. For wildlife and for spotting wildlife, rain is essential in a dry area like southern Morocco as it brings life to the parched lands. However, everyday life is not accustomed to rain and heavy and prolonged precipitation can be a nuisance or even dangerous.

Wadis only flow directly after rain. These flows can be as flash floods and often carry debris and rocks. These can be extremely dangerous to casual visitors, as the leading edge of the flood can travel at great speed and arrive without warning. As a simple rule, if it is raining do not enter a wadi either to walk or to camp. Please note too that flood surges can appear many kilometres away from the actual rainfall.

In rare occasions, rain can be substantial. Then it can lead to road closures and travel disruptions. Rock falls and mud washing onto the roads are frequent and in most instances in a few hours the water goes away and the roads re-open. Exceptionally, as in November 2014, all passes across the High Atlas Mountains were blocked and they didn't reopen for three weeks.

Even without these cataclysmic events, mudslides and rock falls can temporarily block routes and interfere with carefully made plans. If travelling in the mountains during the winter, retain some flexibility in your plans to accommodate such forced changes.

Guides – solicited and unsolicited

It used to be very common to be approached by a guide, or by someone who introduces himself as a guide. Even children frequently acted as guide. This has substantially reduced in the last decade as tourists have become more common and children are in school, but it remains not unusual to be approached by locals wishing to act as unsolicited guides, or simply because they have links to a shop/café or have goods to sell.

In towns, it is generally best to avoid assistance. Most towns have even legislated against such unofficial guides and have registered a small number of official ones instead. However, navigating a medina or souk can be very confusing to a visitor. Remember that, although all of the guides are likely to have ties with some of the shops or cafés they can still have valuable information about local history of a place, or where specific goods, food and water can be bought.

In the countryside the guides can be useful, as they often have local information on places to stay or sites to see – things you won't find in guidebooks. However, it is unusual for them to have any real value to the visiting naturalist specifically. Specialist knowledge on finding certain birds, plants or reptiles is not in the standard repertoire of these guides.

There are exceptions of course. There is a long history of local nomads knowing where high profile desert species are. Pharaoh Eagle Owl roost sites are often only found with local assistance. Egyptian Nightjar and Houbara Bustard are two other species for which the chances of seeing will rise immeasurably with local knowledge. However, if you find a guide to show you these birds, it is unlikely that he has any valid information on other species groups.

There are no easy answers to help in spotting a good guide from a bad one. In most places they will find you much quicker than you find them. You can ask on the online forums for recommendations, especially for day trips in the Erg Chebbi and M'hamid areas, or at your accommodation. Whoever you select, remember they are part of the local scene and by employing them you will be supporting the locals understanding the value of these special places and fauna within them. Normally, the fees are modest and you only pay on results.

Regardless of your trust in them or otherwise, do not use guides who offer to show you nesting sites, dig animals out of burrows, or disturb roosting owls or nightjars. If they try, walk away and do not pay. It is important to give a clear signal that any disturbance of the wildlife is totally unacceptable

On entrance fees and private land

In most places, ownership of land is not an intrusive issue. Most areas are unfenced and there is still a nomadic lifestyle with the expectation that livestock can go anywhere and people can therefore do so too.

Farming plots are often only demarcated by stones or irrigation runnels, and therefore there is no physical fencing or boundaries to limit access to the majority of areas in this book. All this gives the impression of open access, which again is not quite the case. Much of the land is privately owned and you should treat it as such even if it appears open access.
Royal preserves and forests are normally fenced and access is only by invitation. Commercial farms and greenhouses, especially around Agadir, Taroudant and Marrakech also do not welcome visitors. However, there is no reason to access them either, as there is little wildlife to be found.
Although most areas are free to access, if approached, be friendly and explain why you are there. Most people are welcoming. Remember the crops are their food and their livelihood so don't walk through them. Irrigation is the life blood of the whole area so don't interfere with the channels, walk in them or modify the diverting sluices.
There are few places where an entrance fee to a site is required. Instead, there is often a small fee to park your car. This can be a formal parking charge or, more frequently, simply paying a minder to look after your car. This is not a rip-off or a tourist trap, but simply part of the local economy and brings added security for you as they will look after the parking area.

Responsible Tourism

'Take nothing but your photos, leave nothing but your footprint' is a well-known phrase that summarises the nature of responsible tourism. It goes without saying that as a visitor to a natural area, you have a responsibility to leave your surroundings and everything in it undisturbed. But maybe it is less obvious what is and what isn't permissible in the case of southern Morocco. So here is what you should be aware of when visiting this area.
Ecotourism and an interest in the natural world are still strange concepts to most Moroccans. They do understand the importance of vegetation, erosion and water preservation but the fact that people are prepared to travel to see barely visible local creatures is a mystery to them. This brings with it often a curiosity of why you are there and what you are doing.
A decade ago, this would be almost impossible to ignore, and children especially would suddenly appear even in the remotest of settings and hassle for sweets, pens and money. But since tourism has grown and schooling has been mandated this has become less of an issue.
Still, a number of locals will try to hustle a few dirhams from visitors. Finding key bird species and selling fossils are the most notable examples of this. These can be good ways of immediately giving something back to the indigenous peoples, but use the opportunity to go beyond a simple financial transaction to understanding about

their lives, the ecosystem and what is and what is not good in terms of behaviour. Fortunately, most restaurants use local seasonal produce. Be accepting of what is available and don't ask for food that obviously needs to be imported. Bush meat is rarely seen, but there is a history of eating reptiles, especially Sandfish (a type of skink, see pages 51 and 123), that should be dissuaded if proposed. Spiny-tailed Lizards are sometimes eaten, their tails being considered a delicacy, however they rarely offered. It is, by contrast, not unusual to see tethered brightly coloured male lizards being held captive at tourist hotspots, the intention is that you have your photo taken with then in return for a few Dirhams. This obviously should be declined. Additionally, supporting local Argan producers, most of whom are organic (even if not officially labelled as such), helps to maintain the threatened and unique habitat of the Argan forest. In a more indirect manner, buying local crafts also supports

Ecotourism code of Conduct

We appeal to every naturalist, birdwatcher and nature photographer to abide by this code of conduct in the interests of birds, wildlife and their environment.

- Learn patterns of animal behaviour – know when not to interfere with an animal's life cycle
- Acquaint yourself with the fragility of the ecosystem – stay on trails that are intended to lessen impacts.
- When out in the field, use good judgement – treat the wildlife, plants and places as if you were their guest.
- Treat other observers and photographers courteously – ask before joining others already in the area.
- Keep distance from birds to avoid stressing or exposing them to danger, exercise restraint and caution during observation, photography, sound recording or filming. Use appropriate lenses to photograph wild animals – if an animal shows stress, move back and use a longer lens.
- Keep well back from burrows, nests, colonies, roosts, display areas and important feeding sites. Do not handle birds, chicks or eggs unless for recognised research activities.
- Before advertising the presence of a rare species of plant or animal, evaluate the potential for disturbance, its surroundings and other people in the area, and proceed only if access is obtained from private landowners. Unless officially publicised, the sites of rare nesting birds should be divulged only to the proper conservation authorities.
- Tactfully inform others if you observe them engaging in inappropriate or harmful behaviour – people often endanger animals unknowingly. If this doesn't help, report inappropriate behaviour to proper authorities.
- Be a role model – educate others by your actions; enhance their understanding.
- Support the protection of important bird habitat.

low intensity agriculture and a harmony with the environment. Conversely, buying goods and food that is not local should be avoided wherever possible.
The biggest negative impact of people is the rubbish that is left behind. Rubbish disposal is a big issue and there is little formal recycling. Provision of public bins is rare and the separation of paper, plastics, glass etc is in its infancy (and only in the cities). Reducing your need for disposable items is the best way to minimise your impact. Also consider where you leave any rubbish that you create. Look for any 'eurobin' collection points or ask at your accommodation.

Walking in the Atlas Mountains

In general, Moroccans do not walk for pleasure and there are no recreational paths. All the paths that exist are therefore for practical reasons of access to villages or moving livestock between grazing sites.

In the High Atlas Mountains, an industry has been built up to support the demand by foreign hikers for walking routes. The existing paths have been linked and there is a network of trails that allow you to make single day hikes but also fully supported multi-day routes across the Alpine region. Some of these paths are well-marked, but there is an industry of trail guides and mules for those who want a more supported experience. Certainly, an attempt to climb Jebel Toubkal cannot be recommended without a guide. Most of the trail heads are within easy reach of Marrakech and centres in Imlil and Ourika are popular with those who want to experience the peace of the mountains away from the crowds. Walking between the remote mountain villages is a good way to experience this.

Note that this is still a remote region. Although it is possible to walk on your own, there are issues in terms of water, food, accommodation and support if something were to go wrong. Water is probably the biggest issue. Although there are surface streams in the higher areas, it is best to consider the water unsafe to drink due to the number of sheep and goats grazing the upper slopes. This means that water needs to be carried with you or you need knowledge of the springs with clean water. Note that there is little in the way of shade and UV levels are extreme at these high altitudes. Also, temperatures can be very high in summer. Heat stroke is a real problem and reducing your core temperature, which is essential, can be very difficult. There is no formal mountain rescue service in the High Atlas and if something goes wrong you will need local support to work it out. Medical support is really only available in the large towns. For these reasons, we advise against longer treks in the High Atlas Mountains without a professional guide.

In terms of weather, heat is obviously not the only issue. Snow is possible at any season, and certainly until April the upper slopes can be swept with freezing rain and snow even when it appears bright and sunny on the steppes below. Dressing appropriately and treating the mountains with respect is crucial to enjoying them.

The Anti-Atlas Mountains are even more extreme in every sense. These mountains are more arid and there are fewer tracks, with none marked as trails. There are fewer villages and little accessible water. Should anything go wrong you are really on your own – a long way from medical aid. This is hard core trekking and scrambling and has its devotees. Some guides are starting to offer guided routes here, mainly focused around Jebel Aklim and Jebel Sanghro. Shorter walks are available for the experienced, and the adventurous.

Maps

As would be expected for an ex-French colony, Morocco is well served with Michelin maps from scales of 1:1,000,000 for the whole country to 1:200,000 for specific areas. The same information is also covered by the *viamichelin* website (www.viamichelin.com).
Google maps and other free apps such as map.me allow for downloading maps so that they can be used offline from an internet connection. A word of warning, the travel times given often turn out to be optimistic and not all tracks in the field are shown on these maps. Vice versa, the app maps suggest the existence of small roads or drivable tracks that are in reality not suitable to navigate with a normal car. For the proposed routes, the maps in the book suffice, and in the majority of locations are close to the main roads. Certainly, for nowhere on the routes in this book is it essential to have a 4-wheel drive. The areas in the Sahara around Erg Chebbi and M'Hamid should really only be accessed with a guide, and certainly not in a lone vehicle. Help will be remote if it is needed.

Additional information

Recommended reading

Apart from the usual guidebooks and field guides we recommend the following books and websites.
Walking: Most websites on walking are focused on the High Atlas Mountains and are promotional vehicles for various local trekking companies. Getting an overview of what is available and where to go can be difficult. One such attempt to assist visitors is *Moroccan Atlas - The Trekking Guide* by Alan Palmer (Trailblazer Publications; ISBN-13: 978-1905864591). A trek route map is also available *Morocco & High Atlas* (Terraquest; ISBN-13: 978-8361155577). Less information is available on the Anti-Atlas, however, *Walks and Scrambles in the Moroccan Anti-Atlas* by David Wood (Cicerone; ISBN-13: 978-1852848095) offers a range of walks, mainly in the vicinity of Tafraout.

Flora: Although online resources are improving substantially, there remains a rapidly changing taxonomy and no real printed resource to fall back on. In the absence of this, the best source of local information is website Plant Biodiversity of south-western Morocco (**www.teline.fr/en**).

Reptiles and Amphibians: The beautifully produced, but expensive *Amphibians and Reptiles of Morocco* by Gabriel Martinez de Mármol et al (Edition Chimera; ISBN 978-3-89973-117-0) is the new standard for the country. The website **www.moroccoherps.com** is produced by the same authors and is not as complete but serves as a good introduction.

Mammals: The standard field guide for the Western Palearctic is *Mammals of Europe, North Africa and the Middle East* by Stephanie Aulangnier et al (Helm; ISBN-13: 9781408113998). It also covers this region. The taxonomy adopted is a little out of date in places and you will need to supplement the information with recent data from the internet. The website coordinated by Jon Hall, **www.mammalwatching.com**, is a good source for mammal fans and includes trip reports and taxonomy.

Birds: The definitive European field guide, *Collins Bird Guide* by Lars Svensson (Harper Collins, ISBN-13, 9780007268146) fortunately also covers the whole of Morocco. This is also available as a smartphone app, that has songs and calls as a bonus. For those who want a more detailed look at the special birds of this area *Morocco: sharing the birds* by Arnoud van den Berg (The Sound Approach: ISBN 9789081093392) gives a deep insight to the endemics and related species. The website Maghreb Ornitho (**www.magornitho.org**) keeps you up to date with local news and information on all things bird related. Observation.org and eBird.org are two online resources for bird sighting and can be a wealth of information of what is around, including hotspots check lists and bar charts at **www.ebird.org/ebird/hotspots**. For additional bird calls and songs **www.xeno-canto.org** is very useful, especially as a few species here are not included in the Collins app.

Butterflies and dragonflies: The standard guide of this area is the *Collins Butterfly Guide* by Tolman and Lewington (Harper Collins; ISBN-13: 780953139941). For Morocco itself this can be supplemented by more in-depth review of the Butterflies in Morocco, which is solely available in French, *Les Papillons de Jour au Maroc* by Michel R Tarrier and Jean Delacre (Biotype: Collection Parthenope; ISBN 9782914817165) however note that this does not include the skippers. There are updates given on Michel Tarrier's website, **www.micheltarrier.com**

For dragonflies we recommend *A Field Guide to the Dragonflies of Britain & Europe* (2nd Edition) by Dijkstra & Lewington (Bloomsbury Wildlife; ISBN-13: 978-1472943958). There are no specialist texts for the other insects and mix of books regarding the species of the Mediterranean and specialist websites is the way forward.

Observation tips

Nearby destinations worth a visit

The Middle Atlas is another area that is distinct and easily accessible from Marrakech, even though most visitors approach this area from the northern cities of Rabat, Casablanca or Fes.

Being further north, the desert ecosystem is absent, and the lower mountains may not seem as attractive to the first-time visitor as the High Atlas. However, it is home to a number of endemic species and landscapes that are scarce or not present further south. The prime amongst the latter are the forests of Atlas Cedar. These are home to Barbary Macaques and in late spring and summer, to Atlas Pied Flycatchers. A whole range of flora is endemic to the area, but most species are closely related to Mediterranean ones and therefore are something for the connoisseur.

The Middle Atlas lakes also have a range of endangered waterfowl that is not represented further south. There is an internationally important population of White-headed Duck and both Red-crested Pochard and Red-knobbed Coot are plentiful. Midelt sits between the High Atlas and the Middle Atlas and the steppes here, although similar to those in our area, hold a viewable population of the almost mythical Dupont's Lark.

Instead of heading north, the more adventurous traveller could also head further south along the coast to the area formally known as Western Sahara. Dahkla is a centre of kite surfing, so tourists are not as scarce here as perhaps you would think. This edge of the Sahara holds species not found further north and are true desert dwellers. African orientated reptiles, a few special birds (e.g. Cricket Warbler, Golden Nightjar, Dunn's Lark and Black-crowned Sparrow Lark) and special mammals are all possible (including Golden Wolf, Striped Hyena and Sand Cat). It is really only in the last decade that this area has been explored at all, and the area as a whole remains internationally sensitive.

Finding snakes, lizards, scorpions and the like

Reptiles and scorpions are most easily found when they are sunning themselves early in the day, or in and around burrows in sandy soil or in crevices or under stones in rocky areas. Turning stones can be a good way of finding a whole range of geckos, agamas, lizards and scorpions.

Care is needed as some creatures that hide here are poisonous and potentially even deadly. Never hold the turned stone in your hand as something might be on it! Place the stones back exactly where you found them and do it quickly so as not to disturb the creatures you've found for too long and make them into something else's easy meal.

Evening is the best time to search for reptiles in the field. The temperatures may still be high and as dusk turns to early evening you have the possibility of a mix of diurnal and nocturnal reptiles. Road surfaces that hold warmth after the sun has set can be popular with reptiles. Underground cisterns and other tanks can also attract amphibians, snakes and larger lizards as they use them to escape the heat of the day.

Birdwatching the arid steppes and Sahara

Finding birds in the steppes and desert is often a challenge. Population densities are very low and outside of the breeding season they can be highly nomadic. Not all areas are equally attractive to them, so one place can have not a single bird whilst another one that looks identical has multiple birds of various species. The adaptation of each species is slightly different and therefore there is not a single place where all the birds may be found.

Nevertheless, a careful examination of the landscape is key to finding the hotspots. Looking for the change in rock type or following the wash out lines and vegetation can show where the food is and therefore where the birds are most likely to be. During migration, birds can be plentiful and congregated in places with vegetation, especially if water is present. However, there may not be any representatives of the highly adapted desert specialists that you have travelled here to see. They are in the more extreme habitats where only they can eke out a living.

Visits just after dawn and again at dusk are the most productive, as birds are more active than in the middle of the day. However, in contrast to what you are used to in Europe, dawn itself can be eerily quiet. This is the coldest part of the day and many birds prefer it to be a bit warmer before they get moving. In late spring and summer, the temperature rises at an alarming rate and with it comes heat shimmer, mirages and chromatic changes in the harsh light can make viewing difficult.

Using your vehicle as a hide is a good way of watching birds, and certainly of finding those hotspots. However, once you've found a promising place, slowly walking across the habitat can be just as successful for larks and wheatears. Most desert species are ambivalent to watchers, as long as you are quiet. With patience you can often get superb views. Sitting on a vantage point and scanning with binoculars, or even better with a telescope, can also be very productive, especially in establishing where the birds are. The majority of the species also cannot survive without water to drink. Water sources are hotspots for birds. Notably the sandgrouse will travel miles to preferred watering holes. The best are undoubtedly small remote pools far from any other sources of water. Even dripping taps will do! But remember, not all species drink and even those that do will not need to drink every day.

Guided Birding excursions

There are relatively few natural history guides and those that are there are predominantly focussed on birds. Most speak some English or French (or both) and can arrange for the package of vehicle and guiding. Mainly they operate either around Marrakech or in the desert areas around Erg Chebbi and M'hamid. Recently, it appears that some are offering their services on the coast around Essaouira and Agadir. For offshore trips from Agadir, the best opportunity is to join a sports fishing charter or charter a boat yourself. A number of companies have offered places on boats over the last decade, but these are mainly with skippers and their birding skills are limited. Basic ingredients for chum can be collected from fishermen the day before. Look for names that are recommended on the European bird forums including www.birdforum.net.

Birdwatching list

The numbers between the brackets () refer to the routes from page 139 onwards. In addition to the ones listed below, there is also a wide range of vagrants that can make birding here both exciting and pioneering.

Shelducks and ducks: Ruddy Shelduck is plentiful south of High Atlas and big flocks can build up inland (6, 11, 13, 18, 22, 24 and 25). Common Shelduck are scarce and exclusively coastal (24 and 25). Dabbling ducks are more plentiful than diving ducks and can be found throughout the winter, particularly Teal, Shoveler and Pintail (6, 11, 22, 24 and 25). Flocks of Garganey are found on migration wherever there is water. Marbled Duck potentially breeds, but most head further north in spring and are best searched for in the winter (6, 11, 24 and 25). A few diving ducks can be found, mainly Pochard and Tufted Duck, sometimes accompanied by small numbers of Ferruginous Duck. They are normally on the coastal estuaries (22, 24 and 25). but if rains are good, also far inland (e.g. 11). Sea ducks are almost unheard of, but occasionally Common Scoters are found offshore.

Partridge and quail: The Barbary Partridge is widespread except in the most arid parts and can be plentiful around agricultural areas. These same places are also attractive to Quail that pass through on migration.

Grebes: Great Crested Grebe is relatively common both inland and on the coast (6 and 24). Little Grebe is found in lowland areas, particularly in the Souss Valley (15,18 and 25). In winter, it may be joined by dispersing Black-necked Grebes that breed in the Middle Atlas Lakes.

Gannet, shearwaters and petrels: A number of species pass offshore attracted by the conditions created by the Canary Current. From shore the most likely species to be seen are Gannet and Cory's Shearwater. By taking a boat, a whole host of species becomes more likely including North Atlantic breeders such as Madeiran and White-faced Storm-Petrels, Cape Verde, Balearic and Manx Shearwaters and perhaps a migrant Great or Sooty Shearwater from further afield.

Flamingos, cormorants, spoonbills, ibises, herons and egrets: The numerous waterways and the coastal estuaries attract water birds, although few stay to breed.

Greater Flamingos are present year-round at a few sites on the coast (22, 24 and 25) and inland (11) but no evidence of breeding has been found. Cormorants are also found inland as well as the coast. It is only here that you can find the distinctive, white-breasted Moroccan form (22, 24 and 25). Spoonbill is mainly present on passage, as are Glossy Ibis, Purple and Squacco Herons. Little Egrets can be found in all months, as can Cattle Egrets, the latter being widespread in agricultural areas rather than being tied to wetlands. In the last decade or so, Great Egrets have started to appear, no doubt originating from the range expansion in Spain.

The most iconic of these species is without doubt the Northern Bald Ibis. The coast both north and south of Agadir is among the very few places in the world where it is found (22 and 25).

Storks: White Stork is resident throughout the year and can be supplemented in winter with birds from further north. Breeding birds can be seen nesting in most towns and villages. The Black Stork is mainly a winter visitor and passage migrant and can be found most frequently by the coast or by inland waters (6 and 25).

Eagles: Of the resident eagles, Bonelli's is the most frequently encountered and occurs mainly on the southern edge of the High Atlas (2, 3, 4, 5, 7 and site E on page 159) but also on the coast (25). Golden Eagle is a scarce resident of the High Atlas. Short-toed and Booted Eagles are both migrants and summer visitors, although the latter species will winter in some years south of High Atlas (6, site C on page 174). They are widespread, however the Argan forests are the best places for them (17, 18, site C on page 210). Tawny Eagle is no longer breeding, however occasional birds do wander, especially into the Souss (17, site C on page 210).

Other birds of prey: Although Griffon, Rüppell's and Egyptian Vultures are seen infrequently,this is not an area to search for them and no breeding birds are known. Bearded Vulture is also incredibly rare but is known to have bred in the Toubkal Massif and probably still does so. Harriers of all the European species are known from the area. Marsh Harrier breeds and is a familiar bird on the coast and wherever there is water. Hen and Pallid Harriers are winter visitors (the latter is rare but increasing) and Montagu's passes through on migration. Osprey winters on the coast and most estuaries have one or two birds (22, 24 and 25), Black-winged Kite is resident and can be found in the Souss Valley (18, site C on page 210, site E on page 211). Black Kite is a common migrant, but does not stay to breed. Both Sparrowhawk and Goshawk are most likely to be encountered on the northern High Atlas forested slopes (2, 3, C on page 149). Lastly, the cirtensis form of 'Long-legged' Buzzard here is likely to have its taxonomic status changed in the near future as it is increasingly regarded as a distinct subspecies of Common Buzzard. They are widespread, but certainly commoner south of the High Atlas Mountains. The Dark Chanting Goshawk, once one of the key birds of the Argan forest with an endemic subspecies, is now probably extinct.

Falcons: Common Kestrel is a widespread resident and Lesser Kestrel a summer visitor and migrant that breeds just north of this region. Eleonora's Falcon breeds on an island off Essaouira (site A on page 240) and may be seen elsewhere on the coast during the summer and autumn. The same coast holds breeding Barbary Falcons (now considered a subspecies of Peregrine Falcon). In winter, Barbary Falcons can be found across the whole region. Lanner Falcon is also widespread but occurs in very low numbers. Although it could turn up almost anywhere, the best places to look are in the High Arid Steppes or in the Sahara (9, site D on page 194).

Gallinule, rails and crakes: Moorhen and Coot are common wetland birds, Red-knobbed Coot is rather scarce but in winter it is worth searching any coot flocks especially at Oued Massa (25), Dayet Srij (11) or Ouarzazate reservoir (6). A few Western Swamphen (Purple Gallinule) winter as far south as here and can be looked for on the coast. Spotted, Little and Baillon's Crakes all pass through and as always, they are difficult to find. The inland rivers are often the best places for them (Iriri and Aoulouz).

Bustards: Houbara is a scarce inhabitant of the gravel plains close to the Algerian border and one species that you will probably need help from local guides to stand any chance of finding.

Waders: Although normally considered to be coastal birds, many waders cross the area in a broad front during migration. Inland, Wood, Green and Curlew Sandpipers will join the more numerous Ringed, Little Ringed and Kentish Plovers and Ruff. Black-winged Stilt and Avocet are limited to the larger water bodies and the coast (6, 11, 22, 24 and 25). Many of the estuaries attract large flocks of wintering Curlew, Whimbrel, Godwit, Redshank and Greenshank. Stone Curlew is a breeding species in the steppes (6) and drier areas of the Souss Valley and will form large flocks in the non-breeding season. One of the iconic species of the south is the Cream-colored Courser which can be found both on the High Steppe (8) and the Sahara (10, 11, 14).

Skuas, gulls and terns: All of the Western Palearctic skuas are possible on the Atlantic coast but only the Arctic Skua can be said to be regular, particularly during migration when the number of terns builds up (Arctic Skuas chase terns for food). Yellow-legged and Lesser Black-backed Gulls are frequent on the coast. Audouin's Gull is a common non-breeding visitor and the area around Tamri is a particular favourite (22). Slender-billed Gulls are uncommon and a few Little Gulls can be found, especially in late winter in the same areas. Kittiwake and Sabine's Gulls are true pelagic species and therefore only possible from a boat off Agadir. Terns are common along the coast in both spring and autumn with Caspian, Common, Little and Gull-billed Terns being numerous at times (22, 24). The most plentiful is Sandwich Tern and these often hang around the whole winter. Lesser Crested Tern can also join the tern flocks, especially in the autumn around Tamri and Oued Souss (22, 24) and West African Crested Tern has started drifting up the coast after breeding. No doubt, both are taking advantage of the cold offshore current (24). Black Tern tends to join the tern flocks on the coast. In contrast, Whiskered Tern can be found across the area and seem to be fond of Dayet Srij (11).

Sandgrouse: Normally best seen in their morning flights or at their target waterholes, five species are possible. By far the most widespread is the Black-bellied Sandgrouse, which is sometimes joined by Pin-tailed Sandgrouse from further north (8, site A on page 193). In the Sahara both Spotted and Crowned Sandgrouse are the most plentiful species (11, 14). Lichtenstein's Sandgrouse is the scarcest, and this species is best searched for in the remote areas of the Anti-Atlas (20).

Pigeons and doves: Collared Doves are ubiquitous in the towns and villages, but as you go further south, they are increasingly replaced by Laughing Dove. Wood Pigeon are common in the agricultural areas. Care is needed to find pure wild Rock Dove (most populations interbreed with feral pigeons). The southern edge of the High Atlas is the best place to look them (7; site A and B on page 173, and site E on page 175). Turtle Dove pass through as a passage migrant, and still good numbers can be seen of this declining species, especially in autumn.

Cuckoos: Both Common Cuckoo and Great Spotted Cuckoo are passage migrants, although some of the latter species remain to breed in the Souss valley (18, sites B and C pages 208-210).

Owls: The Pharaoh Eagle Owl is a species from the southern edge of the High Atlas southwards to the Sahara edge. Roost sites are often known by local Berbers. The local Maghreb Owl has recently been separated from Tawny Owl as a distinct species and is a scarce resident on the wooded northern slopes of the High Atlas and in the Souss Valley (site B on page 157 and site D on page 210). Barn Owl is another scarce local resident, most often seen in lowland areas. Little Owl is plentiful and widespread. Scops Owl is a scarce migrant through the area. Short-eared Owl is a fairly numerous migrant, or perhaps, as it migrates during the day, just more visible than the nocturnal Scops Owl.

Nightjars: Egyptian Nightjar is a Sahara species that returns in February and leaves in October. Roost sites are known to a few guides. Red-necked Nightjar is more widespread in the coastal edge (24, site A on page 232) and lowland steppe (sites C, D and E on page 210-211) but is little reported. European Nightjar is a passage migrant and rarely encountered.

Swifts: Little Swifts are birds of inland towns and are present all year around. Pallid Swift arrives earlier in the year than the more familiar Common Swift but both are a familiar sight, often in mixed flocks in towns and especially over water. White-rumped Swift appears to be increasing and a look out for this late arriving migrant should be made in the High Atlas, particularly around Imlil (2) where it is known to breed. Finally, the rather enigmatic (in Moroccan terms at least) Plain

Swift needs to be mentioned. There are records of them wintering along the coast from Essaouira to Agadir, and even breeding around Tamri, however there still remain few conclusive records.

Bee-eaters, rollers and hoopoes: Both European and Blue-cheeked Bee-eaters stay to breed. Whilst European is one of the early migrants, with most passing through to Europe, the Blue-cheeked Bee-eater is a later migrant, mainly appearing from April onwards in the far south (11, 12, 13, 14, 20 and 21). Roller is also a passage migrant in this part of Morocco, breeding further north in the country. Hoopoes are resident and widespread.

Woodpeckers: Although Great Spotted Woodpecker is widespread, it is the endemic Levaillant's Woodpecker that is the main interest. It is a species of the High Atlas Mountain river valleys (2, 4 and site B on page 157) and after breeding it heads further up the mountains appearing often above the tree line searching for ants.

Larks: Morocco is an area of diversity for larks and up to fifteen species have been recorded in this area. The confusing three Galerida larks include the widespread Crested and Thekla's Larks and the recently 'split' Saharan specialist, the Maghreb Lark (the latter on 10, 11, 14 and site D on page 194). Temminck's Larks are plentiful in the High Arid Steppes (8, 9) but higher up the Atlas Mountains they are replaced by Horned Lark. Two breeding species are big draws: the Hoopoe Lark and the Thick-billed Lark. Both are charismatic in their own ways and both inhabit similar habitats (8, 9, 10, 11 and 14). The Desert Lark is a species of rocky areas and commonest on the High Arid Steppes (6) whilst the similar-looking Bar-tailed Lark prefers the sandy areas of the Sahara (10,11 and14). Dunn's Lark remains a scarce nomadic visitor to the area. Of the short-toed larks, most Greater are migrants through the area, but Lesser (Mediterranean) Short-toed breed on the coast (25).

Swallows and martins: Barn Swallow and House Martin are common throughout, whilst Sand Martins are a passage migrant attracted to wet areas. Red-rumped Swallow is a familiar species across the lower arid steppes and the Souss Valley, whilst the Brown-throated Martin is only reliably present in the coastal estuaries (25, site A on page 240). Crag Martin is a resident species of the mountains, but in the far south these can be joined by Pale Crag Martin (19, 20, and 21) during the summer months.

Pipits and wagtails: With the exception of Yellow Wagtail, which is a numerous migrant, the other pipits and wagtails are found in small numbers. White Wagtail and Meadow Pipit are primarily winter visitors, however the Moroccan *subpersonata* form of White Wagtail is found south of the High Atlas from the Sahara to the coast, being limited to river valleys. Red-throated Pipit is a scarce winter visitor and migrant. Tree Pipit is also a migrant. Water Pipit can be found in the High Atlas at high altitude, where Grey Wagtail (1, 2 and 5) is found near the rivers. Tawny Pipit is a lowland breeder, being most numerous by the coast (22, 24 and 25).

Dippers and accentor: Both the Dipper and the Alpine Accentor are mountain specialists with relict populations in the Alpine zone of the High Atlas (1).

Wrens and bulbuls: Wren has a limited range in the High Atlas (2, 4) whilst the Common Bulbul is a familiar bird in gardens and parks across well-vegetated lowland areas.

Thrushes: Blackbird is widespread and common, but the other species of thrushes need to be searched for. Mistle Thrush is a species of the Sub-alpine and Alpine meadows in the High Atlas (1, 2, 4 and 5). Song Thrush is a winter visitor in low numbers and mainly to the coast and lowland area. Ring Ouzel is also a winter visitor and prefers the open juniper woodland in the Sub-alpine zone (4). Blue Rock Thrush is resident and can be common on the southern slopes of the High Atlas and across the High Arid Steppes (2, 4, 6 and sites A, B, C, D and E on pages 173-175). Rock Thrush is a scarce local migrant and breeds in the alpine zone of the High Atlas.

Nightingales, chats, redstarts and allies: Nightingale is a widespread migrant and will sing in the well-vegetated valleys even to the edge of the Sahara. Stonechat, Robin and Bluethroat winter on the coast, in the Souss Valley and even into the High Arid Steppes. Rufous-tailed Scrub Robin is another migrant breeder across the area (11, 19 and 20). Whinchat is a migrant and rather scarce. Of the redstarts, Moussier's is a local breeder in the High Atlas Mountains reaching the Alpine zone (2, 4 and site E on page 159), but winters across the Arid Steppes to the north and south (e.g. 6 and sites A, B, C on pages 156-157 and sites B and C on pages 173-174). Black Redstart is widespread in towns and villages, whilst Common Redstart is a migrant that can be found across the whole region.

Wheatears: Wheatears are a conspicuous group and include nine species. Black Wheatear is a species of the mountains and rocky ravines (2, 7). The White-crowned Wheatear favours stony steppes and Sahara to the south of the High Atlas (6, 10, 12). The same steppe areas are home to the endemic Maghreb Wheatear (9, site A on page 173), previously regarded as a race of Mourning Wheatear. Red-rumped and Desert Wheatears are fond of the High Arid Steppes (6, 8, 9, 10), but can also be found in sandier areas of the Sahara. That latter region attracts an increasing number of Isabelline Wheatears in recent years (11, 14). Western Black-eared Wheatear and Northern Wheatear are both migrants through the area and can be widespread then. However, the other endemic, Atlas (Seebohm's) Wheatear is a local breeder in the mountains up to the Alpine zone and winters further south. It tends to arrive later than the initial passage of Northern.

Warblers and babblers: Zitting Cisticola is a widespread species especially along waterways and the coast (22, 24 and 25). A similar range is followed by Cetti's Warbler. Reed Warblers are represented by both the African and European forms, variously regarded as races or two distinct species. The former is resident in the

Souss and at the coast (18, 22, 24 and 25) whilst the latter is a widespread migrant. Sedge and Great Reed Warblers are also migrants, the latter being very scarce. Moustached Warbler is a scarce winter visitor, again to the coast (22, 24 and 25). Chiffchaff is a ubiquitous winter visitor. Willow Warbler, Western Bonelli's Warbler and Iberian Chiffchaff are all migrants.

Eleven species of *Sylvia* warblers are present in the area, most being migrants that pass on a broad front, but can be easiest to see on the edge of the Sahara in autumn (11,12, 14 and sites C and D on page 194). Dartford Warbler is a species that is believed to be solely a winter visitor from further north. Sardinian Warblers are common and widespread residents. African Desert Warbler is a bird of the Halfa grass in the Sahara (11, 14). Tristram's Warbler winters in the same general area but breeds in the Sub-alpine zone and dry, south-facing slopes of the High Atlas Mountains (4, site E on page 159). Another species that is a short-distance migrant is the Scrub Warbler, which summers on rocky slopes on the High Arid Steppes (21 and site A on page 193), but reaches the Sahara in winter (10,11). Western Olivaceous Warblers are mostly passing migrants, but a few breed, especially on the coast (25). Its sister species, the Eastern Olivaceous Warbler, is a breeding species on the edge of the Sahara, particularly favouring tamarisks on the edge of palmeries. Melodious Warbler is solely a migrant.

Finally, Fulvous Babbler is also a species of the palmeries and desert edge and can be found around Erg Chebbi and in the Drâa and Souss valleys (11, 12, 14 and site C on page 210 and site E on page 211).

Crests: Firecrest is a relatively scarce inhabitant of the High Atlas forest all the way up to the tree line (4, site E on page 151).

Flycatchers: Atlas Flycatcher (a recent 'split' from Pied Flycatcher) is very scarce in the High Atlas. Breeding has been proven in Imlil and on the R307 crossing of the Massif. Spotted and Pied Flycatchers can be very common on passage especially in the autumn at migration hotspots (3, B on page 149, E on page 151).

Tits: African Blue Tit is a species of the northern part of the coast up to the tree line of the High Atlas (2, 3, 4), where it is often joined by Coal Tit. Great Tit is found in the Souss Valley and lower orchards.

Nuthatches and treecreepers: Both Nuthatch and Short-toed Treecreeper are scarce species of the High Atlas pine forests.

Shrikes: Great Grey Shrikes are a common sight across the country. Woodchat Shrike is a migrant that passes on a broad front across the area and can be common on the coast (22, 24, 25). Black-crowned Tchagra is another coastal species, found especially around well-vegetated estuaries where it is more often heard than seen (25).

Crows and allies: Maghreb Magpie (a recent 'split' from Common Magpie) is present in agricultural areas and along the coast (24, 25 and site A on page 156).

Jay is a scarce bird of the High Atlas forests. In the Alpine zone both Red-billed and Alpine Choughs can be found (1, 2, 5). In the mountains the Northern Raven can be plentiful but it is replaced in the Sahara by the Brown-necked Raven (11, 14 and site, D on page 186).

Starlings: Spotless Starling is common in agricultural areas especially on the Haouz Plain and the Souss Valley. Golden Oriole is a migrant through the area in March and April and then back south again in September.

Sparrows: Desert Sparrow is a species of palmeries and tamarisks on the edge of sand dunes. It is limited to Erg Chebbi and M'hamid (11 and 14). House Sparrow is common. Spanish Sparrow is a bird of agricultural areas (25, site A on page 156) and tied to stork nests for breeding. Rock Sparrow is widespread in the High Atlas in the Sub-alpine zone and higher (2, 4) and will form large flocks in winter (1).

Finches and allies: Serin is common throughout. Chaffinches (the Moroccan race africana) are commonest in the High Atlas pine forests and can be joined by Brambling and Siskin in winter (1, 2). The local subspecies of Common Crossbill is tied to the Aleppo pines in the same areas. Where deciduous trees are present in the mountains, Hawfinch can be found. The endemic African Crimson-winged Finch is a bird of the Alpine zone and is best looked for at the ski area at Oukaïmeden (1), although in theory it can be present on any of the high peaks. Goldfinch, Greenfinch and Linnet are widespread, especially in lowland agricultural areas. The Trumpeter Finch is a bird of High Steppe and Sahara (8, 9, 10, 11, 12, 13, 14, 19, 20 and 21) and can flock in large numbers out of the breeding season.

Buntings: House Bunting is by far the commonest species and found around buildings and houses throughout. Rock Bunting is found in rocky areas on the edge of the mountains (1, 2). Cirl Bunting and Corn Bunting are found in the agricultural areas in the Souss Valley and along the coast (15, 16 and 25).

ACKNOWLEDGEMENTS

Writing any book and especially a Crossbill guide relating to such a diverse and remote area as Southern Morocco is no easy task and there are a number of special people without whom it would not be possible.

I have to thank (blame) Colin Richardson for getting me hooked on deserts in the first place. Although in a different continent, this love and drive to understand this most extreme of biomes has been with me ever since. I have to thank Brahim Mezane and Lahcen Taouchikht whose practical knowledge of the desert areas makes it a joy to travel with them. I would also like to thank the advice of Jean-Pierre Peltier and Michel Tarrier on flora and butterflies, not only for the dedication that has gone into their websites but also their patience in responding to my questions and requests for assistance. I would also like to thank all the previous pioneers cross the flora and fauna whose hard work and publications have enabled both me and others to build on the foundations they have formed. I will also thank Chris Griffin for his company and humour on recent trips and particularly for the photographic product that illustrates this book.
 I also need to thank the Crossbill team, especially John Cantelo, whose trip with me to the area sparked the initial idea and Dirk Hilbers who has had the thankless task of pushing me to the end of this project through the pandemic.

Lastly I would like to thank my girls, my wife Liz and daughter Rebecca, who have put up with me in the field and during planning other trips and will now see a bit more of me now this two year adventure is complete.

Martin Pitt, November 2022

PICTURE & ILLUSTRATION CREDITS

Crossbill Guides / Hilbers Dirk: 35 (t), 83, 89 (t+b), 211,
van Deijk, Jurriën: 44 (b), 54, 81(t), 109 (t), 113 (t+b), 116 (t), 125, 127 (b), 145 (b), 188, 207 (b), 221
Folkers, Jack: 60, 61, 106
Griffin, Chris: 4 (1st from top), 33 (b), 49 (t), 78, 100, 101 (b), 108, 110 (t), 114, 115, 130, 142, 155 (t), 156, 162, 163, 166 (b), 169 (b), 170, 172 (t), 178, 179, 181 (b), 182 (b), 183, 184, 190, 192, 194 (t+b), 199, 227 (b), 236 (b), 239 (t+b),
Pitt, Rebecca: cover
Pitt, Martin: 4 (2nd, 3rd, 4th from top), 5 (2nd, 3rd, 4th from top); 12, 13, 16, 18, 19, 22, 25, 29, 32, 33 (t), 34, 36, 37, 39 (t+b), 42 (b), 43, 45, 46, 47, 53 (t+b), 55, 56, 58, 59 (t+b), 63, 64, 65, 66, 68, 69, 71 (t+b), 75 (t+b), 77, 85 (b), 92, 93 (t), 105 (t), 121, 128, 132, 134 (b), 135, 136, 140, 143, 146, 149 (b), 150 (t+b), 153 (t), 155 (b), 147, 158, 159, 164, 166 (t), 167, 168, 172 (b), , 173 (t+b), 178-179, 182 (t), 186, 189, 195, 196, 197, 198 (t), 201(t+b), 203, 204, 206 (t+b), 207 (t), 208, 209, 211, 214, 215, 216, 218, 219 (t+b), 222, 224 (t+b), 226, 227 (t), 228, 231 (b), 233, 234, 236 (t), 238, 240, 241, 244
Felix, Rob: 10, 21, 42 (t), 48, 50, 51, 87, 96, 99, 119, 122, 123, 131, 134 (t), 175, 181 (t), 193, 198 (b)
Rowling, Matt: 38 (t+b), 126
Swinkels, Constant: 26, 67, 85 (t), 88, (91 (b), 93 (b), 94, 102, 107, 127 (b), 230 (t), 231 (t)
Wijn, Peter: cover, 5 (top), 17, 35 (b), 40, 44 (t), 49 (b), 81 (b), (92 t), 109 (b), 110 (b), 116 (b), 117, 141, 145 (t), 147, 149 (t), 152, 153 (b), 169 (t), 230

All illustrations by Crossbill Guides / Horst Wolter

SPECIES LIST & TRANSLATION

The following list comprises all species mentioned in this guidebook and gives their scientific, German and Dutch names. Some have an asterisk (*) behind them, indicating an unofficial name. See page 7 for more details.

Plants

English	Scientific	German	Dutch
Acacia, Flat-topped	Vachellia tortilis raddiana	Schirmakazie	Schermacacia
Afessas	Warionia saharae	Atlas-Golddistel*	Atlas-gouddistel*
Asphodel, Branched	Asphodelus ramosus	Ästiger Affodill	Vertakte affodil*
Asphodel, Broken	Asphodelus refractus	Wüsten Affodill*	Woestijnaffodil*
Asphodel, White	Asphodelus tenuifolius	Dünnblättriger Affodil	Dunbladige affodil*
Cedar, Atlas	Cedrus atlantica	Atlaszeder	Atlasceder
Cistanche, Violet	Cistanche violacea	Violette Cistanche	Paarse reuzenbremraap*
Cistanche, Yellow	Cistanche phelypaea	Gelbe Cistanche	Gele reuzenbremraap*
Cyprus, Moroccan	Cupressus atlantica	Atlas-Zypresse	Marokkaanse cipres
Daffodil, Hoop-pettycoat	Corbularia bulbocodium	Reifrock-Narzisse	Hoepelroknarcis
Dock, Bladder	Rumex simpliciflorus	Blasen-Ampfer	Blaaszuring
Fern, Haresfoot	Davallia canariensis	Davallia*	Davallia*
Flower, Spider	Cleome africana	Afrikanischer Spinnenblume*	Afrikaanse kattensnor*
Fritillary, Maroccan*	Fritillaria macrocarpa	Grossfrüchtige Schachblume*	Marokkaanse kievitsbloem*
Fritillary, Spanish	Fritillaria lusitanica	Portugiesische Schachblume	Iberische kievitsbloem
Grass, Halfa	Desmostachya bipinnata	Halfagras	Halfa gras*
Gum, Barbary	Vachellia gummifera	Marokkanischer Akazie*	Marokkaanse acacia*
Juniper, Phoenician	Juniperus phoenicea	Phönizischer Wacholder	Phoenicische jeneverbes
Juniper, Prickly	Juniperus oxycedrus	Stechwacholder	Spaanse jeneverbes
Juniper, Spanish	Juniperus thurifera (var. africana)	Spanischer Wacholder	Spaanse sevenboom*
Laurel, Canary Island	Laurus novocanariensis	Kanaren-Lorbeer	Canarische laurier
Lavender, Fringed	Lavandula dentata	Französischer Lavendel	Tandlavendel
Lavender, Moroccan	Lavandula maroccana	Marokkanischer Lavendel*	Marokkaanse lavendel*
Melon, Desert	Citrullus colocynthis	Koloquinte	Kolokwint
Milkweed, Sodom's Apple	Calotropis procera	Oscher	Sodomsappel zijdeplant*
Nut, Barbary	Moraea sisyrinchium	Mittags-Schwertlilie	Barbarijse lis*
Oleander	Nerium oleander	Oleander	Oleander
Orchid, Dingy Bee	Ophrys fusca	Braune Ragwurz	Bruine orchis
Orchid, Mirror	Ophrys speculum	Spiegel-Ragwurz	Spiegelorchis
Orchid, Omega	Ophrys (omegifera) dyris	Marokkanische Ragwurz	Dyris orchis*
Orchid, Robust Marsh	Dactylorhiza elata	Hohes Knabenkraut	Grote rietorchis
Orchid, Sawfly	Ophrys tenthredinifera	Wespen-Ragwurz	Wolzweverorchis
Orchid, Woodcock	Ophrys scolopax	Schnepfen-Ragwurz	Snippenorchis

English	Scientific	German	Dutch
Orchid, Yellow Bee	Ophrys lutea	Gelbe Ragwurz	Gele orchis
Palm, Date	Phoenix dactylifera	Echte Dattelpalme	Dadelpalm
Palm, Dwarf	Chamaerops humilis	Zwergpalme	Dwergpalm
Pheasant-eye	Adonis annua	Herbst-Adonisröschen	Herfstadonis
Pine, Aleppo	Pinus halepensis	Aleppokiefer	Aleppoden
Pistachio, Wild	Pistacia atlantica	Atlantische Pistazie	Atlas pistache
Poplar, Desert	Populus euphratica	Euphrat-Pappel	Eufraat-populier*
Ramad	Euphorbia calyptrata	Ramad*	Ramad*
Rockrose, Canary	Helianthemum canariense	Kanaren-Sonnenröschen	Canarisch zonneroosje*
Spleenwort, African	Asplenium aethiopicum	Afrikanischer Streifenfarn*	Afrikaanse streepvaren*
Spurge, King Juba's	Euphorbia regis-jubae	König-Juba-Wolfsmilch	Koning Juba wolfsmelk
Thorn, Camel	Vachellia horrida	Kameldorn	Kameeldoorn
Thuja, Barbary	Tetraclinis articulata	Sandarakbaum	Sandarak
Thumb, Desert	Cynomorium coccineum	Malteserschwamm	Maltezer paddenstoel
Traganum	Traganum moquinii	Moquins Traganum	Traganum
Tree, Argan	Argania spinosa	Arganbaum	Arganboom
Tree, Atlas Mastic	See: Pistachio, Wild		
Tree, Dragon	Dracaena draco	Drachenbaum	Drakenbloedboom

Mammals

English	Scientific	German	Dutch
Addax	Addax nasomaculatus	Mendesantilope	Addax
Badger, Honey	Mellivora capensis	Honigdachs	Honingdas
Caracal	Caracal caracal	Karakal	Caracal
Cat, Sand	Felis margarita	Sandkatze	Woestijnkat
Fox, Fennec	Vulpes zerda	Fennek	Fennek
Fox, Red	Vulpes vulpes	Rotfuchs	Vos
Fox, Rüppell's	Vulpes rueppellii	Rüppellfuchs	Zandvos
Gazelle, Cuvier's	Gazella cuvieri	Cuviergazelle	Edmigazelle
Gazelle, Dorcas	Gazella dorcas	Dorkasgazelle	Dorcasgazelle
Genet, Common	Genetta genetta	Ginsterkatze	Genetkat
Gerbil	Gerbillus spec.	Echte Rennmäuse	Gerbil/Renmuis
Gundi, North African	Ctenodactylus gundi	Eigentlicher Gundi	Noord-Afrikaanse goendi
Gundi, Val's	Ctenodactylus vali	Val-Gundi	Woestijngoendi
Hare, Cape	Lepus capensis	Kaphase	Kaapse haas
Hedgehog, Algerian	Atelerix algirus	Algerischer Igel	Trekegel
Hedgehog, Desert	Paraechinus aethiopicus	Äthiopischer Igel	Abessijnse egel
Hyena, Striped	Hyaena hyaena	Streifenhyäne	Gestreepte hyena
Jerboa	Jaculus spec.	Wüstenspringmäuse	Jerboa
Jird, Sundevall's	Meriones crassus	Sundevall-Rennratte	Sundevalls woestijnmuis
Leopard	Panthera pardus	Leopard	Luipaard
Lion	Panthera leo	Löwe	Leeuw
Mongoose, Egyptian	Herpestes ichneumon	Ichneumon	Mangoest
Mouse, Barbary Striped Grass	Lemniscomys barbarus	Berber-Streifengrasmaus	Zebragrasmuis
Oryx, Scimitar-horned	Oryx dammah	Säbelantilope	Algazel
Pipistrelle, Common	Pipistrellus pipistrellus	Zwergfledermaus	Gewone dwergvleermuis
Pipistrelle, Kuhl's	Pipistrellus kuhlii	Weissrandfledermaus	Kuhl's dwergvleermuis

Porcupine, Crested	*Hystrix cristata*	Gewöhnliches Stachelschwein	Gewoon stekelvarken
Rat, Fat Sand	*Psammomys obesus*	Fette Sandratte	Vette zandrat
Sengi, North African	*Petrosaltator rozeti*	Nordafrikanische Elefantenspitzmaus	Noord-Afrikaanse olifantspitsmuis
Serval	*Leptailurus serval*	Serval	Serval
Sheep, Barbary	*Ammotragus lervia*	Mähnenspringer	Manenschaap
Shrew	*Crocidura spec.*	Weisszahnspitzmäuse	Spitsmuizen
Squirrel, African Ground	*Xerus erythropus*	Gestreiftes Borstenhörnchen	Afrikaanse grondeekhoorn
Squirrel, Barbary Gound	*Atlantoxerus getulus*	Atlashörnchen	Barbarijse grondeekhoorn
Wildcat, African	*Felis lybica*	Falbkatze	Afrikaanse wilde kat
Wolf, African Golden	*Canis anthus*	Afrikanischer Goldwolf	Afrikaanse goudjakhals

Birds

English	Scientific	German	Dutch
Accentor, Alpine	*Prunella collaris*	Alpenbraunelle	Alpenheggemus
Avocet, Pied	*Recurvirostra avosetta*	Säbelschnäbler	Kluut
Babbler, Fulvous	*Argya fulva*	Akaziendrosselhäherling	Bruingele babbelaar
Bee-eater, Blue-cheeked	*Merops persicus*	Blauwangenspint	Groene bijeneter
Bee-eater, European	*Merops apiaster*	Bienenfresser	Bijeneter
Bittern, Eurasian	*Botaurus stellaris*	Rohrdommel	Roerdomp
Bittern, Little	*Ixobrychus minutus*	Zwergdommel	Woudaapje
Blackbird, Common	*Turdus merula*	Amsel	Merel
Blackcap, Eurasian	*Sylvia atricapilla*	Mönchsgrasmücke	Zwartkop
Bluethroat	*Luscinia svecica*	Blaukehlchen	Blauwborst
Brambling	*Fringilla montifringilla*	Bergfink	Keep
Bulbul, Common	*Pycnonotus barbatus*	Graubülbül	Grauwe buulbuul
Bunting, Cirl	*Emberiza cirlus*	Zaunammer	Cirlgors
Bunting, Common Reed	*Emberiza schoeniclus*	Rohrammer	Rietgors
Bunting, Corn	*Emberiza calandra*	Grauammer	Grauwe gors
Bunting, House	*Emberiza sahari*	Hausammer	Huisgors
Bunting, Ortolan	*Emberiza hortulana*	Ortolan	Ortolaan
Bunting, Rock	*Emberiza cia*	Zippammer	Grijze gors
Bustard, Great	*Otis tarda*	Grosstrappe	Grote trap
Bustard, Houbara	*Chlamydotis undulata*	Kragentrappe	Westelijke kraagtrap
Buzzard, Common	*Buteo buteo*	Mäusebussard	Buizerd
Buzzard, Honey	*Pernis apivorus*	Wespenbussard	Wespendief
Buzzard, Long-legged	*Buteo rufinus*	Adlerbussard	Arendbuizerd
Chaffinch, Common	*Fringilla coelebs africana*	Buchfink	Vink
Chiffchaff, Common	*Phylloscopus collybita*	Zilpzalp	Tjiftjaf
Chiffchaff, Iberian	*Phylloscopus ibericus*	Iberischer Zilpzalp	Iberische tjiftjaf
Chough, Alpine	*Pyrrhocorax graculus*	Alpendohle	Alpenkauw
Chough, Red-billed	*Pyrrhocorax pyrrhocorax*	Alpenkrähe	Alpenkraai
Cisticola, Zitting	*Cisticola juncidis*	Cistensänger	Graszanger
Coot, Eurasian	*Fulica atra*	Blässhuhn	Meerkoet
Coot, Red-knobbed	*Fulica cristata*	Kammblässhuhn	Knobbelmeerkoet
Cormorant, Continental	*Phalacrocorax carbo sinensis*	Kormoran	Aalscholver

English	Scientific	German	Dutch
Cormorant, North African	*Phalacrocorax carbo maroccanus*	Weissbrust-Kormoran	Marokkaanse aalscholver
Courser, Cream-coloured	*Cursorius cursor*	Rennvogel	Renvogel
Crake, Baillon's	*Porzana pusilla*	Zwergsumpfhuhn	Kleinst waterhoen
Crake, Little	*Porzana parva*	Kleines Sumpfhuhn	Klein waterhoen
Crake, Spotted	*Porzana porzana*	Tüpfelsumpfhuhn	Porseleinhoen
Crane, Common	*Grus grus*	Kranich	Kraanvogel
Crossbill, Red	*Loxia curvirostra*	Fichtenkreuzschnabel	Kruisbek
Cuckoo, Common	*Cuculus canorus*	Kuckuck	Koekoek
Cuckoo, Great Spotted	*Clamator glandarius*	Häherkuckuck	Kuifkoekoek
Curlew, Eurasian	*Numenius arquata*	Grosser Brachvogel	Wulp
Dipper, White-throated	*Cinclus cinclus*	Wasseramsel	Waterspreeuw
Dotterel, Eurasian	*Charadrius morinellus*	Mornellregenpfeifer	Morinelplevier
Dove, Eurasian Collared	*Streptopelia decaocto*	Türkentaube	Turkse tortel
Dove, European Turtle	*Streptopelia turtur*	Turteltaube	Tortelduif
Dove, Laughing	*Spilopelia senegalensis*	Palmtaube	Palmtortel
Dove, Rock	*Columba livia*	Felsentaube	Rotsduif
Duck, Ferruginous	*Aythya nyroca*	Moorente	Witoogeend
Duck, Marbled	*Marmaronetta angustirostris*	Marmelente	Marmereend
Duck, Tufted	*Aythya fuligula*	Reiherente	Kuifeend
Dunlin	*Calidris alpina*	Alpenstrandläufer	Bonte strandloper
Eagle, Bonelli's	*Aquila fasciata*	Habichtsadler	Havikarend
Eagle, Booted	*Hieraaetus pennatus*	Zwergadler	Dwergarend
Eagle, Golden	*Aquila chrysaetos*	Steinadler	Steenarend
Eagle, Short-toed	*Circaetus gallicus*	Schlangenadler	Slangenarend
Eagle, Tawny	*Aquila rapax*	Raubadler	Savannearend
Eagle-Owl, Pharaoh	*Bubo ascalaphus*	Wüstenuhu	Woestijnoehoe
Egret, Great	*Ardea alba*	Silberreiher	Grote zilverreiger
Egret, Little	*Egretta garzetta*	Seidenreiher	Kleine zilverreiger
Egret, Western Cattle	*Bubulcus ibis*	Kuhreiher	Koereiger
Falcon, Barbary	*Falco peregrinus pelegrinoides*	Wüstenfalke	Barbarijse valk
Falcon, Eleonora's	*Falco eleonorae*	Eleonorenfalke	Eleonora's valk
Falcon, Lanner	*Falco biarmicus*	Lannerfalke	Lannerval
Falcon, Peregrine	*Falco peregrinus*	Wanderfalke	Slechtvalk
Finch, African Crimson-winged	*Rhodopechys alienus*	Afrikanischer Rotflügelgimpel	Atlasbergvink
Finch, Trumpeter	*Bucanetes githagineus*	Wüstengimpel	Woestijnvink
Firecrest, Common	*Regulus ignicapilla*	Sommergoldhähnchen	Vuurgoudhaantje
Flamingo, Greater	*Phoenicopterus roseus*	Flamingo	Europese flamingo
Flycatcher, Atlas	*Ficedula speculigera*	Atlasschnäpper	Atlasvliegenvanger
Flycatcher, European Pied	*Ficedula hypoleuca*	Trauerschnäpper	Bonte vliegenvanger
Flycatcher, Spotted	*Muscicapa striata*	Grauschnäpper	Grauwe vliegenvanger
Gannet, Northern	*Morus bassanus*	Basstölpel	Jan-van-gent
Garganey	*Spatula querquedula*	Knäkente	Zomertaling
Godwit, Bar-tailed	*Limosa lapponica*	Pfuhlschnepfe	Rosse grutto
Godwit, Black-tailed	*Limosa limosa*	Uferschnepfe	Grutto
Goldfinch, European	*Carduelis carduelis*	Distelfink	Putter
Goose, Greylag	*Anser anser*	Graugans	Grauwe gans

English	Scientific	German	Dutch
Goshawk, Northern	Accipiter gentilis	Habicht	Havik
Grebe, Black-necked	Podiceps nigricollis	Schwarzhalstaucher	Geoorde fuut
Grebe, Great Crested	Podiceps cristatus	Haubentaucher	Fuut
Grebe, Little	Tachybaptus ruficollis	Zwergtaucher	Dodaars
Greenfinch, European	Chloris chloris	Grünling	Groenling
Greenshank, Common	Tringa nebularia	Grünschenkel	Groenpootruiter
Gull, Audouin's	Ichthyaetus audouinii	Korallenmöwe	Adouins meeuw
Gull, Black-headed	Chroicocephalus ridibundus	Lachmöwe	Kokmeeuw
Gull, Lesser Black-backed	Larus fuscus graellsii	Heringsmöwe	Kleine mantelmeeuw
Gull, Little	Hydrocoloeus minutus	Zwergmöwe	Dwergmeeuw
Gull, Mediterranean	Ichthyaetus melanocephalus	Schwarzkopfmöwe	Zwartkopmeeuw
Gull, Sabine's	Xema sabini	Schwalbenmöwe	Vorkstaartmeeuw
Gull, Slender-billed	Chroicocephalus genei	Dünnschnabelmöwe	Dunbekmeeuw
Gull, Yellow-legged	Larus michahellis michahellis	Weisskopfmöve	Geelpootmeeuw
Harrier, Hen	Circus cyaneus	Kornweihe	Blauwe Kiekendief
Harrier, Montagu's	Circus pygargus	Wiesenweihe	Grauwe kiekendief
Harrier, Western Marsh	Circus aeruginosus	Rohrweihe	Bruine kiekendief
Hawfinch	Coccothraustes coccothraustes buvryi	Kernbeisser	Appelvink
Heron, Black-crowned Night	Nycticorax nycticorax	Nachtreiher	Kwak
Heron, Grey	Ardea cinerea	Graureiher	Blauwe reiger
Heron, Purple	Ardea purpurea	Purpurreiher	Purperreiger
Heron, Squacco	Ardeola ralloides	Rallenreiher	Ralreiger
Hoopoe, Eurasian	Upupa epops	Wiedehopf	Hop
Hoopoe-Lark, Greater	Alaemon alaudipes	Wüstenläuferlerche	Witbandleeuwerik
Ibis, Glossy	Plegadis falcinellus	Braunsichler	Zwarte ibis
Ibis, Northern Bald	Geronticus eremita	Waldrapp	Heremietibis
Jaeger, Parasitic	Stercorarius parasiticus	Schmarotzerraubmöwe	Kleine jager
Jaeger, Pomarine	Stercorarius pomarinus	Spatelraubmöwe	Middelste jager
Jay, Eurasian	Garrulus glandarius	Eichelhäher	Vlaamse gaai
Kestrel, Common	Falco tinnunculus	Turmfalke	Torenvalk
Kestrel, Lesser	Falco naumanni	Rötelfalke	Kleine torenvalk
Kingfisher, Common	Alcedo atthis	Eisvogel	IJsvogel
Kite, Black	Milvus migrans	Schwarzmilan	Zwarte wouw
Kite, Black-winged	Elanus caeruleus	Gleitaar	Grijze wouw
Knot, Red	Calidris canutus	Knutt	Kanoet
Lapwing, Northern	Vanellus vanellus	Kiebitz	Kievit
Lark, Bar-tailed	Ammomanes cinctura	Sandlerche	Rosse woestijnleeuwerik
Lark, Calandra	Melanocorypha calandra	Kalanderlerche	Kalanderleeuwerik
Lark, Crested	Galerida cristata	Haubenlerche	Kuifleeuwerik
Lark, Desert	Ammomanes deserti	Steinlerche	Woestijnleeuwerik
Lark, Dunn's	Eremalauda dunni	Einödlerche	Dunns leeuwerik
Lark, Dupont's	Chersophilus duponti	Dupontlerche	Duponts leeuwerik
Lark, Greater Short-toed	Calandrella brachydactyla	Kurzzehenlerche	Kortteenleeuwerik
Lark, Horned	Eremophila alpestris	Ohrenlerche	Strandleeuwerik
Lark, Lesser Short-toed	Alaudala rufescens	Stummellerche	Kleine kortteenleeuwerik

Lark, Maghreb	*Galerida macrorhyncha*	Maghreblerche	Langsnavelkuifleeuwerik
Lark, Temminck's	*Eremophila bilopha*	Saharaohrenlerche	Temmincks strandleeuwerik
Lark, Thekla	*Galerida theklae*	Theklalerche	Theklaleeuwerik
Lark, Thick-billed	*Ramphocoris clotbey*	Knackerlerche	Diksnavelleeuwerik
Linnet, Common	*Linaria cannabina*	Bluthänfling	Kneu
Magpie, Maghreb	*Pica mauritanica*	Maghrebelster	Maghrebekster
Mallard	*Anas platyrhynchos*	Stockente	Wilde eend
Martin, Brown-throated	*Riparia paludicola*	Braunkehl-Uferschwalbe	Vale oeverzwaluw
Martin, Common House	*Delichon urbicum*	Mehlschwalbe	Huiszwaluw
Martin, Eurasian Crag	*Ptyonoprogne rupestris*	Felsenschwalbe	Rotszwaluw
Martin, Pale Crag	*Ptyonoprogne obsoleta presaharica*	Vale rotszwaluw	Wüstenschwalbe
Martin, Sand	*Riparia riparia*	Uferschwalbe	Oeverzwaluw
Moorhen, Common	*Gallinula chloropus*	Teichhuhn	Waterhoen
Nightingale, Common	*Luscinia megarhynchos*	Nachtigall	Nachtegaal
Nightjar, Egyptian	*Caprimulgus aegyptius*	Pharaonen-Ziegenmelker	Egyptische nachtzwaluw
Nightjar, Red-necked	*Caprimulgus ruficollis*	Rothals-Ziegenmelker	Moorse nachtzwaluw
Oriole, Eurasian Golden	*Oriolus oriolus*	Pirol	Wielewaal
Osprey, Western	*Pandion haliaetus*	Fischadler	Visarend
Ouzel, Ring	*Turdus torquatus*	Ringdrossel	Beflijster
Owl, Eurasian Scops	*Otus scops*	Zwergohreule	Dwergooruil
Owl, Little	*Athene noctua*	Steinkauz	Steenuil
Owl, Maghreb	*Strix mauritanica*	Mauretanischer Waldkauz	Maghrebbosuil
Owl, Short-eared	*Asio flammeus*	Sumpfohreule	Velduil
Owl, Tawny	*Strix aluco*	Waldkauz	Bosuil
Oystercatcher, Eurasian	*Haematopus ostralegus*	Austernfischer	Scholekster
Partridge, Barbary	*Alectoris barbara*	Felsenhuhn	Barbarijse patrijs
Petrel, White-faced Storm	*Pelagodroma marina*	Weissgesicht-Sturmschwalbe	Bont stormvogeltje
Petrel, Wilson's Storm	*Oceanites oceanicus*	Buntfuss-Sturmschwalbe	Wilsons stormvogeltje
Phalarope, Grey	*Phalaropus fulicarius*	Thorshühnchen	Rosse franjepoot
Pigeon, Common Wood	*Columba palumbus*	Ringeltaube	Houtduif
Pintail, Northern	*Anas acuta*	Spiessente	Pijlstaart
Pipit, Meadow	*Anthus pratensis*	Wiesenpieper	Graspieper
Pipit, Red-throated	*Anthus cervinus*	Rotkehlpieper	Roodkeelpieper
Pipit, Richard's	*Anthus richardi*	Spornpieper	Grote pieper
Pipit, Tawny	*Anthus campestris*	Brachpieper	Duinpieper
Pipit, Tree	*Anthus trivialis*	Baumpieper	Boompieper
Pipit, Water	*Anthus spinoletta*	Bergpieper	Waterpieper
Plover, Common Ringed	*Charadrius hiaticula*	Sandregenpfeifer	Bontbekplevier
Plover, European Golden	*Pluvialis apricaria*	Goldregenpfeifer	Goudplevier
Plover, Grey	*Pluvialis squatarola*	Kiebitzregenpfeifer	Zilverplevier
Plover, Kentish	*Charadrius alexandrinus*	Seeregenpfeifer	Strandplevier
Plover, Little Ringed	*Charadrius dubius*	Flussregenpfeifer	Kleine plevier
Pochard, Common	*Aythya ferina*	Tafelente	Tafeleend
Pratincole, Collared	*Glareola pratincola*	Rotflügel-Brachschwalbe	Vorkstaartplevier
Quail, Common	*Coturnix coturnix*	Wachtel	Kwartel

English	Scientific	German	Dutch
Rail, Water	Rallus aquaticus	Wasserralle	Waterral
Raven, Brown-necked	Corvus ruficollis	Wüstenrabe	Bruinnekraaf
Raven, Northern	Corvus corax tingitanus	Nordafrikanischer Kolkrabe	Noordafrikaanse raaf*
Redshank, Common	Tringa totanus	Rotschenkel	Tureluur
Redshank, Spotted	Tringa erythropus	Dunkler Wasserläufer	Zwarte ruiter
Redstart, Black	Phoenicurus ochruros	Hausrotschwanz	Zwarte roodstaart
Redstart, Common	Phoenicurus phoenicurus	Gartenrotschwanz	Gekraagde roodstaart
Redstart, Moussier's	Phoenicurus moussieri	Diademrotschwanz	Diadeemroodstaart
Robin, European	Erithacus rubecula	Rotkehlchen	Roodborst
Robin, Rufous-tailed Scrub	Cercotrichas galactotes	Heckensänger	Rosse waaierstaart
Roller, European	Coracias garrulus	Blauracke	Scharrelaar
Ruff	Calidris pugnax	Kampfläufer	Kemphaan
Sanderling	Calidris alba	Sanderling	Drieteenstrandloper
Sandgrouse, Black-bellied	Pterocles orientalis	Sandflughuhn	Zwartbuikzandhoen
Sandgrouse, Crowned	Pterocles coronatus	Kronenflughuhn	Kroonzandhoen
Sandgrouse, Lichtenstein's	Pterocles lichtensteinii	Wellenflughuhn	Lichtensteins zandhoen
Sandgrouse, Pin-tailed	Pterocles alchata	Spiessflughuhn	Witbuikzandhoen
Sandgrouse, Spotted	Pterocles senegallus	Senegal-Flughuhn	Sahelzandhoen
Sandpiper, Common	Actitis hypoleucos	Flussuferläufer	Oeverloper
Sandpiper, Curlew	Calidris ferruginea	Sichelstrandläufer	Krombekstrandloper
Sandpiper, Green	Tringa ochropus	Waldwasserläufer	Witgat
Sandpiper, Marsh	Tringa stagnatilis	Teichwasserläufer	Poelruiter
Sandpiper, Wood	Tringa glareola	Bruchwasserläufer	Bosruiter
Serin, European	Serinus serinus	Girlitz	Europese kanarie
Shearwater, Balearic	Puffinus mauretanicus	Balearensturmtaucher	Vale pijlstormvogel
Shearwater, Cape Verde	Calonectris edwardsii	Gelbschnabelsturmtaucher	Kaapverdische pijlstormvogel
Shearwater, Cory's	Calonectris borealis	Gelbschnabelsturmtaucher	Kuhls pijlstormvogel
Shearwater, Great	Ardenna gravis	Grosser Sturmtaucher	Grote pijlstormvogel
Shearwater, Manx	Puffinus puffinus	Atlantiksturmtaucher	Noordse pijlstormvogel
Shearwater, Sooty	Ardenna grisea	Dunkler Sturmtaucher	Grauwe pijlstormvogel
Shelduck, Common	Tadorna tadorna	Brandgans	Bergeend
Shelduck, Ruddy	Tadorna ferruginea	Rostgans	Casarca
Shoveler, Northern	Spatula clypeata	Löffelente	Slobeend
Shrike, Great Grey	Lanius excubitor algeriensis	Raubwürger	Klapekster
Shrike, Great Grey	Lanius excubitor elegans	Raubwürger	Klapekster
Shrike, Red-backed	Lanius collurio	Neuntöter	Grauwe klauwier
Shrike, Woodchat	Lanius senator	Rotkopfwürger	Roodkopklauwier
Siskin, Eurasian	Spinus spinus	Erlenzeisig	Sijs
Skua, Great	Stercorarius skua	Skua	Grote jager
Skylark, Eurasian	Alauda arvensis	Feldlerche	Veldleeuwerik
Snipe, Common	Gallinago gallinago	Bekassine	Watersnip
Snipe, Great	Gallinago media	Doppelschnepfe	Poelsnip
Snipe, Jack	Lymnocryptes minimus	Zwergschnepfe	Bokje
Sparrow, Desert	Passer simplex	Wüstensperling	Woestijnmus

English	Scientific	German	Dutch
Sparrow, House	Passer domesticus	Haussperling	Huismus
Sparrow, Rock	Petronia petronia barbata	Steinsperling	Rotsmus
Sparrow, Spanish	Passer hispaniolensis	Weidensperling	Spaanse mus
Sparrowhawk, Eurasian	Accipiter nisus	Sperber	Sperwer
Spoonbill, Eurasian	Platalea leucorodia	Löffler	Lepelaar
Starling, Spotless	Sturnus unicolor	Einfarbstar	Zwarte spreeuw
Stilt, Black-winged	Himantopus himantopus	Stelzenläufer	Steltkluut
Stint, Little	Calidris minuta	Zwergstrandläufer	Kleine strandloper
Stint, Temminck's	Calidris temminckii	Temminckstrandläufer	Temmincks strandloper
Stonechat, European	Saxicola rubicola	Schwarzkehlchen	Roodborsttapuit
Stone-curlew, Eurasian	Burhinus oedicnemus	Triel	Griel
Stork, Black	Ciconia nigra	Schwarzstorch	Zwarte ooievaar
Stork, White	Ciconia ciconia	Weissstorch	Ooievaar
Swallow, Barn	Hirundo rustica	Rauchschwalbe	Boerenzwaluw
Swallow, Red-rumped	Cecropis daurica	Rötelschwalbe	Roodstuitzwaluw
Swamphen, Western	Porphyrio porphyrio	Purpurhuhn	Purperkoet
Swift, Alpine	Tachymarptis melba	Alpensegler	Alpengierzwaluw
Swift, Common	Apus apus	Mauersegler	Gierzwaluw
Swift, Little	Apus affinis	Haussegler	Huisgierzwaluw
Swift, Pallid	Apus pallidus	Fahlsegler	Vale gierzwaluw
Swift, Plain	Apus unicolor	Einfarbsegler	Madeiragierzwaluw
Swift, White-rumped	Apus caffer	Kaffernsegler	Kaffergierzwaluw
Tchagra, Black-crowned	Tchagra senegalus	Senegaltschagra	Zwartkruintsjagra
Teal, Eurasian	Anas crecca	Krickente	Wintertaling
Tern, Arctic	Sterna paradisaea	Küstenseeschwalbe	Noordse stern
Tern, Black	Chlidonias niger	Trauerseeschwalbe	Zwarte stern
Tern, Caspian	Hydroprogne caspia	Raubseeschwalbe	Reuzenstern
Tern, Common	Sterna hirundo	Flussseeschwalbe	Visdief
Tern, Gull-billed	Gelochelidon nilotica	Lachseeschwalbe	Lachstern
Tern, Lesser Crested	Thalasseus bengalensis	Rüppellseeschwalbe	Bengaalse stern
Tern, Little	Sternula albifrons	Zwergseeschwalbe	Dwergstern
Tern, Royal	Thalasseus maximus	Königsseeschwalbe	Koningsstern
Tern, Sandwich	Thalasseus sandvicensis	Brandseeschwalbe	Grote stern
Tern, West African Crested	Thalasseus albididorsalis	Afrikanische Königsseeschwalbe	Afrikaanse koningsstern
Tern, Whiskered	Chlidonias hybrida	Weissbart-Seeschwalbe	Witwangstern
Thrush, Blue Rock	Monticola solitarius	Blaumerle	Blauwe rotslijster
Thrush, Mistle	Turdus viscivorus	Misteldrossel	Grote lijster
Thrush, Song	Turdus philomelos	Singdrossel	Zanglijster
Tit, African Blue	Cyanistes teneriffae	Kanarenmeise	Tenerifepimpelmees
Tit, Coal	Periparus ater atlas	Tannenmeise	Zwarte mees
Tit, Great	Parus major	Kohlmeise	Koolmees
Treecreeper, Short-toed	Certhia brachydactyla	Gartenbaumläufer	Boomkruiper
Vulture, Bearded	Gypaetus barbatus	Bartgeier	Lammergier
Vulture, Egyptian	Neophron percnopterus	Schmutzgeier	Aasgier
Vulture, Griffon	Gyps fulvus	Gänsegeier	Vale gier
Wagtail, Grey	Motacilla cinerea	Gebirgsstelze	Grote gele kwikstaart
Wagtail, Moroccan	Motacilla alba subpersonata	Marokkanische bachstelze	Marokkaanse kwikstaart

TOURIST INFORMATION & OBSERVATION TIPS

English	Scientific	German	Dutch
Wagtail, Western Yellow	*Motacilla flava*	Schafstelze	Gele kwikstaart
Wagtail, White	*Motacilla alba alba*	Bachstelze	Witte kwikstaart
Warbler, African Desert	*Curruca deserti*	Saharagrasmücke	Afrikaanse woestijngrasmus
Warbler, African Reed	*Acrocephalus baeticatus*	Zimtrohrsänger	Kortvleugelkarekiet
Warbler, Cetti's	*Cettia cetti*	Seidensänger	Cetti's zanger
Warbler, Dartford	*Curruca undata*	Provencegrasmücke	Provençaalse grasmus
Warbler, Eastern Olivaceous	*Iduna pallida reiseri*	Blassspötter	Oostelijke vale spotvogel
Warbler, Eurasian Reed	*Acrocephalus scirpaceus*	Teichrohrsänger	Kleine karekiet
Warbler, Garden	*Sylvia borin*	Gartengrasmücke	Tuinfluiter
Warbler, Melodious	*Hippolais polyglotta*	Orpheusspötter	Orpheusspotvogel
Warbler, Moltoni's	*Curruca subalpina*	Moltonis Grasmücke	Moltoni's baardgrasmus
Warbler, Sardinian	*Curruca melanocephala*	Samtkopf-Grasmücke	Kleine zwartkop
Warbler, Sedge	*Acrocephalus schoenobaenus*	Schilfrohrsänger	Rietzanger
Warbler, Spectacled	*Curruca conspicillata*	Brillengrasmücke	Brilgrasmus
Warbler, Streaked Scrub	*Scotocerca inquieta*	Wüstendickichtsänger	Maquiszanger
Warbler, Subalpine	*Sylvia cantillans*	Weissbart-Grasmücke	Baardgrasmus
Warbler, Tristram's	*Curruca deserticola*	Atlasgrasmücke	Atlasgrasmus
Warbler, Western Bonelli's	*Phylloscopus bonelli*	Berglaubsänger	Bergfluiter
Warbler, Western Olivaceous	*Iduna opaca*	Isabellspötter	Westelijke vale spotvogel
Warbler, Western Orphean	*Curruca hortensis*	Orpheusgrasmücke	Orpheusgrasmus
Warbler, Western Subalpine	*Curruca iberiae*	Iberien-Bartgrasmücke	Westelijke baardgrasmus
Warbler, Willow	*Phylloscopus trochilus*	Fitis	Fitis
Wheatear, Atlas	*Oenanthe seebohmi*	Seebohm-Steinschmätzer	Seebohms tapuit
Wheatear, Black	*Oenanthe leucura*	Trauersteinschmätzer	Zwarte tapuit
Wheatear, Black-eared	*Oenanthe hispanica*	Mittelmeer-Steinschmätzer	Blonde tapuit
Wheatear, Desert	*Oenanthe deserti*	Wüsten-Steinschmätzer	Woestijntapuit
Wheatear, Isabelline	*Oenanthe isabellina*	Isabellsteinschmätzer	Izabeltapuit
Wheatear, Maghreb	*Oenanthe halophila*	Berber-Steinschmätzer	Westelijke rouwtapuit
Wheatear, Northern	*Oenanthe oenanthe*	Steinschmätzer	Tapuit
Wheatear, Red-rumped	*Oenanthe moesta*	Fahlbürzel-Steinschmätzer	Roodstuittapuit
Wheatear, White-crowned	*Oenanthe leucopyga*	Sahara-Steinschmätzer	Witkruintapuit
Whimbrel	*Numenius phaeopus*	Regenbrachvogel	Regenwulp
Whinchat	*Saxicola rubetra*	Braunkehlchen	Paapje
Whitethroat, Common	*Sylvia communis*	Dorngrasmücke	Grasmus
Wigeon, Eurasian	*Anas penelope*	Pfeifente	Smient
Woodlark	*Lullula arborea*	Heidelerche	Boomleeuwerik
Woodpecker, Great Spotted	*Dendrocopos major*	Buntspecht	Grote bonte specht
Woodpecker, Levaillant's	*Picus vaillantii*	Atlasgrünspecht	Levaillants specht
Wren, Eurasian	*Troglodytes troglodytes*	Zaunkönig	Winterkoning
Wryneck, Eurasian	*Jynx torquilla*	Wendehals	Draaihals

Reptiles and Amphibians

English	Scientific	German	Dutch
Adder, Puff	*Bitis arietans*	Puffotter	Gewone pofadder
Agama, Bibron's	*Agama impalearis*	Atlasagame	Atlasagame
Agama, Böhme's	*Trapelus boehmei*	Böhme's Agame*	Böhme's agame*

Chameleon, Common	*Chamaeleo chamaeleon*	Chamäleon	Gewone kameleon
Cobra, Egyptian	*Naja haje*	Uräusschlange	Egyptische cobra
Eater, Sahel Egg	*Dasypeltis sahelensis*	Sahel-Eierschlange	Sahel-eiereter*
Frog, Moroccan Painted	*Discoglossus scovazzi*	Marokkanischer Scheibenzüngler	Marokkaanse schijftongkikker
Frog, North African Water	*Pelophylax saharicus*	Sahara-Wasserfrosch	Saharakikker
Frog, Painted	*Discoglossus pictus*	Gemalter Scheibenzüngler	Schijftongkikker
Frog, Stripeless Tree	*Hyla meridionalis*	Mittelmeer-Laubfrosch	Mediterrane boomkikker
Gecko, Algerian Dwarf	*Tropiocolotes algericus*	Algerischer Sandgecko	Algerijnse dwerggekko*
Gecko, Anderson's Short-fingered	*Stenodactylus petrii*	Nordafrikanischer Dünnfingergecko	Petri's dunvingergekko*
Gecko, Böhme's	*Tarentola boehmei*	Böhmes Gecko	Böhmes gekko
Gecko, Helmethead	*Tarentola chazaliae*	Helmkopfgecko	Helmgekko
Gecko, High Atlas Day	*Quedenfeldtia trachyblepharus*	Atlas-Tagesgecko	Atlas-daggekko
Gecko, Moorish	*Tarentola mauritanica*	Maurischer Gecko	Muurgekko
Gecko, Moorish Short-fingered	*Stenodactylus mauritanicus*	Wüsten-Dünnfingergecko	Moorse dunvingergekko*
Gecko, Moroccan Day	*Quedenfeldtia moerens*	Marrokanischer Tagesgecko	Marokkaanse daggekko
Gecko, Oudri's Fan-footed	*Ptyodactylus oudrii*	Marokkanischer Fächerfingergecko	Marokkaanse waaierteengekko*
Gecko, South Morocco Lizard-fingered	*Saurodactylus brosseti*	Marokkanischer Echsenfingergecko	Marokkaanse hagedisteengekko*
Lizard, Atlas Dwarf	*Atlantolacerta andreanskyi*	Atlas-Eidechse	Atlashagedis*
Lizard, Bosc's Fringe-fingered	*Acanthodactylus boskianus*	Afrikanischer Fransenfinger	Bosc's franjeteenhagedis*
Lizard, Common Fringe-fingered	*Acanthodactylus erythrurus*	Europäischer Fransenfinger	Moorse franjeteenhagedis
Lizard, Dumeril's Fringe-fingered	*Acanthodactylus dumerilii*	Dumérils Fransenfinger	Dumerils franjeteenhagedis*
Lizard, Golden Fringe-fingered	*Acanthodactylus aureus*	Gold-Fransenfinger	Gouden franjeteenhagedis*
Lizard, Long-footed Fringe-fingered	*Acanthodactylus longipes*	Langfüssiger Fransenfinger	Langpootfranjeteenhagedis*
Lizard, Margarita's Fringe-fingered	*Acanthodactylus margaritae*	Margaritas Fransenfinger*	Margarita´s franjeteenhagedis
lizard, Moroccan Ocellated	*Timon tangitanus*	Marokko-Perleidechse	Marokkaanse parelhagedis
Lizard, Moroccan Rock	*Scelarcis perspicillata*	Brilleneidechse	Brilhagedis
Lizard, Moroccan Spiny-tailed	*Uromastyx nigriventris*	Marokko-Dornschwanz	Marokkaanse doornstaartagame
Lizard, Olivier's Small	*Mesalina olivieri*	Oliviers Wüstenrenner	Oliviers woestijnrenner*
Lizard, Pasteur's Small	*Mesalina pasteuri*	Pasteurs Wüstenrenner	Pasteurs woestijnrenner*
Lizard, Simon's Small	*Mesalina simonii*	Simons Wüstenrenner	Simons woestijnrenner*
Lizard, Small-spotted	*Mesalina guttulata*	Gefleckter Wüstenrenner	Gevlekte woestijnrenner*
Lizard, Spotted Fringe-fingered	*Acanthodactylus maculatus*	Gefleckter Fransenfinger	Gevlekte* franjeteenhagedis

English	Scientific	German	Dutch
Lizard, Vaucher's Wall	Podarcis vaucheri	Südiberische Mauereidechse	Moorse muurhagedis
Monitor, Desert	Varanus griseus	Wüstenwaran	Woestijnvaraan
Newt, Sharp-ribbed	Pleurodeles waltl	Spanischer Rippenmolch	Ribbensalamander
Psammodromus, Large	Psammodromus algirus	Algirischer Sandläufer	Algerijnse zandloper
Sandfish, Western	Scincus albifasciatus	Senegal-Skink	Westelijke zandskink*
Skink, Coastal	Chalcides mionecton	Küsten-Walzenskink	Kust-parelskink*
Skink, Many-scaled	Chalcides polylepis	Marokkanischer Walzenskink	Marokkaanse parelskink*
Skink, Mountain	Chalcides montanus	Marokkanischer Gebirgs-Walzenskink	Berg-parelskink*
Skink, Orange	Eumeces algeriensis	Berberskink	Berberskink
Skink, Senegal Sand	Chalcides sphenopsiformis	Senegal-Keilschleiche	Senegalese zandskink*
Snake, Algerian Whip	Hemorrhois algirus	Algerische Zornnatter	Algerijnse Toornslang
Snake, Brown House	Boaedon fuliginosus	Braune Hausschlange	Bruine huisslang
Snake, Forskal's Sand	Psammophis schokari	Forskals Sandrennnatter	Afrikaanse zandrenslang
Snake, Moorish Diadem	Spalerosophis dolichospilus	Marokkanische Diademnatter*	Marokkaanse diadeemslang*
Snake, Southern Smooth	Coronella girondica	Girondische Glattnatter	Girondische gladde slang
Snake, Viperine	Natrix maura	Vipernatter	Adderringslang
Toad, African Green	Bufotes boulengeri	Nordafrikanische Wechselkröte	Afrikaanse groene pad
Toad, Brongersma's	Barbarophryne brongersmai	Atlaskröte	Atlaspad*
Toad, Moroccan	Sclerophrys mauritanica	Berberkröte	Berberpad
Toad, Southern Common	Bufo spinosus	Mittelmeer-Erdkröte	Westelijke gewone pad
Tortoise, Common	Testudo graeca	Maurische Landschildkröte	Moorse landschildpad
Turtle, Kemp's Ridley	Lepidochelys kempii	Atlantik-Bastardschildkröte	Kemps zeeschildpad
Turtle, Loggerhead	Caretta caretta	Unechte Karettschildkröte	Dikkopschildpad
Turtle, Sahara Pond	Mauremys (leprosa) saharica	Sahara-Wasserschildkröte	Sahara-moerasschildpad
Viper, Horned	Cerastes cerastes	Wüsten-Hornviper	Hoornadder
Viper, Lataste's	Vipera latasti	Stülpnasenotter	Wipneusadder
Viper, Moorish	Daboia mauritanica	Atlasotter	Atlasadder
Viper, Sand	Cerastes vipera	Avicennaviper	Avicenna-adder
Viper, Saw-scaled	Echis pyramidum	Ägyptische Sandrasselotter	Egyptische zaagschubadder

Invertebrates

English	Scientific	German	Dutch
Argus, Southern Brown	Aricia cramera	Südlicher Sonnenröschen Bläuling	Moors bruin blauwtje
Black-tip, Greenish	Elphinstonia charlonia	Grüner Weissling*	Groen marmerwitje
Blue, African Babul	Azanus jesous	Grosser Akazien-Bläuling	Groot acaciablauwtje
Blue, African Grass	Zizeeria knysna	Amethist- Bläuling*	Amethistblauwtje
Blue, Allard's	Plebejus allardi	Kretania allardi	Barbarijs saffierblauwtje

Blue, Amanda's	*Polyommatus amandus*	Vogelwicken-Bläuling	Wikkeblauwtje
Blue, Atlas	*Polyommatus atlantica*	Atlas Wundklee-Bläuling*	Atlasturkooisblauwtje
Blue, Black-eyed	*Glaucopsyche melanops*	Schwarz-Auge Blauling*	Spaans bloemenblauwtje
Blue, Common Tiger	*Tarucus theophrastus*	Andalusischer Christusdorn-Bläuling*	Moors christusdoornblauwtje
Blue, Desert Babul	*Azanus ubaldus*	Kleiner Akazien-Bläuling	Klein acaciablauwtje
Blue, False Baton	*Pseudophilotes abencerragus*	Morischer Quendel-Bläuling	Moors tijmblauwtje
Blue, Long-tailed	*Lampides boeticus*	Grosser Wander-Bläuling	Tijgerblauwtje
Blue, Lorquin's	*Cupido lorquinii*	Morischer Zwerg-Bläuling	Moors dwergblauwtje
Blue, Mediterranean Tiger	*Tarucus rosaceus*	Marokkanischer Christusdorn-Bläuling*	Groot christusdoornblauwtje
Blue, Southern	*Polyommatus celina*	Mittelmeer-Hauhechelbläuling*	Mediterraan icarusblauwtje
Blue, Spotted Adonis	*Lysandra punctifera*	Marokkanischer Himmelblauer Bläuling*	Gestipt adonisblauwtje
Blue, Vogel	*Maurus vogelii*	Marokkanischer Bläuling*	Marokkaans bruin blauwtje
Blue-eye	*Erythromma lindenii*	Pokaljungfer	Kanaaljuffer
Bluet, Common	*Enallagma cyathigerum*	Gemeine Becherjungfer	Watersnuffel
Bluet, Desert	*Enallagma deserti*	Wüsten-Becherjungfer	Woestijnsnuffel
Bluetail, Oasis	*Ischnura fountaineae*	Oasen-Pechlibelle	Oaselantaarntje
Bluetail, Sahara	*Ischnura saharensis*	Sahara-Pechlibelle	Saharalantaarntje
Brimstone	*Gonepteryx rhamni*	Zitronenfalter	Citroentje
Brown, Moroccan Meadow	*Hyponephele maroccana*	Marokkanische Ochsenauge*	Marokkaans grauw zandoogje
Brown, Moroccan Wall	*Lasiommata meadewaldoi*	Marokkanischer Braunauge*	Marokkaanse rotsvlinder*
Cascader, Ringed	*Zygonyx torridus*	Wasserfall-Kreuzer	Watervallibel
Cleopatra	*Gonepteryx cleopatra*	Mittelmeer-Zitronenfalter	Cleopatra
Clubtail, Yellow	*Gomphus simillimus*	Gelbe Keiljungfer	Gele rombout
Copper, Moroccan	*Lycaena phoebus*	Marokkanischer Feuerfalter*	Marokkaanse vuurvlinder
Copper, Purple-shot	*Lycaena alciphron*	Violetter Feuerfalter	Violette vuurvlinder
Damselfly, Mediterranean	*Coenagrion caerulescens*	Südliche Azurjungfer	Zuidelijke waterjuffer
Darter, Desert	*Sympetrum sinaiticum*	Blasse Heidelibelle	Woestijnheidelibel
Darter, Red-veined	*Sympetrum fonscolombii*	Frühe Heidelibelle	Zwervende heidelibel
Demoiselle, Copper	*Calopteryx haemorrhoidalis*	Rote Prachtlibelle	Koperen beekjuffer
Dropwing, Orange-winged	*Trithemis kirbyi*	Gefleckter Sonnenzeiger	Oranje zonnewijzer
Dropwing, Red-veined	*Trithemis arteriosa*	Rotader-Sonnenzeiger	Rode zonnewijzer
Dropwing, Violet	*Trithemis annulata*	Rotviolette Segellibelle	Purperlibel
Emerald, Orange-spotted	*Oxygastra curtisii*	Gekielte Smaragdlibelle	Bronslibel
Emperor, Blue	*Anax imperator*	Grosse Königslibelle	Grote keizerlibel
Emperor, Lesser	*Anax pathenope*	Kleine Königslibelle	Zuidelijke keizerlibel
Emperor, Vagrant	*Anax ephippiger*	Schabrackenlibelle	Zadellibel
Featherleg, Barbary	*Platycnemis subdilatata*	Maghreb-Federlibelle	Berberbreedscheenjuffer

TOURIST INFORMATION & OBSERVATION TIPS

Festoon, Spanish	Zerynthia rumina	Spanischer Osterluzeifalter	Spaanse pijpbloemvlinder
Fritillary, Aetherie	Melitaea aetherie	Aetherie-Scheckenfalter	Moorse parelmoervlinder
Fritillary, African Knapweed	Melitaea punica	Afrikanischer Flockenblumen-Scheckenfalter	Barbarijse knoopkruid-parelmoervlinder
Fritillary, Cardinal	Argynnis pandora	Kardinal	Kardinaalsmantel
Fritillary, Desert	Melitaea deserticola	Wüsten-Scheckenfalter	Woestijnparelmoervlinder
Fritillary, Moroccan High Brown	Argynnis auresiana	Atlas Perlmutterfalter*	Atlasparelmoervlinder*
Fritillary, Spotted	Melitaea didyma	Roten Scheckenfalter	Tweekleurige parelmoervlinder
Glider, Wandering	Pantala flavescens	Wereldzwerver	Wanderlibelle
Goldenring, Atlas	Cordulegaster princeps	Atlas-Quelljungfer	Atlasbronlibel
Grayling, Austaut's	Hipparchia hansii	Atlas-Samtfalter*	Atlasheivlinder
Grayling, Dark Giant	Berberia lambessanus	Kleiner Berber-Samtfalter*	Kleine berberzandoog
Grayling, False	Arethusana arethusa	Rotbindiger Samtfalter	Oranje steppevlinder
Grayling, Giant	Berberia abdelkader	Grosser Berber-Samtfalter*	Grote berberzandoog
Grayling, Moroccan	Pseudochazara atlantis	Marokkanischer Samtfalter*	Marokkaanse heremiet
Grayling, Moroccan Rock	Hipparchia caroli	Marokkanischer Waldportier*	Marokkanse boswachter*
Grayling, Striped	Hipparchia fidia	Streifen-Samtfalter*	Gestreepte heivlinder
Grayling, Tree	Neohipparchia statilinus	Eisenfarbiger Samtfalter	Kleine heivlinder
Groundling, Northern Banded	Brachythemis impartita	Nördlicher Treuer Kurzpfeil	Noordelijke bandgrondlibel
Hairstreak, False Ilex	Satyrium esculi	Südlicher Eichenzipfelfalter	Spaanse eikenpage
Hairstreak, Moroccan	Tomares mauretanicus	Grüner Zipfelfalter*	Barbarijse klaverpage
Hairstreak, Provencal	Tomares ballus	Ballus-Zipfelfalter	Groene klaverpage
Heath, Moroccan Dusky	Coenonympha fettigii	Atlas-Wiesenvögelchen*	Atlashooibeestje*
Heath, Vaucher's	Coenonympha vaucheri	Marokkanischer-Wiesenvögelchen*	Marokkaans hooibeestje
Hermit, Southern	Chazara prieuri	Südlicher Berghexe*	Bonte heremiet
Hooktail, Green	Paragomphus genei	Afrikanische Sandjungfer	Groene haaklibel
Lady, Painted	Vanessa cardui	Distelfalter	Distelvlinder
Locust, Moroccan	Dociostaurus maroccanus	Marokkanische Wanderheuschrecke	Marokkaanse sprinkhaan
Pasha, Two-tailed	Charaxes jasius	Erdbeerbaumfalter	Aardbeiboomvlinder
Pennant, Black	Selysiothemis nigra	Teufelchen	Zwarte korenbout
Pincertail, Faded	Onychogomphus costae	Braune Zangenlibelle	Moorse tanglibel
Pincertail, Large	Onychogomphus uncatus	Grosse Zangenlibelle	Grote tanglibel
Satyr, Moroccan Sooty	Satyrus atlantea	Dunkeler Samtfalter*	Donkere saterzandoog
Scarlet, Broad	Crocothemis erythraea	Feuerlibelle	Vuurlibel
Silver-line, Allard's	Cigaritis allardi	Grosser Silberlinie*	Grote zilverstreep